Japanese Horror Cinema and Deleuze

Japanese Horror Cinema and Deleuze

Interrogating and Reconceptualizing Dominant Modes of Thought

Rachel Elizabeth Barraclough

BLOOMSBURY ACADEMIC
NEW YORK • LONDON • OXFORD • NEW DELHI • SYDNEY

BLOOMSBURY ACADEMIC
Bloomsbury Publishing Inc
1385 Broadway, New York, NY 10018, USA
50 Bedford Square, London, WC1B 3DP, UK
29 Earlsfort Terrace, Dublin 2, Ireland

BLOOMSBURY, BLOOMSBURY ACADEMIC and the Diana logo
are trademarks of Bloomsbury Publishing Plc

First published in the United States of America 2022
Paperback edition published 2023

Copyright © Rachel Elizabeth Barraclough, 2022

For legal purposes the Acknowledgements on p. xi constitute
an extension of this copyright page.

Cover design: Eleanor Rose
Cover image: a still from *Kairo* (2001), Dir. Kiyoshi Kurosawa. © Daiei Eiga / Hakuhodo / Collection Christophel / ArenaPAL; www.arenapal.com

All rights reserved. No part of this publication may be reproduced or transmitted in any form or by any means, electronic or mechanical, including photocopying, recording, or any information storage or retrieval system, without prior permission in writing from the publishers.

Bloomsbury Publishing Inc does not have any control over, or responsibility for, any third-party websites referred to or in this book. All internet addresses given in this book were correct at the time of going to press. The author and publisher regret any inconvenience caused if addresses have changed or sites have ceased to exist, but can accept no responsibility for any such changes.

Library of Congress Cataloging-in-Publication Data
Names: Barraclough, Rachel Elizabeth, author.
Title: Japanese horror cinema and Deleuze : interrogating and reconceptualizing dominant modes of thought / Rachel Elizabeth Barraclough.
Description: New York : Bloomsbury Academic, 2022. | Includes bibliographical references and index. |
Summary: "An analysis of Japanese horror films from the 1990s and 2000s using Deleuzian concepts"– Provided by publisher.
Identifiers: LCCN 2021042213 (print) | LCCN 2021042214 (ebook) | ISBN 9781501368295 (hardback) | ISBN 9781501368301 (epub) | ISBN 9781501368318 (pdf) | ISBN 9781501368325 (ebook other)
Subjects: LCSH: Horror films–Japan–History and criticism. | Motion pictures–Philosophy. | Deleuze, Gilles, 1925–1995–Influence. | Motion pictures–Japan–History–21st century.
Classification: LCC PN1995.9.H6 B37 2022 (print) | LCC PN1995.9.H6 (ebook) | DDC 791.43/6164–dc23
LC record available at https://lccn.loc.gov/2021042213
LC ebook record available at https://lccn.loc.gov/2021042214

ISBN:	HB:	978-1-5013-6829-5
	PB:	978-1-5013-7502-6
	ePDF:	978-1-5013-6831-8
	eBook:	978-1-5013-6830-1

Typeset by Integra Software Services Pvt. Ltd.

To find out more about our authors and books visit www.bloomsbury.com and sign up for our newsletters.

CONTENTS

List of Illustrations vii
Acknowledgements xi
Note on Japanese names and terms xii

Introduction: A boom, a crash and a death rattle 1
    Chapter summary 7

Part one   Theory

1 Theoretical intersections: National, transnational and global flows and the Japanese horror genre 13
    National, transnational and world cinema 13
    Japanese horror cinema 28

2 Theoretical transformations: The perspectives of Gilles Deleuze 43
    The Deleuzian taxonomy 43
    Theoretical transformations: National, transnational and world cinema 61
    Transforming thought: The horror genre and psychoanalysis 69

Part two   Case studies

3 The 'any-space-whatever', 'becoming-woman' and *Ju-On: The Grudge* (2002) 75
    Assemblages and any-spaces-whatever 76
    Subjective fluidities: Becoming-woman 90

4 Auteurship, adaptation and the molecularity of *Audition* (1999) 109

   Auteurship and industrial assemblages 111

   Audition the novel: Adaptation and transmedia relations 122

   Audition the film: Mapping molecularity and drifts 134

5 *Kairo* (*Pulse*) (2001): Cosmicism and 'becoming-machine' 157

   The living characters 161

   The spirits and becoming-machine 167

Conclusion: Reconceptualizations of Japanese horror and beyond 207

Notes 216
Bibliography 229
Filmography 238
Index 241

ILLUSTRATIONS

1 The opening montage, a collection of stills, *Ju-On: The Grudge* (Shimizu, 2002) 80

2 Becoming Kayako: Takeo threatens us with a box-cutter, *Ju-On: The Grudge* (Shimizu, 2002) 82

3 Izumi and Yūji stare at each other across a temporal void, *Ju-On: The Grudge* (Shimizu, 2002) 85

4 Izumi sees her deceased father in her home's shrine room, *Ju-On: The Grudge* (Shimizu, 2002) 87

5 Kayako covered in blood, signifying her abject femininity, *Ju-On: The Grudge* (Shimizu, 2002) 93

6 Kayako's shadowy force engulfs a security guard in Hitomi's building, *Ju-On: The Grudge* (Shimizu, 2002) 96

7 Kayako in a more discernible form, *Ju-On: The Grudge* (Shimizu, 2002) 97

8 Extreme close-up of Katsuya's face, *Ju-On: The Grudge* (Shimizu, 2002) 98

9 Kayako becomes Katsuya, *Ju-On: The Grudge* (Shimizu, 2002) 100

10 One of the flashback images, Sachie holds her hands to her face, *Ju-On: The Grudge* (Shimizu, 2002) 101

11 Kayako becomes Rika's reflected image, *Ju-On: The Grudge* (Shimizu, 2002) 102

12 Kayako bursts from Rika's blouse, *Ju-On: The Grudge* (Shimizu, 2002) 103

13 Kayako watching Rika in a much more human-like form, *Ju-On: The Grudge* (Shimizu, 2002) 104

14 Rika in more traditional, feminine dress, *Ju-On: The Grudge* (Shimizu, 2002) 107

15 Left: A long, drawn out, static shot of Shigeharu and his son, *Audition* (Miike, 1999). Right: A similar static, long shot from Ozu's *Tōkyō Monogatari* (Tokyo Story) (1953); Miike's possible inspiration 112

16 Shot of an auditionee from the perspective of Shigeharu and Yoshikawa, *Audition* (Miike, 1999) 137

17 Shots of Shigeharu (right) and Yoshikawa (left) during the audition montage, *Audition* (Miike, 1999) 138

18 Shot of the male operator of the camera (left), *Audition* (Miike, 1999) 139

19 Low-quality footage from the operated camera, *Audition* (Miike, 1999) 140

20 Voyeuristic shot from the operated camera of an auditionee's breasts, *Audition* (Miike, 1999) 140

21 A collage of the range of bodies, colours, tones, textures, expressions and movements on show in the fast paced sequence at the end of the first part of the audition montage, *Audition* (Miike, 1999) 141

22 The successful designer auditionee transposed from the novel to the film, *Audition* (Miike, 1999) 143

23 Another character transposed from the book to the film, the suicidal, mentally unstable yoga instructor, *Audition* (Miike, 1999) 143

24 Shigeharu stares warily down the staircase leading to The Stone Fish, a bar in Ginza, *Audition* (Miike, 1999) 145

25 First person sequence leading down the narrow passageway towards the bar, *Audition* (Miike, 1999) 146

26 Three dismembered fingers, an ear and a writhing tongue lie beneath barstools within the bar, *Audition* (Miike, 1999) 146

27 Asami inserts needles into Shigeharu's chest, intoning the words '*Kiri, Kiri, Kiri*', *Audition* (Miike, 1999) 148

28 Shigeharu's dismembered foot, *Audition* (Miike, 1999) 148

29 The child Asami pets the bestial man in this anomalous, recollection-image, *Audition* (Miike, 1999) 152

30 Asami becomes Shigeharu's secretary, *Audition* (Miike, 1999) 153

31 Asami also becomes Shigehiko's young girlfriend, Misuzu, *Audition* (Miike, 1999) 154

32 Michi taking care of Junko, *Kairo (Pulse)* (Kurosawa, 2001) 163

33 The experimental computer programme within Harue's lab, *Kairo (Pulse)* (Kurosawa, 2001) 165

34 A black, shadowy spirit Ryosuke encounters, *Kairo (Pulse)* (Kurosawa, 2001) 168

35 The *yūrei* Junko encounters, *Kairo (Pulse)* (Kurosawa, 2001) 169

36 Harue embracing the invisible force in her apartment, *Kairo (Pulse)* (Kurosawa, 2001) 171

37 The computer programme displaying the more fluid, malleable orbs, *Kairo (Pulse)* (Kurosawa, 2001) 184

38 The electronic device through which a spirit transfers and transcodes itself, *Kairo (Pulse)* (Kurosawa, 2001) 189

39 The blurred, pixelated spirit Ryosuke encounters, *Kairo (Pulse)* (Kurosawa, 2001) 190

40 A close-up of the pixelated spirit, *Kairo (Pulse)* (Kurosawa, 2001) 191

41 Taguchi appearing where the stain, left after his suicide, once was, *Kairo* (*Pulse*) (Kurosawa, 2001) 198

42 The abandoned factory floor, *Kairo* (*Pulse*) (Kurosawa, 2001) 200

43 The mise-en-abyme image featuring Taguchi, *Kairo* (*Pulse*) (Kurosawa, 2001) 201

44 The pixelated figure Toshio first sees, *Kairo* (*Pulse*) (Kurosawa, 2001) 204

45 The discernible face of the spirit Toshio encounters, *Kairo* (*Pulse*) (Kurosawa, 2001) 204

ACKNOWLEDGEMENTS

First, I would like to thank and dedicate this book to my family, mum, dad, Angela and Derek. Thank you all for your encouragement and support throughout the writing of this book. It certainly would not be here today, in this current form, without you.

I would also like to thank my colleagues and supervisors at the University of Lincoln, Dr Dean Lockwood and Mr Dave McCaig, for your friendship, guidance and support throughout my postgraduate studies and beyond.

A special thank you also to Dr David Deamer and Professor Jay McRoy for helping to shape the book through your expertise, comments and suggestions. I am very grateful for the time you took to review my work.

Finally, I would like to thank staff (current and former) at The University of Bradford, Dr Ben Roberts, Dr Karen Thornton, Dr Mark Goodall and Mr William Godfrey especially, for all your support and encouragement during my undergraduate degree and in the early stages of my career. I certainly would not be where I am today without you all.

NOTE ON JAPANESE NAMES AND TERMS

Japanese names have been rendered with family name first followed by given name in respect of Japanese naming conventions. Accents on English renderings of Japanese words have also been used.

Introduction: A boom, a crash and a death rattle

In the late 1990s and early 2000s, a slew of Japanese horror films emerged to great domestic and international success. With the release of *Ringu* in 1998, the Japanese horror boom (or 'J-horror' as it was affectionately known) was widely considered by critics to have reanimated what was becoming a stagnant, 'putrefying' (Kermode, 2003) international genre. The unique stylistic and thematic attributes of these films remapped the parameters of the genre both domestically and globally, breaking it free from the cycle of producing remakes and sequels to previously successful horror films (a notable tendency within the American horror film market) and allowing it to creatively diverge down different lines of flight. Japanese horror films, from *Ringu* to *Battle Royale* (2000), *Kairo* (*Pulse*) (2001), *Ju-On: The Grudge* (2002) and *Chakushin Ari* (*One Missed Call*) (2003), amongst others, have inspired filmmakers globally, with some (most prolifically in America) even creating direct remakes of these texts (such as *The Ring* (2002), *The Grudge* (2004) and *One Missed Call* (2008)).

Because of the widespread popularity and influence of Japanese horror films from this period, it is no wonder that they have been the focus of extensive research and scholarship. There have been many insightful commentaries on these films (and their remakes) which have produced new contributions to knowledge, including Collette Balmain's *Introduction to Japanese Horror Film* (2008) and Jay McRoy's *Japanese Horror Cinema* (2005) and *Nightmare Japan: Contemporary Japanese Horror Cinema* (2008) to name a few. To date, scholarship on Japanese horror cinema from this period has been dominated by a particular ontology of thought: the hermeneutic. Hermeneutics, as a methodological discipline, 'offers a toolbox for efficiently … [interpreting] human actions, texts and other meaningful material' (Mantzavinos, 2016), this includes all media texts. The term 'hermeneutics' is derived from Hermes, the Greek mythological deity and messenger of the gods, who relayed information in the form of Holy Scriptures to the mortals for them to interpret. These scriptures, as with all religious texts, were believed to have another layer of hidden meaning which needed to be inferred by the interpreter. The various hermeneutic theories and concepts, pertaining to different aspects and representations within film, are thus tools for reading hidden, allegorical and moral meanings. Therefore, each hermeneutic theory or concept applied within an analysis seeks to establish truths of a text.

Whilst much of hermeneutic thought is very sophisticated and has proven to be extremely fruitful to many strands of film scholarship, these truths of meaning established can be too generalizing and simplistic as they may occlude alternative thoughts and knowledges that we could derive from film texts. Because of the dominance of hermeneutics within various strands of film scholarship, there are other dimensions to a film, particularly the affective,[1] that we are not yet fully attuned to and which might reveal new, developmental knowledges about a film. It is the aim of this book to explore these alternative dimensions in relation to Japanese horror cinema, challenging and incrementally transforming the hermeneutic concepts that have informed understandings of it in the past. To achieve such developments in thought on Japanese horror cinema from the boom years, this book mobilizes the taxonomy of the philosopher Gilles Deleuze, whose work is antithetical to hermeneutic modes of thought.

Hermeneutic film scholarship, as Deleuze highlights in his texts *Cinema 1: The Movement-Image* (2005) and *Cinema 2: The Time-Image* (2013), predominantly conceptualizes cinema in terms of movement-images, linear, abstracted, cause and effect models of time and narrative structure. Although there are different types of interconnected movement-images which are explored in more detail later, the most prominent of these, the large form action-image, conceptualizes cinema as beginning with a situation which creates forces directly leading to actions from characters, which in turn reconstitute the situation or the encompassing milieu. Through such a linear conceptualization of film it is easy for scholars to derive singular, unifying languages, meanings or semiotics from them as all other possibilities or potentialities of narrative and time are negated. There is only one true narrative, with conclusive outcomes and derived meanings, within movement-image cinema.

Not all cinema can be conceptualized in this way, however. What Deleuze (2013) terms time-image cinema (of which, this book asserts, there are some exemplary texts within Japanese horror cinema from the late 1990s to early 2000s), an a-temporal, non-linear and often incoherent form, which, for extended periods, takes place within an affective, multipotential zone of indetermination, is incompatible with this model. Within time-image cinema, time is not measured and conceptualized through the movements of characters on-screen, instead a whole image of time or duration is presented, revealing to us the possibilities of multiple, potential abstractions. Presenting the whole of duration means that audiences and characters on-screen become suspended, their sensory-motor continuity is disrupted and they exist within an affective state, unable to comprehend (only feel) their surroundings and the forces that flow through them. Characters and audiences become suspended in the interval between perception and action. Affect is transmitted at this point of indetermination, where all potential actions, outcomes and meanings are possible as one singularity has not yet been realized. As Deleuze discusses: 'affection is what occupies the interval, what occupies it without filling it in or filling it up. It surges in the centre of indetermination, that is to say in the subject, between a perception which is troubling in certain respects and a hesitant action' (2005: 67). Within movement-image cinema, this point of indetermination is quickly transitioned through and action and outcome are realized; however this is not the case within the time-image. Instead, in time-image cinema, characters and audiences are placed within 'a purely optical and sound situation' which 'does not extend into action, any more than it is induced by action. It makes us grasp, it is supposed to make us grasp, something intolerable and unbearable ... It is a matter of something too powerful, or too unjust, but sometimes also too beautiful, and which henceforth outstrips our sensory-motor capacities' (Deleuze, 2013: 18).

Time-image cinema, for Deleuze, emblematized in Italian Neorealist and French New Wave Movement, arose in Europe in the wake of the Second World War, which is perceived as a break in linear time or a traumatic event, where previous, linear regimes of understanding the world are disrupted. This break affected cinema, creating a crisis within the movement-image and leading to the emergence of a new, expressive form, the time-image. This book contends that there are other such breaks throughout world history which have led to profound re-emergences of the time-image. Relevant to this text and to the Japanese horror films studied here is the break experienced in Japanese society when the economy collapsed in 1990, leading to the *Heisei* recession (the recession was punctuated by other traumatic, disruptive events in Japan, as is detailed throughout this book). This particular break arguably led to the production of time-images which can be found within (and potentially beyond) the plethora of Japanese horror texts that emerged in the late 1990s and early 2000s. These time-images are especially useful devices for rendering specific breaks in linear time and their disruptive effects, allowing audiences to register them affectively upon the body rather than process them cognitively, which often becomes too difficult a task.[2] It may be that the codes and conventions of horror are also particularly useful tools for these renderings as they are explicitly engineered to instigate visceral, affective responses in audiences.

Because of the time-images' association with breaks in linear time, their non-linearity and their affectiveness, hermeneutic models are insufficient for drawing out meanings from these films. Therefore, these need to be augmented with alternative ontologies of thought which diverge from the hermeneutic. Deleuzian perspectives, as well as identifying these more complex, a-temporal cinematic forms in the first place, offer a way for concepts and ideas to be developed about them. Meanings, ideas and understandings that arise from film texts, unlike within hermeneutic conceptualizations, are transformative and unfixed under Deleuzian thought. This is due to the relational, fluid way in which Deleuze understands bodies (including organic or human as well as machinic bodies like cinema), spaces and thought. He perceives them as perpetually interconnecting or forming new, affective assemblages with each other,[3] which can last for varied periods of time and produce new understandings or ways of being and functioning. Understandings of filmic texts mutate in response to the flows of affects that are transmitted to the human body from the film and from any number of other interconnections with other bodies which form a part of an assemblage, making up a unique experiential encounter with a film text. However, it is crucial that the assemblage is not understood as simply a one-way flow of affective energy, where only the organic, human body of the audience is impacted by film and other bodies it forms assemblages with. All bodies or nodes within an assemblage have the propensity to both transmit and absorb affect, meaning that connections within assemblages and transformations instigated can be exceptionally creative and complex in each instance. Through producing filmic case studies, which analyse three Japanese horror texts in-depth, this book aims to map out some of the assemblages that these films form (including assemblages with hermeneutic thought), which in turn will lead to explorations of some of the transformations and fluidities, in terms of meaning, thought and being, that could occur.

The first of the three films studied here is *Ju-On: The Grudge*, an icon of the Japanese horror boom, which tells the tale of two vengeful spirits, murdered by the patriarch of their family, who haunt their former home, condemning all who encounter them to death. The second study focuses upon Miike Takashi's *Audition* (1999), which, diverging from the supernatural themes of *Ju-On: The Grudge*, follows the story of film producer Aoyama Shigeharu (Ishibashi Ryo) who sets up an audition to find a new wife. Upon meeting Yamazaki Asami (Shiina Eihi), however, she is not all that she first appears to be and she proceeds to torture and mutilate Shigeharu for seemingly taking advantage of the ambitions of young women to be actresses. The final film under consideration in this book is Kurosawa Kiyoshi's *Kairo* (*Pulse*) which follows a range of characters living within a metropolis as they attempt to survive an apocalypse brought about by the proliferation of the internet. The internet creates a bridge between the world of the living and the realm of the dead, allowing ghosts to cross over and infiltrate the living characters' environments. Those who meet a spirit begin to exhibit strange, depressive behaviours and eventually commit suicide. As this begins to happen en-masse, the bustling city soon becomes hauntingly empty.

By focusing upon these films, this book situates itself primarily amongst two broad areas of scholarship: horror cinema studies and the interlinking fields of national, transnational and world cinema studies.[4] Consideration of perspectives, theories and bodies of thought from each of these fields is threaded throughout the book and its three filmic case studies. Wider notions, from other areas of film scholarship, are also explored within specific case studies, from auteur studies to adaptation studies, cosmic horror and post/transhumanism. A broad range of hermeneutic ideas from these fields are considered in an assemblage with Deleuzian thought and are transformed at various intersections. This book does not advocate a removal of the hermeneutic from scholarly considerations as there is an inherent tension between molar regimes and the molecular within the time-image cinema discussed here and potentially beyond.[5] Deleuze himself, despite challenging hermeneutic modes of thought, would not promote its eradication from scholarship. Through his and Félix Guattari's notion of 'the art of dosages' (1987),[6] the need to retain 'small rations' of molar regimes, significance and subjectification within analyses, in order to produce effective challenges to and transformations of these dominant realities and their perspectives, is expressed. Eradicating or taking a sledgehammer to hermeneutic thought is not, Deleuze and Guattari (1987) argue, conducive to the reform of these dominant regimes, the fine file or small doses of molecular thought must be used to transform them. Aligning with this notion, this book aims to introduce deterritorializing elements to hermeneutic perspectives on Japanese horror cinema and thus open up scholarship to new potentialities or becomings of thought.[7] As is explored in detail later within this book, various strands of film scholarship, including horror, national and transnational cinema studies, have already been opened up to more molecular ways of thinking. This book therefore aims to search for a position in and amongst these stirrings.

Considering films as molecular, blocks of affect as well as bodies crossed by various hermeneutic groundings can transform understandings of texts, their representations and significations. In particular, regarding the hermeneutic in relation to affective dimensions of the film may indicate possible molar groundings from which these films depart. For instance, a film may appear to represent patriarchally constrained women; however, by considering the affective dimensions of the text it may become apparent that it actually departs from this representation and the woman becomes a much more fluid, multifaceted character. Similarly, a film space may appear to be nationally encoded (a space geographically and culturally identifiable); however, it may, at points, become ungrounded or deterritorialized from such notions through the time-image and the affective indetermination it fosters.

Furthermore, conceptualizing the audience as engaging in an affective way with film has potential implications for the way in which audiences are understood under hermeneutic perspectives, as fully formed, static, subjective beings. Perhaps we can re-envision audiences as more subjectively fluid and mutable when they engage with film.

One might be forgiven for questioning why, in this book, such transformations in thought are sought to be established via Japanese horror cinema from the late 1990s and early 2000s. Since the boom, Japanese horror has lapsed in popularity and has seemed to become creatively stagnant. Low quality sequels to previously popular series such as *Ringu* (which currently has eight Japanese films, five international remakes and two television series), *Chakushin Ari (One Missed Call)* (of which there are two sequels, a Japanese-American coproduced remake and a ten-episode TV drama series) and *Ju-On: The Grudge* (which has to date accumulated thirteen feature films, four of which were produced in America, and a recent Netflix series) are churned out in an attempt to recapture the furore and success of the boom. Nevertheless, with the *Ringu* franchise being revisited as recently as 2017 (through Gutiérrez's film *Rings*) and *Ju-On: The Grudge* in 2020 (through Pesce's feature film, *The Grudge*, and the short series being promoted on Netflix), it appears that the global audience love affair with Japanese horror is not quite over yet. Indeed, critics also continue to focus their attention on the horror outputs of Japan with some even forecasting a 'return to form for the genre' (William, 2016). Such a resurgence is predicted to be heralded by recent films such as Nakamura Yoshihiro's *Zan'e: Sunde wa ikenai heya (The Inerasable)* (2016) and Kurosawa Kiyoshi's *Kuriipii: Itsuwari no rinjin (Creepy)* (2016) which have formed, through their generic conventions, themes, motifs, representations and structures, interconnections with Japanese horror films from the boom years. If we are to continue to see a preoccupation with Japanese horror forms in cinema and other media more widely, or indeed a renaissance of the genre, then a resurgence and a reformation of scholarship should also take place. Rather than summoning the conceptual ghosts of Japanese horror scholarship past, there is a prime opportunity to incrementally develop and transform thought on this cinema. It is also hoped that the transformations in thought that are generated here will have wider implications for scholarship beyond the study of Japanese horror cinema. Wider interventions into the fields of horror studies, national, transnational and world cinema scholarship (as well as research into posthumanism and transhumanism, auteur and adaptation studies) will be produced here, which will hopefully serve as catalysts for others working in these fields. Giving a broad overview of how these incremental transformations in thought will be achieved, what follows is a chapter summary.

Chapter summary

Part One of this book develops the theoretical and methodological foundations necessary for the exploration of the three case studies. Chapter 1 considers the intersections between different strands of hermeneutic thought that have characterized the study of Japanese horror cinema in the past. In particular, how Japanese horror texts can be understood through concepts of national, transnational and world cinema as well as theories related to the horror genre and psychoanalysis, are considered within this chapter. It is important that such hermeneutic conceptualizations are maintained, to a degree, within Deleuzian explorations of Japanese horror texts, which is why a thorough consideration of them is imperative here. As becomes clear, particularly within Chapter 2 of this book, which provides an essential, detailed account of some of Deleuze's key ideas, explorations of cinema through his taxonomy should not involve an eradication of hermeneutic thought from purview. The way in which incremental transformations to thought are achieved is through exposing hermeneutic concepts to the ungrounding, transformative properties of the Deleuzian taxonomy. How exactly hermeneutic concepts, pertaining to the horror genre, psychoanalysis and national, transnational and world cinema, can be transformed through Deleuzian thought is explored in detail in the latter half of the second chapter.

Establishing the methodological and theoretical groundwork in the first part of this book allows the second part to be dedicated to the exploration of film texts. In three separate studies, each exploring a different film, the methodologies, ideas and theories outlined in Part One are put to work. A case studies approach is a particularly appropriate method for this book in order to combat criticisms previously made about Deleuzian studies by various scholars. It has been suggested that ideas generated by Deleuzian perspectives within scholarship are sometimes ethereal and insubstantial with little known or demonstrable applicability. This critique may have manifested from the fact that studies which explore the taxonomy of Deleuze and the development of his thought in great depth, outweigh studies that actually apply Deleuzian methodologies to analyses of films. As Eugenie Brinkema argues, rather than incising or applying these methodologies to particular examples, Deleuzian film scholars, to date, have often tended to repeatedly intone a polemic, sometimes with the resultant effect of 'deforcing and deflating … that very concept' (2014: XIII). Nevertheless, there are notable exceptions within scholarship, including the work of David Martin-Jones (2006, 2011) who similarly utilizes a case studies approach in the analysis of film.

Whilst three-film case studies provide, by no means, an exhaustive account of Japanese horror cinema, limiting the number of filmic examples ensures that they can be explored in greater depth via the methodologies developed here. The incremental transformations to a range of concepts that aim to be produced in this book, it is hoped, will have a much wider applicability to studies beyond this. Within this study, Japanese horror cinema is a generative device, a machine that is utilized to create extensions, developments and transformations in thought which will hopefully have utility within other types of scholarship.

The three case studies in this book were selected from a wide range of Japanese horror films, firstly because these texts each played an integral part in the worldwide Japanese horror boom of the late 1990s and early 2000s. They constituted extremely popular titles which fuelled global interest in Japanese culture and Japanese horror. It is particularly important for this book that the case studies have a discernible transnational audience reach as it aims to extend and transform transnational thought and understandings about the ways in which films travel and interconnect with audiences and cultures beyond national borders. Because of their popularity, these films constitute some of the most widely considered within hermeneutic based, Japanese horror cinema studies. This again is a particularly important factor for this book which seeks to transform and complexify well-established, widely recognized hermeneutic perspectives on Japanese horror cinema. If it is so that the most radical thought under Deleuze can be produced by retaining a consideration of hermeneutic perspectives, 'by way of collaboration, [or] sometimes as a point of departure' (Deamer, 2014: 13), then it makes sense to explore those films which have been most widely analysed under such regimes.

Chapter 3, the first case study found in Part Two of the book, explores Shimizu Takashi's *Ju-On: The Grudge*, perhaps the most widely viewed of the films. The chapter explores the film's a-temporal, rhizomatic narrative sequences which allow different, once clearly demarcated layers of temporality and existentiality to intermingle. This, as is discussed, is arguably expressive of (Japanese) societal conditions today, rendering the ungrounded, fragmented experiences of people after a break with linear time has occurred. *Ju-On: The Grudge* is perhaps most adept at deterritorializing and allowing for transformations of gendered and psychoanalytical ideologies of the female to emerge, due to the strong presence of woman in the film. Concepts such as the monstrous-feminine, amongst others, become ungrounded within our understandings of the representations of the film and the figure of woman becomes much more fluid and multifaceted. As the chapter considers, the characters (particularly the women) in this film can perhaps be most usefully understood through Deleuze's notion of 'becoming-woman'. The becoming-woman is a fluid, mutable being not dictated by the gender dichotomy, who inspires deterritorializations and transformations in subjectivity amongst others, including the audience who form relationalities with these characters.

The concept of becoming-woman is also mobilized in Chapter 4 to discuss a character within Miike Takashi's *Audition*, the seemingly iconic, femme fatale, Asami. Rather than just considering how ideologies pertaining to female subjectivity become ungrounded here, *Audition* offers the opportunity, through the prevalence of the character Shigeharu, to explore in more depth how molar concepts of masculinity are perhaps also ungrounded and transformed.

Audition, more so than *Ju-On: The Grudge* perhaps, expresses complex relationships between molar concepts and molecularities. This is perhaps because of the spatial, bodily and conceptual relations that it forms with the source novel it has been derived from. The source novel is arguably more linear and territorialized within hermeneutic concepts than the film, thus, many of its conceptualizations may drift into experiences of the film. Nevertheless, if the two texts are conceptualized under Deleuze as relational spaces or bodies, the film, as a more a-temporal, deterritorializing media product, similarly has the potential to drift more fluid, molecular conceptualizations of being and space to the reading of the novel. Relational perceptions of these two media ecologies therefore, as is explored, help to transform the hierarchical, demarcating language of adaptation studies, which has informed the analysis of adapted film texts such as *Audition*.

Another way in which *Audition* is expressive of complex relationships between molar and molecular facets is through its connections to ideas pertaining to the auteur. The acclaimed director of *Audition*, Miike Takashi, has often been discussed within scholarship under the concept of the auteur, as having a unique style of filmmaking. The author of the novel, Murakami Ryū, can also be considered under this idea, as having a distinct writing style which is carried across his works. Within the *Audition* assemblage then, these two auteurs can be considered as relational or forming connections with one another, each perhaps having both grounding (molar) and ungrounding (molecular) effects upon the other. Such a conceptualization of relationality between auteurs may help to introduce intervention within the field of auteur studies, allowing for transformation of the idea of the auteur as a static, distinct being with their own unique, unchanging creative style. Instead, auteurs can be understood as fluid beings whose creative outputs mutate and transform in response to the interconnections they form with other bodies, auteurs and their creative products.

Perhaps some of the most fluid, ungrounded and mutable beings can be found within the film *Kairo* (*Pulse*), the focus of the final study in Chapter 5. The living characters of the film, unlike those of the other texts case studied here, are largely relational, ungrounded beings when we first encounter them on screen, where very few hermeneutic meanings can be attributed to them. This, as is discussed, has implications for the mapping of the transformed, hermeneutic understandings that can be generated in an analysis of these characters under Deleuzian perspectives.

The spirits (or non-living characters) we encounter within *Kairo* (*Pulse*), however, can be considered as even more heterogeneous, relational beings, as they do not belong to just one subjectivity or even one ontology. Instead, they are extremely malleable, flitting between different existentialities through the interconnections with other bodies and space they form (most notably the internet). To understand these spirits a shift away from the familial or traditional hermeneutic readings is required. New, contemporary perspectives on cosmic horror, posthumanism and transhumanism are drawn upon in this chapter to formulate new understandings of these spirits. These bodies of thought are interesting in that, through concepts such as 'becoming-machine' (posthumanism/transhumanism), a transformative, deterritorializing idea and the weird, cosmic being (which can only be felt upon the body), they possess distinct Deleuzian inflections of thought. Such perspectives then represent particularly important interventions in thought which cannot fail to be addressed in this book. As highlighted within this case study, however, the utility of more traditional, familial, hermeneutic concepts to understandings of the spirits should not be forgotten. This is a point which the following chapter also emphasizes in respect of understandings of all the filmic case studies more broadly.

PART ONE

Theory

1

Theoretical intersections: National, transnational and global flows and the Japanese horror genre

Before new lines of thought can be produced, an exploration of the assemblages of thought that have previously coalesced at the site of Japanese horror cinema must take place. Whilst not all modes of thought, concepts and commentaries can be accounted for in this book, this chapter seeks to outline some of the foundational ideas that have broadly informed understandings of Japanese horror cinema. In particular, these centre around the overriding themes of national, transnational and world cinema, as well as horror cinema and psychoanalysis.[1]

National, transnational and world cinema

Perhaps some of the most developmental, vibrant areas of research in recent years have been the interconnecting fields of national, transnational and world cinemas. Whether focusing on a specific instance of national, transnational or world cinema, or producing a more general mapping out of the field, there is a plethora of interesting, exciting work continuing today.

Traditionally, since the 'early days of the institutionalization of film as an academic discipline' (Hjort and Mackenzie, 2000: 2), scholarship, particularly from the West, has analysed films from all over the world under the paradigm of the national. This is perhaps largely due to the development of national film industry frameworks across the world since cinema's inception and thus the dominance of nationally based production contexts. Such nationally based industries are primarily funded and maintained by state governments in various ways. The state, the main proponents of the national imaginary and its community, can influence and shape the cinematic output of the industry, tailoring it (to different extents) to its specific ideologies of the nation. As Chaudhuri (2005: 3) argues, 'a nation-state's involvement in cinema can take the form of state investment, state protection, industrial assistance, intervention, [and] national festivals with prizes' which motivate the production of certain films.

Under ideologies of the national, films produced within a particular territory are perceived to reflect its culture and its people. As Athique argues, 'films were seen as naturalistically indicative of a nationally specific aesthetic and, by extension, as presenting a literal forming of the cultural identity, behaviours and beliefs of the producing society' (in Khorana, 2013: 107). Regarding Japanese cinema studies in particular, texts such as Donald Richie's *Japanese Cinema: Film Style and National Character* (1971), Keiko McDonald's *Reading a Japanese Film: Cinema in Context* (2006) and Colette Balmain's *Introduction to Japanese Horror Film* (2008) each explore national paradigms (some, particularly Balmain's text, do contain transnational inflections, however), discussing how various Japanese films are reflective of Japanese people, arts and culture. Within these texts, such arts as *noh*, *bunraku* and *kabuki* theatre, as well as woodblock prints (*ukiyo-e*) and *rokyoku* (storytelling with a *shamisen* instrument accompaniment) (Raine, in Miyao, 2014: 103), are perceived to influence the narratives, themes and aesthetics of various films.[2] That is, of course, if they are not direct adaptations of theatre plays (like Nakagawa Nobuo's *Tōkaidō Yotsuya Kaidan* (*Ghost Story of Yotsuya in Tōkaidō*) (1959)). As Richie states, when cinema was first introduced to Japan in 1897 it was perceived to be 'a new form of theatre' (2005: 22).

Folktales and religious concepts too (from *Shintōism* and Buddhism most commonly) are perceived to be encoded within Japanese cinema, alongside various moral, communal values (notions of filial piety and obligation to family members and superiors, for instance), which are understood to be shared amongst and distinct to the Japanese people. Richie, in particular, takes the stance that 'much of what is considered most typical in Japanese aesthetics stems from zen [Buddhism]' (Singer, in Miyao, 2014: 40). This perspective is at odds, however, with Noël Burch's famous text, *To the Distant Observer: Form and Meaning in the Japanese Cinema* (1992). While these texts are 'united in posing Japanese cinema as an outgrowth of deep-rooted Japanese traditions' (Singer, in Miyao, 2014: 39), Burch contrastingly stresses 'a genealogical link between Japanese cinema and kabuki' (Miyao, 2014: 40–41), along with other traditional arts, such as *noh* theatre.

The disparity between the two highlights the problem with essentializing and generalizing cultures and cinemas under national paradigms. They are more multifaceted than scholars (particularly of the past) perhaps anticipate, taking influence from multiple different sources. The issue with over-essentialization is one which film scholarship today (particularly transnational cinema studies) seeks to address. A redress of such essentializing perspectives has been positioned by some scholars as particularly significant for Japanese cinema studies. As Bordwell argues, 'in no area of film studies do generalizations about national temperament circulate so blithely as in this one. We constantly encounter claims about what the Japanese are ... and what they are like' (1979, cited in Singer, in Miyao, 2014: 47–8). The drawbacks of such generalizing studies, however, should not cloud the interesting and useful contributions to knowledge that national cinema studies make.

Using the national paradigm, films and societies from all over the world can be easily categorized and understood by scholars, critics, marketers, distributors and audiences alike. The national paradigm gives films and the cultures they derive from a language, a framework from which their themes, aesthetics representations and differences from other bodies of film and culture (proclaiming their 'otherness') can be understood. This model is therefore a very useful implementation within analyses of cultures and cinemas, as nations each have their own separate, comprehensive networks of ideologies, detailing unique traits, cultural discourses and rituals, which come to be rendered in communications such as cinema.[3]

The utility of the model of the national and its dominance within the film studies field, however, does not only derive from its ability to reveal the encoded national-cultural specificities of a cinema and the individual films that make it. As Crofts (in Church-Gibson and Hill, 1998) argues, national cinemas can be qualified as such and analysed in several ways, other than exploring their encoded national-cultural specificity. Highlighting the diversity that can exist within studies of national cinema, Crofts asserts that national cinemas can be analysed in terms of: 'production', 'audiences', 'discourses', 'textuality', 'the cultural specificity of genres' and 'nation-state cinema movements' (Church-Gibson and Hill, 1998).

Such models as the national also, despite their hermeneutic core, are nevertheless able to become flexible and mutate, transforming their utility to suit changing contexts. This is a particularly important observation when one considers the ungrounded nature of today's global, transnational societies. As Smith argues, nations are often understood as unchanging; however, they 'can also signify a gradual movement of change and transformation, or an accumulation of layers of past states' (2001: 29).[4] Thus, the idea of national cinema, as an extension of the concept of nation, too, can be conceptualized as unfixed or transformative. Illustrating this, in the 1970s and 1980s, through influxes of psychoanalysis, semiotics and feminism in film theory, scholars began to understand that analysis should be 'a matter of problematising notions of the national, while sustaining national cinema as a descriptive category' (Hjort and Mackenzie, 2000: 3). Therefore, national cinema was reconceptualized in a more fluid, mutable manner, as a site of conflict where the nation's transformations in state or movements over time could be represented, understood and debated. Films then were no longer understood 'to simply represent or express the stable features of a national culture' and became one of 'the loci for debates about a nation's governing principles, goals, heritage and history' (Hjort and Mackenzie, 2000: 4). The ideologies of nation within a film were now understood to not be pre-given, static and determined, but flexible, and open to interpretation by filmmakers and audiences. As Hill argues, national cinema was reconceptualized as being 'characterised by questioning and inquiry' and 'critical of inherited notions of national identity ... [not assuming] the existence of a unique, unchanging "national culture"' (1992, cited in Higson, in Hjort and Mackenzie, 2000: 70-1).

Under this reconceptualization, however, alternative interpretations of nation formed within films would still have to remain strictly within the given 'parameters set by the culture and traditions of the nation in question and its distinctive heritage' (Smith, 2001: 20). Alternative manifestations of nation and national identity within this reconceptualization then are not particularly radical or ungrounding and a fundamental coherence and progression of the nation is perceived to be maintained. Thus, this particular conceptualization of national cinema was not quite as flexible as it first appeared and arguably, in light of the hybridized, multicultural natures of many nations today would need to be mutated further to contribute significantly to understandings of cinema and nation today.

Contributing to these developments within concepts of national cinema during the 1970s and 1980s, two seminal texts emerged, Benedict Anderson's *Imagined Communities* (2006) and Ernest Gellner's *Nations and Nationalism* (2009). Perhaps the most important premise, highlighted especially in Anderson's work, is the idea that nations are 'imagined communities' where the members of 'even the smallest nation will never know most of their fellow members, meet them, or even hear of them, yet in the minds of each lives the image of their communion' (2006: 6). In other words, nations and nationalisms are invented, imagined and fabricated by the nation state and its people who conceptualize that each member lives within the territorial boundaries of the nation participate in the same cultural events and discourses and resonate with or adhere to the ideologies which pertain to the nation's cultural identity. Central to the construction and maintenance of national imagined communities are understandings of how each one is distinct from others. As Anderson states 'nations ... cannot be imagined except in the midst of an irremediable plurality of other nations' (1983, cited in Higson, 1989: 38). Notions of differentiations bring a sense of unity and cohesion to the national community.

However, national communities, as they are imagined, can be constructed or understood differently amongst individual members or groups of members. Over time, understandings of the make-up of the national community and its identity (both official, state and public conceptions) can also mutate in response to certain events or developments. However, under this conceptualization (as mentioned above) strict parameters for understanding the nation and the national community are in place so that differing ideologies of national identity and belonging are still compatible with each other and not damaging to an overall sense of unity and cohesion.

Within Japan, the notion of the imagined, national community is exemplified within the term *kokutai* which expresses 'the Japanese nation as a racially homogenous entity linked by blood to a single imperial family' (Taylor-Jones, 2013: 203). Under this concept, Japanese people find commonality in their ethnic background and their reverence of the figure of the emperor. Terms such as *Nihonjinron* and *Nihonbunkaron*, expressing the unique character of Japanese people and culture respectively and how they differ from other peoples and cultures around the world, also emblematize Anderson's (2006) notion of the imagined community. These ideologies construct imaginary images of how Japanese people are united through their shared, unique qualities and their experiences of a distinct national culture.

Imagined notions of communion, especially, can be effectively communicated through cinema. Scholars of the national and national cinema aligning with 'social communication theory', 'the bedrock of national cinema studies' (Schlesinger, in Hjort and Mackenzie, 2000: 29), highlight how cinema and other such communications are integral to the formulation and maintenance of imagined nations. As Karl W. Deutsch argues 'the essential aspect of the unity of a people … is the complementary or relative efficiency of communication among individuals' (1966, cited in Schlesinger, in Hjort and Mackenzie, 2000: 19). Such communicative devices band the nation people together and create feelings of comradeship, solidarity and shared experience. Often, such communications of the national become invisible, habitual or 'banal', as Billig (1995) argues, so that nation people no longer ascribe such a significance or meaning to them, making the nation appear natural, ingrained within culture and as the only conceivable way to formulate conceptions of community and ways of life.

Smith (2001, 2007), developing upon Anderson (2006), discusses the ways in which nations are constructed and how national cinema draws upon a panoply of symbols and representations to reify the nation and create an imagined sense of community amongst audiences. In particular, cinema invokes collective memories of past golden ages, 'which may be political and economic, ages of wealth, power and splendour … they may be religious, times of ascetic faith and saintliness and wisdom … or they may be cultural and artistic, when great thinkers, writers and artists congregated in cities and empires' (Smith, 2001: 140). Within cinema, the spirit and values of these ages are often attempted to be recaptured and made relevant to the modern era. Furthermore, films may also invoke concepts of boundaries and territories and foster the growth of attachments to notions of a historic homeland and its poetic landscapes and architecture. They may also cultivate myths of election, where divine protection and blessing or a special task or mission are conferred upon the nation people (Smith, in Sturm, Young and Zuelow, 2007: 21), or relate to 'the cult of the glorious dead' (Smith, 2001: 144) and represent heroic figures and their acts of self-sacrifice for the sake of the nation. Within cinema, national heroes do just take not only the form of military personnel but also sports figures or geniuses within the arts and sciences.

Illustrating this, within the Japanese *Jidaigeki* (period drama) genre of films, a past golden age of feudalism (typically during the *Edo* or *Tokugawa* period between 1603 and 1868) is invoked. This links the Japanese people of the present with a glorious history, where men and women had clearly defined roles and places within society, people lived in harmony with nature and the Japanese landscape and the heroic *samurai* protected the nation people and the prosperous *shogunate* (the military government). Through these renderings, cinema may also play a part in generating the strong, emotional resonances the nation people feel and come to associate with invocations of their nation, something which 'only religions had previously been able to encompass' (Smith, 2001: 2).

According to Gellner (2009), national cultures are often derived from earlier, folk cultures, which the nation then reimagines and reshapes, creating an impression that the national culture is constant. However, unlike Anderson (2006), Gellner (2009) argues that the formation of nation states 'is the inevitable outcome of industrialization' (Schlesinger, in Hjort and Mackenzie, 2000: 21). Nations provide a stable societal basis with 'political centralization ... [and] a costly educational infrastructure' (Gellner, 2009: 110) which standardizes and homogenizes the thoughts and skills of the nation people. National structures provide the right, cohesive environment for the dissemination of generic training to the nation people which is required for functioning and working within an industrialized society.

Higbee reiterates and extends Gellner's (2009) idea, stating that 'the origins of nation are perceived in Western thought to be "coeval with the birth of universal history" (a linear collective past) and the development of post-enlightenment discourses of progress, modernity, liberty and humanism that coincide in the nineteenth century with the rise of industrialism and democracy' (in Bâ and Higbee, 2012: 86). In other words, as Anderson (2006) himself also asserts, the concept of nation was formed when functional, linear conceptions of time, through clock and calendar, were formed. Where a coherent past informs the present and leads into the future (a historicism), where everyday life is marked by national, state-sanctioned calendric events (for instance, bank holidays) and measured by specified periods of work and leisure. Concepts of national linear time, organization and belonging therefore, help to create and maintain coherent, progressive, productive, as well as democratic societies.

Gellner (2009), Anderson (2006) and many other scholars of the national and national cinema also agree upon the idea that cultural products constitute a 'necessary shared medium' (Gellner, 2009: 36) through which these ideologies of linear, progressive national time and cohesion are disseminated. Cinema has been conceptualized as a 'device for the presentation of simultaneity in homogenous empty time' (Anderson, 2006: 25) where the community steadily moves through history.

As part of the functioning of this device, to maintain the cohesion of the nation, cinema must also help to refute all other notions and constructions of community and identity. It must position its notion of community and identity (the national) as the only true, viable construction for progression. Something, which, due to accelerations in the processes of globalization, continues to become increasingly difficult, as evidenced by the emergence of new forms of scholarship on transnational and world cinema.

Within scholarship, there has recently been a shift away from the national towards considerations of world cinema and the transnational, where films and the cultures they are produced within are perceived to be much less static and contained and more fluid, hybrid and border-defying. A multitude of texts, from Chaudhuri (2005), Ezra and Rowden (2006) to Ďurovičová and Newman (2010), attest to this scholarly shift. This development has occurred in conjunction with accelerations in the forces of globalization, which have caused nations and cultures to become even more closely interconnected.[5] Particularly since such infrastructures as transportation and communication have advanced, the flow of people, materials and ideas between nations has increased. Naturalizing many of these border-crossing elements, individual nations become more diverse and multicultural and the indigenous becomes less visible. As Iwabuchi notes, 'cross border interaction, fusion and mobility ... seriously put the clearly demarcated national cultural borders into question' (2015: 1). Travel, immigration and the sharing of goods across national boundaries have led to the formation of more multifaceted and multicultural societies, where one encounters many different conceptualizations of community and being in the world. Speaking about Japan specifically, Tezuka theorizes that 'banal cosmopolitanism' has largely replaced 'banal nationalism', where 'everyday life is largely sustained by producing and consuming goods and symbols from and for many different and faraway parts of the world' (2012: 2).

Cinemas, reflecting and commenting upon the nature of societies around the world, are also affected by these transformations and appropriate these transnational flows into their language. In particular, the processes of globalization have ungrounded understandings of film industries as being embedded within nations and cultures, being influenced by local structures, ideologies and conditions, and contributing to national aims related to culture, industry and the economy. Instead, industrial processes (design, production, distribution and marketing) are much more dispersed and less wedded to national structures and ideologies.

Some scholars of transnational cinema have also conceptualized that film, as a medium, is losing any national particularities that it may have had and that a 'global cine-literacy' (Ezra and Rowden, 2006: 4) has formed. This is where cinema's mechanisms and its visual flows can be apprehended and understood worldwide, regardless of an audience's cultural positioning, nationality or spoken language. Rather than drawing upon nationally specific ideas and concerns, it is perhaps more profitable for producers and directors to draw upon universal themes and issues which are pertinent to large numbers of people living within multicultural, capitalist, transnational societies. For instance, films which render the processes of globalization and technologization, and how they have transformed and effected societies and peoples, potentially have a very strong transnational resonance and appeal. This, whilst celebrated by some, is not viewed positively by all scholars and commentators. As Appadurai highlights, there is a large body of work which argues that films, inscribing such a transnational outlook and language, are 'stunted by the forces of commoditization, industrial capitalism, and the generalized regimentation and secularization of the world' (1996: 6) which requires films to be thoroughly culturally and ideologically cleansed to create empty forms of entertainment and spectacle. This is linked to another criticism which is aimed at those scholars who argue for the formulation and understanding of a global film language and cine-literacy. It can be perceived that such formulations and concepts align too closely with the mores, trends and languages of Hollywood films. As Esfandiary states, 'this vision [of a global film language] seems to imply the compliance of artists from around the world with the norms and values of a dominant intellectual discourse and aesthetic tradition originating from particular, yet powerful, geo-political and geo-cultural formations' (in Bâ and Higbee, 2012: 102–3). Hollywood cinema has been so globally successful that it is perhaps considered by many to be *the* model for transnationality which other cinema industries aspire to emulate. Formulating such transnational ideas of film then, some scholars warn, can simply work to (re)perpetuate America and Hollywood's cultural dominance, positioning them as the centre of all cinematic flows and other cinemas as disparate, weak peripheries (Nagib, in Dennison and Lim, 2006: 30).

Concepts of nation and a reflective national cinema are now, however, seemingly inadequate frameworks for understanding the current make-up of societies and their cinemas. They privilege 'only a limited range of subject positions' (Higson, 1989: 44) and present little more than a fragment of the potential forms and constructions of community and subjectivity that exist. It seems there is no longer a singular truth of national time when nations have been opened to the temporalities of others, and no coherent, shared cultural identity exists amongst the populace, who now embrace many different forms of identity.

There now exists hybrid cultures and subjectivities, where notions of ethnic absolutism, cultural purity, essentialized concepts of nations and dichotomous relationships between them (e.g. notions of the West versus the East) 'have become increasingly untenable as ... histories, cultures and peoples become inextricably intertwined' (Dennison and Lim, 2006: 4). As Homi K. Bhabha argues, hybrid cultures create a 'third space which enables other positions to emerge ... it displaces the histories that constitute it, and sets up new structures of authority, new political initiatives, which are inadequately understood through received wisdom' (1990, cited in Iwabuchi, 2002: 51) such as paradigms of the national. Within these hybrid cultures and subjectivities, multicultural systems of cross-pollination proliferate, where new, alternative ideologies, customs, ways of being, images, narratives, representations and themes perpetually amalgamate with those already established within a particular territory. Thus, cultures and individual subjectivities are endlessly appendable (González, in Shohat and Stam, 2003: 316), never fully formed and always in a state of indetermination, transforming themselves constantly.

Cinema, reflecting these transformations, has become increasingly hybrid, mutable, creative and complex itself. Blurring the boundaries between different cultures, nations and various forms of identity, so that it is difficult, if not impossible, to assign a fixed, homogenous national character to it. Iwabuchi refers to this process of appropriation and mutation as 'transculturation', where 'the asymmetrical encounter of various cultures results in the transformation of an existing cultural artifact and the creation of a new style' (2002: 40). We can perceive this occurring within genre cinema for instance, where models, themes, codes and conventions travel are received and reshaped by various cultures to suit their contexts. South Korean, Taiwanese and Hollywood remakes of Japanese horror films could be understood as part of this process for instance. As Walter vividly explains in her discussion of horror cinema: 'terrifying images and horrifying tales circulate from one region and home to another ... and are culturally reshaped in an ever-spinning fractal of tropes and transformations, both changing and being changed by the cultures they encounter' (in Och and Strayer, 2014: 28).

This shift towards world cinema and transnational approaches does not mean, however, that the national has been completely eradicated from scholarly purview. In fact, many scholars working within these areas, including Iwabuchi (2015) Higson (in Ezra and Rowden, 2006), Hjort and McKenzie (2000) and Vitali and Willemen (2006), advocate a retention and transformation of concepts of the national within explorations of how cinema travels and crosses national boundaries. Recognition of the continuing importance of concepts of national cinema as well as its limitations is perceived by many such scholars to be integral. This is particularly so as many nation states, in response to the cultural transformations that globalization has brought, endorse projects, such as within cinema, which attempt to reassert a sense of indigenous, cultural identity.[6] As Iwabuchi argues, nationalism 'does not recede but hangs around by working closely with cultural globalization processes' (2015: 9). In fact, national frameworks have perhaps become more robust in light of accelerations of globalization, which sees state powers regulating national media systems and markets, acting as gatekeepers to the types of global flows the nation indulges in.

Cinema itself constitutes one such global flow which may be varyingly accepted within different national territories and thus there has been much scholarly attention given to the reception of world films within different cultures. Many studies have looked at how to understand the resonance that particular films have amongst diverse audiences and whether or not their reception in different cultures challenges existing power structures of international film distribution (where, for many years, Hollywood has dominated). For Instance, commenting upon the growing, global popularity of East Asian media in recent years, Iwabuchi argues that it is 'dubious whether the rise of East Asian media cultures radically challenges existing configurations of global cultural power' (2010: 407). This is because East Asian firms often integrate themselves within existing transnational power structures and distribution networks, which involves adapting to hegemonic principles already in place. Discussing Japan as a particular case, Iwabuchi argues that as part of this adaptation, Japanese cultural products must undergo 'a process that involves removing some of their "Japaneseness" [cultural, racial and ethnic characteristics] to make them more acceptable to American and European audiences' (2010).

Nevertheless, the result is not a straightforward homogenization of culture. The local is not wholly displaced within these globalized East Asian media cultures, rather, it is reworked through a process termed 'glocalization' where products and their locally specific processes of meaning construction are adapted to the local particularities of the space in which they are being sold.[7] Within this process there is a 'turn from the notion of a straightforward globally homogenizing cultural dominant toward the idea of an orchestrated heterogenization under the sign of globalizing forces' (Iwabuchi, 2002: 43). Here the local/national and the global have become intertwined, making dichotomies between the two inadequate to forming understandings of culture. These processes of glocalization are particularly significant within Japan as it perceives itself as participating in a 'strategic hybridism' where it 'absorbs foreign cultures without changing its national/cultural core ... its essence and wholeness' (Iwabuchi, 2002: 53–4). However, there are many uncontrollable forces of globalization and transformations incurred which cannot be territorialized under the hermeneutic concepts of nation or negotiated by it. As is discussed in the next chapter particularly, it is perhaps a falsity that there is a stable, unchanging cultural essence in Japan.

Not all cultural products can be understood as 'glocalized' or 'glocalizing', however. In some instances, Iwabuchi (2015) argues, rather than attempting to create more culturally 'odorless'[8] products, the nation and its culture become the common unit of exchange. Within global flows of media culture especially, 'local distinctiveness and differences are expressed to each other' (2015: 11). Media products are received by other territories in a nationalized packaging, which has the result of strengthening stereotypical ideologies about national identities or causing a 'cultural thickening'. Nation states and media producers have become aware of this cultural thickening discourse and have sought to exploit it to enhance their international reputations and to generate economic profits and tourism. This has led to something Iwabuchi terms 'nation branding', where the state 'is urged to play an active role in the production of attractive national cultural odor' (2015: 14), through media and other cultural products, which then compete against other nation brands in the international arena.

These nation brands do not just engage with and create meaning for international audiences, however. Locally, these discourses provide 'new narratives for domestic consumption' (2015: 18), encouraging domestic audiences to live the national brand and become its ambassadors. As these nation brands draw upon pre-established, stereotypical ideologies about a nation and its culture, one would assume that expressing these to domestic audiences would create a resurgence in nationalistic, patriotic sentiment and a strengthening of the national imagined community. However, as Iwabuchi (2015) highlights, this may not be the case and it is possible that such nation brands and their products only produce superficial attractions to nation and do not facilitate the creation of any significant meaning. This may be in part due to the fact that nations today are much more multicultural in nature and thus such expressions of unity, homogeneity and common experience have no useful, grounding function within society.

As Iwabuchi (2015) highlights, within Japan, this nation branding discourse is emblematized within the 'J-cool' (Japanese cool) pop-culture products of the 1990s and 2000s. It first became clear that Japan was increasingly being understood globally as an attractive national brand when Douglas McGray (2002), an American journalist, pronounced that Japan was becoming a new cultural superpower, challenging the dominance of America in the global market. Products such as anime, manga, video games, consumer electronics, J-pop music and significantly, Japanese horror films, were (and still are to this day) all avidly consumed by global (but particularly Western) consumers. These J-cool products have been 'specifically assembled and packaged to target the Western market' (Choo, in Fung, 2013: 12). For instance, much of Japanese horror cinema's appeal in the West arguably stemmed from its highly marketed, perceived differences from standard Hollywood horror fare and the unique references to Japanese culture and folklore the films contain. This has led, however, to accusations of self-Orientalism on the part of the Japanese producers of these consumables. Fully aware of the appeal of their products amongst Western audiences and consumers, producers knowingly encode them with Orientalist[9] stereotypes, attempting to invoke and play-up to pre-established conceptions and ideas about Japan. In the case of horror cinema, producers, marketers and distributors arguably attempted to invoke Japan as a place which is 'weird and wonderful, sublime and grotesque' (Shin, in Choi and Wada-Marciano, 2009: 86–7). This is partially why Iwabuchi (2015) argues that such products only produce superficial connections with the Japanese nation and its ideologies, as the vision of nation and culture encoded within these products is essentialized, perverted and, many would say, fantastical.

Whether superficial or not, what is particularly interesting about J-cool products, Allison (2009) asserts, is their ability to create strong affective resonances amongst international audiences, turning Japan into a site associated with particularly strong intensities of feeling. This affective power of J-cool products, Allison (2009) suggests, may contribute to the strength of Japan's image and its prowess in co-opting peoples and groups from other nations into admiring it and emulating its creed and ways of being.

This, however, constitutes just one way in which to conceptualize transnational flows of culture and film, how they are constructed and positioned in terms of dissemination and marketing. There are other ways in which to understand such flows beyond this nationally focused concept as not all cultural products, travelling transnationally, will be positioned by the state or through marketing as part of the nation brand. There is also no guarantee that audiences will receive cultural products within the framework of the nation brand and they may have divergent readings of this framing. Ungroundings of the nation brand framework are likely to be produced when the audience engages with the contents of products, which are often much more complex and multifaceted than simple invocations of the brand, the homogenous, unified nation and its culture. As Iwabuchi argues, Japanese cultural exports cannot be entirely constituted in terms of the nation brand, just as they 'cannot be constituted entirely in terms of the disappearance of visible Japanese cultural presence' (2002: 76).

Cultural products, from Japan specifically, are therefore crossed by a myriad of complex territorializing and deterritorializing forces at many different levels, from production and content, to marketing and distribution, and the nuance of this needs to be accounted for within scholarship. Through these products we can 'consider how seemingly contradictory vectors of globalizing forces – decentering-recentering, diversifying-homogenizing, and transnationalizing-nationalizing – are working simultaneously and interconstitutively' (Iwabuchi, 2015: 2). The complexity and fluidity of these forces and how they relate to any one cultural product, as this book argues in the next chapter, can be most adequately understood by mobilizing Deleuzian thought.

Some recent works within these interconnected fields have already adopted distinct Deleuzian leanings (allusions to his thought), or else have directly engaged with his philosophy, in attempts to develop perspectives on national, transnational and world cinema. For instance, Dennison and Lim and contributors to their edited volume, *Remapping World Cinema: Identity, Culture and Politics in Film* (2006), formulate alternative ways of looking at transnational cinema. They argue that perspectives on cinema have, by and large, been envisioned through national paradigms as 'genealogical trees, one tree per country' where 'their elaborate root and branch structures are seldom shown as intermingled' (Andrew, in Dennison and Lim, 2006: 21). This is a problematic way to envision cinemas today which connect and communicate (form assemblages) with the cinemas of other cultures in a multitude of ways. They prefer to utilize a world systems approach which, most importantly, encapsulates the idea that particularly dominant cinemas (such as Hollywood) are simply cinemas amongst others.[10] Alluding to some of the fundamentals of Deleuzian thought, collectively, they argue for a centreless, interconnected approach to the study of cinema. This can help capture how global contexts, processes of filmmaking, flows of cinema and film aesthetics and themes are much more complex than essentializing, hermeneutic concepts for understanding cinema can account for.

Other similar works to this which, likewise, have distinct Deleuzian leanings, include Bâ and Higbee (2012), Iwabuchi (in Chua and Erni, 2005), Ezra and Rowden (2006) and Shohat and Stam (1994, 2003). These texts perceive nations, communities and societies (and thus the cinemas that are borne from them) as constituted in a 'densely woven web of connectedness, within a complex and multivalent relationality' (Shohat and Stam, 2003: 1). This allows for discussions around 'issues of multiculturalism, colonialism and race [and how these manifest in cinema] within a web of relationality from multiple vantage points' (Bâ and Higbee, 2012: 6). These texts, like Deleuzian philosophy, refute binaristic thinking and seek to more adequately capture the reality of the flowing and dialogical global economic, industrial, cultural and social landscapes of today, which, of course, impact film cultures worldwide. Proximity and interconnection, as Iwabuchi identifies, is redefined through this way of thinking as 'a dynamic process of becoming' (in Chua and Erni, 2005: 28) rather than as a static condition. In other words, relationalities between cultures, societies and peoples, whether through cinema or by some other means, are transformative in nature. As Iwabuchi (Chua and Erni, 2005) further illustrates, within each cultural encounter or at each meeting point between previously distinct cultures and temporalities, the nature of the merging, the feeling of proximity or resonance will take on a different form.

Perhaps the most significant study to mobilize Deleuzian thought in a detailed discussion of the processes of globalization and the fluid nature of Western cultures and societies today is Steven Shaviro's *Post Cinematic Affect* (2010). Shaviro's (2010) text, like this book, sets out to explore how these processes and conditions are affectively mapped[11] within various contemporary media texts. Shaviro posits that we are witnessing the emergence of a novel media regime, 'and indeed of a different mode of production, than those which dominated the twentieth century' (2010: 2). He argues that the proliferation of digital technologies and 'neo-liberal economic relations' has given rise to new ways of manufacturing media and articulating lived experiences. Indeed, these new modes of expression are, Shaviro (2010) argues, required, as transformations within societies, cultures and economies mean they cannot be understood entirely under previously well-established, hermeneutic theories.[12] These new modes of media expression similarly then cannot be understood through traditional methods without limitations. Thus, new regimes of thought must be utilized.

Texts under this novel media regime provide 'indices of complex social processes, which they transduce, condense, and rearticulate in the form of what can be called, after Deleuze and Guattari, "blocs of affect"' (2010). In other words, media texts, under this alternative regime, produce affective renderings, or as Shaviro (2010) terms them, affective maps, of complex societal, economic and political conditions, transformations and flows. These aspects of modern society, too difficult to be represented and understood solely through molar regimes (like the hermeneutic), can be, instead, apprehended upon the body and understood at this level.[13]

These texts also affectively map our subjective positionings (or lack of) and transformations within these complex processes. We, as Shaviro argues, perhaps become more flexible, mutable beings, able to transform ourselves, 'to take any shape as needed, [with] a capacity to adapt quickly and smoothly to the demands of any form or any procedure' (2010: 14) and any fluctuating environment. Many scholars of globalization and transnationality agree with Shaviro (2010) in this regard. For instance, Appadurai argues that 'in the context of flexibility demanded by contemporary global capitalism, there has been a great deal of compression of time and space, and the body comes to be seen as a chaotic, hyperflexible site, ridden with contradictions and warfare' (1996: 85). This flexibility and mutability of subjectivity means that, as Appadurai (1996) suggests, once again, hermeneutic conceptualizations of identity and societal positions become largely insufficient. Thus, a new mode of thought, the affective, must be utilized to produce developed understandings.

Shaviro (2010) suggests that these affective media products do not just render such fluid subjectivities, however, they might even help produce them. As he states, these texts may 'help and train us [the audience or consumers of these media] to endure – and perhaps also to negotiate – the unthinkable complexity of cyberspace, or the unrepresentable immensity and intensity of the world space of multinational capital' (2010: 138).

Illustrating this in his discussion of the film *Boarding Gate* (2007), Shaviro suggests how the character of Sandra (Asia Argento), creating interconnections with the audience, may constitute an inspirational model for navigating contemporary, 'unrepresentable' globalized spaces. Sandra flits between several cities, from Paris to Hong Kong, as she tries to escape her violent, crime-ridden past. Such environments of 'transnational capital', argues Shaviro (2010), force Sandra to become flexible, versatile and resourceful, transforming her subjectivity perpetually. Sandra is also an affective character who 'registers in her body all the transactions and exchanges ... that flow through her and define the space around her' (2010: 59) as she cannot navigate her environments or understand them through linear, hermeneutic paradigms. In 'the non-places of transnational capital, our sensory-motor schemata jam, or break' (Deleuze, 2013, cited in Shaviro, 2010: 59), thus Sandra cannot develop coherent understandings of her surroundings which can lead to decisive, meaningful action (this jamming or breaking of the sensory-motor schemata is discussed in more detail in the following chapter). Sandra then expresses these affects to the viewing audience through her postures, movements and expressions. This 'mode of precarious, intermittent, [affective] and "just-in-time" subjectivity', Shaviro argues, 'however damaged and limited it may be, is the only one possible in our world of ceaseless modulations of control, and delirious financial and libidinal flows' (2010: 60). Rendered on screen, it therefore constitutes a useful model for audiences to emulate so that they too can navigate contemporary, globalized environments more successfully. Characters within the films studied in this book may similarly relay a bodily understanding to us about our position within this global world system. They may also, as is discussed in relation to Kayako of *Ju-On: The Grudge* especially, be inspirational models for the navigation of these complex, fluctuating systems. However, this book takes issue with Shaviro's (2010) suggestion that this 'intermittent', 'just-in-time' way of being is the only mode of subjectivity possible within contemporary, globalized societies. This ties to a wider concern this book has with the polemic Shaviro (2010) creates.

The polemic Shaviro (2010) establishes in his work is one which prioritizes an analysis of the molecular, deterritorializing elements of film and other media texts. As such, it exaggerates the extent to which media free themselves from molar ideas. Shaviro (2010) removes considerations of molar facets that still potentially inform contemporary experiences of society, forces of globalization and the transformations they undergo. At times we still experience our spaces, our ways of being, as territorialized, filled with molar meanings, at others we experience them as fluid where such linear understandings of them are difficult to pin down. One could argue, as Shaviro (2010) and others do, that 'appropriation, loss, deterritorialization, and cultural ambivalence are coming to be seen as more or less permanent conditions and not simply as transitional states' (Ezra and Rowden, 2006: 109), qualifying his molecular mode of thought. However, this is to underestimate the force of grounded, molar understandings and senses of being in and amongst these deterritorializing forces. Unlike Shaviro (2010) then, this book discusses in detail how Japanese horror films render the nuances, tensions and transformations that such molecular, deterritorializing forces create when they encounter molarities, such as concepts of nation, which persist in modern societies.

The utility of Shaviro's (2010) polemic, not only for this book, but for wider scholarship on globalization and national, transnational or world cinema, should not be understated, however. Its skilful adaptation of Deleuzian perspectives poses a particularly exciting prospect for opening up scholarship in these areas to reconceptualization and alternative ways of thinking. Indeed, scholarship, for instance, in the form of Iwabuchi (2015) and Cazdyn (In Miyao, 2014), who consider notions of embodiment and the experiential (for Cazdyn, as these manifest in the medium of film) as providing alternative ways to understand the make-up of contemporary societies and how these spaces are negotiated, have perhaps been inspired by Shaviro's (2010) work. David Martin-Jones' (2006, 2011) works (one of which predates Shaviro's (2010) seminal text) are also significant in how they generate new thought on national, transnational and world cinemas by mobilizing Deleuzian philosophy. His works, in particular, are utilized more in the next chapter. The existence of such work should not detract, however, from the fact that there are still too few studies in this field which appropriate Deleuzian perspectives.

It is not only approaches and ideas pertaining to national, transnational and world cinemas that can be developed through Deleuzian thought, however. Another area of scholarship which can be incrementally transformed is the field of horror cinema and the interlinking field of psychoanalysis.

Japanese horror cinema

As within other nations and societies across the globe, Japanese culture and arts have a long, well-established history of producing horror. Scholars have noted the presence of the horrific in traditional folktales, literature, religions (such as *Shintōism* and Buddhism) as well as in theatre (such as *Noh* and *Kabuki*), all of which have come to influence depictions of horror on-screen. Whilst scholars, such as Balmain (2008), Kinnia (2009) and McRoy (2005, 2008), discuss these influential cultural forms in order to uncover the truths of Japanese horror films (where their tales and artistry originate from and what meanings we can derive from them as part of such traditions), in fact, they unintentionally reveal that there is no coherent, singular truth to them that can be established. They reveal that Japanese horror films are potentially impacted by multiple, different societal ecologies and media forms.

One of the most common links that scholars make between Japanese culture and horror genre codes and conventions is how the unique conceptualization and aesthetic of the ghost is derived from Japanese religions, especially *Shintō*. *Shintōism* is thought to contribute to a supposed profound belief in the existence of ghosts amongst the Japanese population, leading to images of more substantial, impactful spirits within culture. This more profound belief stems from *Shintōism*'s conceptualization that *Kami* (spirits) inhabit and shape our own world. *Kami* can be elements of the landscape (living and non-living), such as mountains or waterfalls, and also forces of nature, such as earthquakes or storms, who can influence the course of humanity. *Kami* can also be evil and can exact punishments upon humans for not carrying out their duties, such as performing purification rituals to protect themselves and the *Kami* around them (BBC, 2009). It can be argued that the *Onryō*[14] that are depicted within Japanese horror films such as *Ju-On: The Grudge*, *Ringu*, *Apartment 1303* (2007) and *Chakushin Ari* (*One Missed Call*) are emblematic of this idea. Becoming evil *Kami* following their deaths, they punish those who encounter them, have had some part in their deaths, have failed to give them the appropriate burial rights or who neglect to remember them in the correct manner after their deaths.

In conjunction with this, the influence of *Noh* theatre on the conceptualization of the ghost within Japanese cinema is also often cited. Richard Hand (in McRoy, 2005: 20), for instance, argues that the *Shura-mono* (ghost), *Shunen-mono* (revenge) and *Kyōjo-mono* (mad woman) repertoire of plays, especially, have inspired Japanese horror films. The numerous tales of women betrayed by the men they love,[15] who are consumed by resentment and transform into monstrous demons, serpents or spirits to exact revenge[16] can be said to have inspired numerous ghost films throughout Japanese cinematic history, including within the Japanese horror boom years (in the late 1990s and early 2000s).

In relation to *Kabuki* theatre, once again many of its narrative and thematic elements have been said to have impacted Japanese horror cinema specifically. Early Japanese cinema generally, however, has been understood to have been influenced prolifically by *Kabuki* theatre. As McDonald argues, three definitive elements were derived from theatre in early cinema, 'its use of *onnagata* (female impersonators), [as only men were permitted to perform in *Kabuki* plays], *benshi* (commentators), [who narrated the scenes], and centre-front long shots following strict continuity [and mimicking the viewpoint of an audience of theatre-goers]' (2006: 2). In terms of *Kabuki*'s influence upon Japanese horror cinema, the *aragoto* or 'rough business' repertoire of plays (Hand, in McRoy, 2005: 20), which often included supernatural themes, has been discussed. Many such *Kabuki* plays, particularly in the early days of Japanese cinema, were even adapted straight to screen, highlighting the irrefutability of this form's influence. For instance, the supernatural play *Yotsuya Kaidan*, first performed in 1825, has provided the template for over thirty screen adaptations (Balmain, 2008: 54). The play, which tells the tale of Oiwa, a woman killed by her husband, who returns as a spirit to haunt and punish him, was most famously adapted to screen by Nakagawa Nobuo in *Tōkaidō Yotsuya Kaidan* (*The Ghost Story of Yotsuya*) in 1959. However, *Ju-On: The Grudge*, for instance, could be considered as a modern-day *Yotsuya Kaidan* tale, bringing the fundamental theme of the wronged-woman, murdered by her husband, out of its feudal era setting and into the twenty-first century.

Interestingly, *Kabuki* theatre has also been upheld by scholars of Japanese horror cinema as a source for some of the more brutal, gory elements of the genre. As Hand (in McRoy, 2005: 21) discusses, characteristic sequences in the more brutal *Kabuki* plays include scenes of torture, as well as *korishiba* (violent/murder scenes), self-mutilation, *seppuku* (suicide) and *tachiwara* (elaborate fight sequences). These aspects of the form establish a distinct quality in Kabuki that is known as *zankoku no bi* (aesthetics of cruelty). Japanese horror films such as *Battle Royale*, with its frequent depictions of creative, yet callous, murders of high-school students, *Audition* with its scenes of torture and dismemberment, and *Jisatsu Saakuru* (*Suicide Club*) (2001), with its disturbing and gory presentations of mass suicide, amongst many others, can be placed within this tradition of depictions of cruelty and brutal violence within Japanese arts.

This notion of the linear development of Japanese horror cinema, stemming from theatre traditions, is, however, too simplistic as the genre is much more nuanced and complex than this, crossed by many different influences and creative forces. Contributing to the creative diversification of Japanese cinema more generally and horror cinema specifically, by the 1920s there was a 'call for more realistic acting styles, modern narratives and an increasing focus on cinema as an art form in its own right, separate from the theatre' (Taylor-Jones, 2013: 11–12). Thus, Japanese theatrical arts should not always be considered as a primary influence upon contemporary Japanese horror cinema, as, since the 1920s, the medium attained the freedom to creatively diverge down myriad paths.

Further highlighting the nuances of the Japanese horror genre, various scholars have also explored the influence of Western, especially American, horror traditions (in both literature and cinema). As Iwabuchi states, 'East Asian media cultures have long dexterously hybridized in local elements while absorbing American cultural influences' (2015: 105). Working upon this principle, scholars have attempted to decode how Japanese horror films have hybridized native generic elements with American genre codes and conventions especially. It has been suggested, for instance, that the slasher/stalker cycle which dominated the American horror genre in the

1970s and 1980s, which includes films like *Halloween* (1978), *Friday the 13th* (1980) and *A Nightmare on Elm Street* (1984) within its repertoire, most notably influenced Shimizu Takashi and his conceptualizations of cinematic horror (McRoy, 2008: 92–3) within *Marebito* (2004), *Ju-On: The Grudge* and *Tomie: Re-birth* (2001). Furthermore, scholars have noted that America's suggestive, restrained horror film cycle of the late 1990s and early 2000s, contemporaneous with the horror film boom in Japan has also been particularly impactful. It has been argued, by scholars like Martin (2009), that films such as *The Blair Witch Project* (1999) have influenced Japanese horror films like *Ringu* and *Ju-On: The Grudge*. In these films, fleeting shadows or glimpses of the spirits leave much of the terror to the audience's imagination rather than an outright revealing of the image of the ghost. Richards (2010) also argues in his book that the prominence of this cycle in America and other parts of the West perhaps led to a positive reception of Japanese horror films at this time amongst audiences and critics.[17]

Gothic horror, originating in eighteenth- and nineteenth-century English literature, has also often been linked to Japanese horror within scholarship. Scholars, such as Balmain (2008), Chiho Nakagawa (in Och and Strayer, 2014), Andrew Hock-Soon Ng (2008) and McRoy (2005, 2008), cite the aesthetic and thematic influences Western gothic cinema has had upon Japanese horror and (in the case of Ng (2008) especially) in wider Asia. For instance, the depictions of dark, foreboding, haunted houses within British films such as *The Innocents* (1961) and *The Haunting* (1963) and the American film *House on Haunted Hill* (1959), which entrap or curse those who enter them, have arguably aesthetically and thematically influenced the Japanese horror genre. Films discussed in this way have included *Ju-On: The Grudge*, with its accursed family home in Tokyo, *Sweet Home* (1989) where a film crew, visiting the former home of an artist, fall foul to a malevolent spirit tormented by the loss of their child, and *House* (1977), which tells the tale of seven schoolgirls, attending to one of their number's sick aunt at her home, who, one by one are devoured by the eponymous house.

Perhaps more influential upon the gothic constructs within Japanese horror cinema, however, are the early Japanese gothic works of literature which, in part inspired by the likes of Edgar Allan Poe and Sir Arthur Conan Doyle, began to emerge around the same time as these prolific Western writers. Interestingly, Ueda Akinari's *Ugetsu Monogatari* (*Tales of Moonlight and Rain*) was the first definitive gothic work to be produced within Japan in 1776. This text, in particular, has inspired many gothic works of cinema and it has also been adapted more wholeheartedly, most notably within Mizoguchi Kenji's film, *Ugetsu Monogatari* (*Tales of Moonlight and Rain*) (1953). Gothic works of literature by authors such as Izumi Kyoka and Akutagawa Ryunosuke, like Western gothic tales, 'share ... [their] subversion of religious and social norms, an obsession with sex and death, and a fear of the supernatural or unknown' (Hughes, 2000: 60). However, rather than drawing upon Christian themes, these Japanese gothic tales often subverted the norms of *Shintōism*, Buddhism and Confucianism.

As each of these accounts of the codes and conventions of the Japanese horror genre highlight, the form develops over time in relation to changing contexts and audience needs. Linking closely to conceptualizations of nation then, genre too is a site of perpetual conflict, development and reconfiguration. The complexity and nuance of Japanese horror films today attest to the form's longevity within culture. The horror genre's continuity may be, as notably theorized by psychoanalyst Julia Kristeva (1982), attributable to a compulsion, belonging to all societies, to therapeutically reject the abject things that pervade them at any given time and due to the decline of religions that previously fulfilled this function. As she notes:

> The various means of purifying the abject – the various catharses – make up the history of religions, and end up with that catharsis par excellence called art, both on the far and near side of religion. Seen from that standpoint, the artistic experience, which is rooted in the abject it utters and by the same token purifies, appears as the essential component of religiosity. That is perhaps why it is destined to survive the collapse of the historical forms of religions.
>
> (1982: 17)

The abject is a term that refers to things (objects or other subjects) which invoke a sense of horror within the subject as they threaten a breakdown in meaning through the loss of distinction between the subject and what is defined as other. This idea that the abject invokes disgust and fear amongst subjects ensures that it is perhaps most appropriately rendered within the horror genre. Kristeva (1982) notes that sewage, the open wound and the corpse are all examples of the abject, things that are rejected by the subject as they work against life and are part of the discourses of death, rot and decay.

Furthermore, following Freud, the founder of psychoanalytical thought, and his theory of the Oedipus complex, Kristeva (1982) notes how the woman and allusions to her sexuality (in images of the vagina, for example) are also abject. They invoke a fear of castration amongst male subjects and the dismantling of patriarchal power. As Creed also argues, 'probably no male human being is spared the fright of castration at the sight of the female genital' (1993: 1). This stems from how the desire for the mother within the Oedipus complex is threatening as the male child fears that the father will punish him for his desire by castrating him. For Lacan, however, contrasting to Freud, the threat of castration is one which comes from the mother herself as, in an act of penis envy, 'it is her wish to castrate the man' (1993: 121). The penis, within patriarchal societies, marking human wholeness, is what grants the male access to the symbolic order. This enables him to be a maker of meaning and law (the law of the father) within the patriarchal social order (dictating the ideal behaviours, functions, roles and domains of people within society), rather than, like the female, a bearer of meaning. Nevertheless, in both interpretations, the abject female must be expelled for the patriarchal order and meaning to continue.

The mirror phase, as theorized by Lacan, explains the genesis and functions of the subjective ego and, following on from this, the Oedipus complex. Lacan conceptualized the mirror phase as a point in an infant's (specifically a male infant's) life when 'an external image of the body (reflected in a mirror or represented to the infant through the mother or the primary caregiver) produces a psychic response that gives rise to the mental representation of an "I"' (Zuern, 1998). In other words, the mirror phase is the point at which the child begins to form a static subjectivity, ego and sense of self which must be perpetually maintained and strived toward throughout their life. Psychoanalysis holds that the maintenance of the subjective self and its boundaries is dependent upon formulating external objects or subjects as 'other' and rejecting them.

Kristeva (1982) highlights that in the womb, the child is indistinguishable from the mother, where bodily fluids are shared, and there perhaps remains a deep, unconscious memory of this union in everyone. This connection with the mother becomes abhorrent, however, when, in the mirror phase, a sense of subjectivity, the ego, is established. The reappearance of bodily substances such as blood, pus, vomit and faeces appears to tap into our unconscious memory of this union and threatens a breakdown of subject and, ultimately, a return to the womb. Thus, the mother and the primal, abject bodily functions and substances associated with her, must be rejected to maintain subjective boundaries. Yet, at the same time that the abject repels, it also attracts. As Creed states, there may be pleasure in breaking with taboo, returning us to 'that time when the mother-child relationship was marked by an untrammelled pleasure in "playing" with the body and its wastes' (1993: 74).

Emblematizing these conceptualizations of abject femininity, within horror cinema, is the monstrous-feminine motif. As theorized by Creed, the monstrous-female refuses to adopt the proper, submissive, domesticated, social and sexual definitions of the feminine role (1993: 132, 134) and she therefore fundamentally challenges the patriarchal order. The monstrous-feminine may manifest in several different ways, for instance, as an archaic mother (such as within *Psycho* (1960), *Carrie* (1976) and *The Birds* (1963)) who will not relinquish control of her child and allow them to take their place within the symbolic order (producing abject ideas about the union of mother and child). Or she may manifest as a femme-castratrice, a violent, subversive woman who brutalizes the man, literally castrating him (as in the case of Jennifer (Camille Keaton) in *I Spit on Your Grave* (1978)) or else penetrating his body with phallic symbols such as knives.

The monstrous-feminine motif, depicted within cinema, becomes part of the male's discourse of making meaning, of redefining the boundaries of subjectivity. It is not only though this motif, however, that patriarchal discourses are at work. Laura Mulvey, for instance, famously argued that all aspects of cinema, under a patriarchal order, come to be part of the male discourse of making meaning, playing on 'socially established interpretation[s] of sexual difference which controls images, erotic ways of looking and spectacle' (1975, in Braudy and Cohen, 2004: 837). Man, through the medium of film, 'can live out his phantasies and obsessions through linguistic command by imposing them on the silent image of woman' (Braudy and Cohen, 2004: 838), including his obsessions with the castration anxiety and, beyond this, his preoccupations with dominance. To create this objectifying gaze, cinema constructs a male protagonist on-screen with whom the camera and the (assumed) male audience identifies with and through whom the audience becomes stitched into the film narrative. This gaze upon the woman produces particularly voyeuristic pleasures amongst the audience, described by Mulvey (Braudy and Cohen, 2004) as scopophilia. In terms of the horror genre, the voyeuristic gaze may often extend into a sadistic-voyeuristic gaze, where the female is subjected to torture or punishment, and where the audience is perceived to take a perverse pleasure in this. These punishments are constructed as justified within many horror films as the women on-screen are perhaps monstrous-females and represent a threat to patriarchal structures and the dominance of men. They may take up and commit reprehensible roles and actions such as appropriating the active investigating gaze or by being sexually independent and promiscuous, 'putting her unsocialized body on display' (Creed, 1993: 42). They threaten to symbolically castrate men from the leading, active roles that have been previously designated to them, making men the submissive being.

This has often been considered, by scholars like Mulvey (1975, in Braudy and Cohen, 2004), to be reflective of how men, within Western societies especially, feel about the instigation of greater rights for women and changing gender roles. Commenting upon America and masculinity, Faludi (1999) argued that, following the Second World War, many men felt emasculated from society and were expected to play the role of a consumer rather than a 'breadwinner'. As she states: 'where we once lived in a society in which men in particular participated by being useful in public life, we now are surrounded by a culture that encourages people to play almost no functional public roles' (1999: 34–5). This emasculation from society, however, rather than being attributed to a growing consumer culture, has been blamed on the rise of feminism and greater women's rights. Demonizations of feminism and women who try to 'to wrest man's power from their grasp' (1999: 14) have pervaded cinema therefore.

Similar discourses of crises in masculinity may be found elsewhere, beyond America and the West, for instance, in Japan. Here, hegemonic constructions of masculine identity, embodied within the 'salaryman' (the modern-day samurai), have been undermined by such events as the economic crash of the 1990s (amongst others discussed later in this book) and by the proliferation of women in the workplace. Such events and perceived issues have led to a rise in depictions, within Japanese cinema, of demonized womanhood. For instance, one notable trope is that of the neglectful, career-focused mother, appearing in films such as *Greatful Dead* (2013) and *Ringu*. The sexuality of women and the power that they now hold as prolific consumers within Japanese society have also been depicted as perverse, abject and threatening within films such as *Audition, Destruction Babies* (2016) and *Kawaki (The World of Kanako)* (2014).

Such monstrous-females within horror films are often also informed by and analysed under the Freudian concept of the 'return of the repressed'. The term pertains to a person's primitive desires (such as sexual desires) which must be repressed and sent to the 'Id' or the unconscious in order for that person to function within every day, civilized society. If such desires were expressed freely, this would be disastrous, however, they do continually threaten to return to consciousness and disrupt the functioning of societal order. As illustrated by scholars like Creed (2005) and Wood (in Nichols, 1985), horror cinema can be perceived as continually rendering such repressions, bringing them to consciousness once more. The repressed elements rendered within horror cinema can be described, following Freud (1919), as uncanny or 'unheimlich', something unsettling and disturbing yet oddly familiar. It is not only unconscious desires, however, which make a return within the horror film. They may represent a multitude of things that a dominant societal order may wish to keep buried. This may include such things as past abuses of women at the hands of patriarchy. Within cinema then, 'return of the repressed scenarios', for instance, can involve women, abused, victimized and forgotten by patriarchal society, who return to the forefront of patriarchal consciousness for revenge, threatening the regime's linear functioning. Nevertheless, as Wood (in Nichols, 1985) notes, within Western horror cinema specifically, the monstrous, abject being is often defeated at the end of a film, returning to its repressed state and thus restoring the linear order.

Beyond the sexual, this discourse of rejection and expulsion of the other also has clear links with other forms of subject formation and demarcation. Within the formulation of national subjectivity, for instance, this process of rejecting what is other from oneself is key. It forms understandings of what demarcates 'us' from 'them' and instils reasons why 'our' national community, its ideologies, its structure, are superior to those of 'others'.[18]

Within products of the horror genre then, there are potentially multiple different ways in which depictions of the abject can be understood. To realize this more fully within scholarship, however, a fundamental change in the way representations of the abject are perceived must occur. Scholarship must move away from the idea that the abject is a static conceptualization within a film and only one, singular meaning or signification can be derived from it.

One way in which conceptualizations of the abject can become more fluid and incorporative of multiplicity is through Deleuzian and Guattarian thought. Indeed, as is discussed further in this section, some recent works in horror film scholarship have begun to utilize (both directly and indirectly) this taxonomy to achieve such reconsiderations of the abject. In *Anti-Oedipus* (2000), Deleuze and Guattari argue that subjectivity is fluid and disagree with the idea that one must align with the system of sexual difference which perpetuates clear demarcations between male and female. Deleuze and Guattari (2000) take issue with Freudian concepts of subject formation and ego-boundaries as they are constructed through the Oedipal complex. It follows then that Deleuze and Guattari would take issue with other, similar dichotomous systems, such as those that nations form counter to one another. This anti-Oedipal thinking opens up interpretations of gendered subjectivity to more becomings where subjectivity can fluctuate perpetually between different positionings. As Deleuze and Guattari state: 'we pass from one field to another by crossing thresholds: we never stop migrating, we become other individuals as well as other sexes, and departing becomes as easy as being born or dying' (2000: 85). Distinctions between male and female subjectivities (in fact, any such fixed positionality), for Deleuze and Guattari, become ill-defined, leaky and contradictory. As notions of what is abject are borne from binaristic conceptualizations of difference and distinction, they too can become fluid and mutable through an intervention of Deleuzian and Guattarian thought. There are multiple ways in which difference and thus abjection can be conceptualized and understood which are aligned with the ways in which subjectivity manifests and fluctuates on-screen.

It is important that these examples of psychoanalytical thought, in particular, are considered in conjunction with Deleuze and his collaborative works with Guattari as studies of Japanese horror cinema, to date, have been pervaded by conceptualizations of static (psycho-sexual) subjectivity and abjection. Balmain, for instance, conceptualizing abjection through a static Japanese national perspective, argues that 'Japan's experiences during World War Two and the allied occupation are a trauma which underlies many, if not all, horror films from the 1950s onwards' (2008: 7). Linnie Blake (2012) concurs with this line of thinking, arguing that the atomic bomb attacks upon Hiroshima on the 6th of August 1945 and then on Nagasaki three days later are wounds upon the Japanese national psyche, which can only be partially healed through re-opening them within Japanese horror cinema through direct or allegorical depictions of the *hibakusha*[19] and the *pika*.[20]

Some of the horror films analysed by such scholars, to demonstrate how the traumatic events of the Second World War are allegorized on-screen, include *Gojira* (*Godzilla*) (1954), which represents the widespread destruction and death the atomic bombs wrought. Also, *Ringu*'s main character, the malevolent spirit Sadako, is an evocation of Sadako Sasaki, a child who suffered and eventually died from radiation poisoning because of the bombing of Hiroshima (Deamer, 2014: 253). Sadako can be understood as an abject rendering of the horrors of war, the *hibakusha*, and all that was destroyed when the United States unleashed the atom bombs. Similarly, Kayako of *Ju-On: The Grudge*, with her blood-spattered skin, has been understood as an abject representation of the *hibakusha*'s suffering.

It is not only these significant events of the Second World War, however, that are rendered as abject within Japanese horror cinema. Many more contemporary traumas and issues within Japanese society have also been understood within scholarship to have become allegorized on-screen. Ko (2004), for instance, discusses how issues with increases in immigration to Japan have been allegorized within the films of director Miike Takashi. She argues that the depictions of breakdowns in bodily boundaries and fragmentation that pervade Miike's work, for example, depictions of severed human heads, arms and feet, allegorize the break-up of the national body or *Kokutai* of Japan. They allegorize the disintegration of the 'notion of an apparent natural or given, self-evident unity' (2004: 36) based upon racial homogeneity.

Also, within McRoy's (2005) edited volume, Eric White argues that the films *Ringu* and *Ringu 2* (1999), through their premise of a malevolent spirit spreading its curse via a video tape, address issues with the growing technologization of Japanese society. He argues these films depict 'a social milieu in which the family matrix no longer provides the exclusive basis for psychological structure' (in McRoy, 2005: 44–5), a particularly worrying development in relation to Japanese youths who are perceived to be becoming increasingly withdrawn and lonely individuals.

These contemporary issues related to multiculturalism, societal and cultural hybridization with other nations, and technologization, that are decoded from Japanese horror films, can actually be understood as interconnected. Each of these anxieties, amongst a multitude of others, are fragments within the experience of the acceleration in the processes of globalization as a whole. Whilst the connections between globalization, multiculturalism and a seeming disintegration of national identity are quite obvious, the technologization of society is also entwined with the processes of globalization. Without the proliferation of digital technologies (particularly the internet), greater, more proximate connections between different nations, territories and their economies would not have occurred. They are vital mediums through which global flows of currency, media and ideas can occur.

Transforming and complexifying such linear, allegorical understandings of Japanese horror cinema and horror films more generally, distinct

Deleuzian leanings and even direct engagements with the taxonomy have recently emerged within research. These works therefore offer the prospect of some interesting developments for thought in this field, aligning with some of the ideas discussed in this book.

Most notably, Anna Powell (2005) has explicitly explored Deleuzian thought in relation to horror cinema. She addresses the prominence of psychoanalytical thought within studies of horror cinema and argues that it could usefully be transformed and extended through the Deleuzian taxonomy. Such a transformation of psychoanalytical thought is particularly important with regards to the study of horror cinema as this, Powell argues, is an affective genre where its codes and conventions are designed 'to arouse visceral sensations and to horrify the viewer' (2005: 2). The taxonomy of Deleuze can offer studies of horror cinema a way to explore the intense bodily reactions that this genre provokes, something which hermeneutic perspectives like psychoanalysis cannot adequately account for. Within her text, Powell (2005) creates interesting accounts of the affective ranges of a variety of horror films which demonstrate the usefulness of Deleuzian approaches to understanding affect, bodies and assemblages.

Powell (2005) furthermore aligns with the perspectives of Deleuze and Guattari in *Anti-Oedipus* (2000) arguing that characters within horror films, particularly the monstrous-feminine, and audiences watching them, do not have to submit to such systems as that of sexual difference and actually fluctuate between many different formulations of identity and ways of being. This idea has the potential to unground and transform the notion of the monstrous-feminine. If such a character's identity is fluid and transformative then it cannot be defined solely as feminine. Thus, the idea that femininity is abject and other is also deterritorialized here as the many different facets of subjectivity that the monster comes to embody can be understood as such, not just femininity.

There are a few other studies, focusing upon Japanese film texts specifically, which similarly conceptualize people's bodies as polynomial or sites of multiple invocations, representations and meanings. These include Taylor-Jones's chapter in Hipkins and Plain's (2007) work, which conceptualizes the body of the female in post-war Japanese cinema as more fluid and mutable, the 'site of a variety of conflicting discourses such as war, economics ... familial values and Japanese cultural history' (2007: 138). Also, Coates's work, discusses the actresses Hara Setsuko and Tanaka Kinuyo, arguing that they had particularly transformative personas, 'able to breakdown and reconstruct ... [themselves] anew' (2016: 34). This is particularly evident if comparisons are made between their performances in filmic works and their personas as depicted in wider media discourses, from the pre-war period, post-war period and during the war itself.

Coates's (2016) work also has some further, Deleuzian inspired insights into the cathartic role of cinema for audiences which may be key to reconceptualizing the functions of horror cinema specifically. Coates (2016) examines a particular peak in film production and cinema attendance in Japanese history, occurring after the Second World War ended. She attributes this peak to an ability of cinema to allow the viewer to reject the abject, or 'process change and resituate their relation to formative concepts such as nation and self' (2016: 2). As part of its processes of narrating and rendering transformation, Coates (2016) argues that within cinema at the time there was a high incidence of repetition of certain imageries, narratives and characterizations, particularly in relation to female representations. Interestingly, within the filmic discourses of Japanese horror cinema from the late 1990s and early 2000s, we see, once again, high incidences of repetitions of certain characterizations, narratives and imagery related to the female. During the post-war period, through repetition, anxieties over 'individual subjectivity, guilt, and war responsibility' could be negotiated at the site of cinema alongside issues related to 'radically reimagined social and gender roles' (2016: 2). Within the contexts of the late 1990s, early 2000s then (as is explored in this book), we perhaps see the repetition of certain imageries and representations which can help negotiate certain anxieties and issues.

Central to such negotiations, Coates (2016) purports, is cinema's affective, intense nature. Utilizing Deleuze's text, *Difference and Repetition* (1968), Coates (2016) argues that repeated images, themes and characterizations are affectively potent. As she states: 'imagined relationships with an actor or character increase in intensity when the actor or character appears frequently, while repetitive narratives and imagery invite both the comforting affect of recognition and the heightened emotional responses created by premonition as to how an on-screen situation will play out' (2016: 3). These affect-laden repetitions, in the post-war period, encouraged viewers to return time and time again to the cinema to negotiate and work through the transformations their societies and positionalities had undergone. The image of the female, then became a particular 'affective tool' or 'a site of affective-performative experience' (Rio, 2008, cited in Coates, 2016: 8), within this discourse.

Another particular site for the concentration of affect, which may well, in some cases, be synonymous with the representation of the female, is the depiction of the abject. Drawing on Kristeva (1982) and her conceptualizations of the abject, Coates argues that 'to be abject ... is ... to be neither subject nor object, but to be pre- or post-subjecthood, as in the state of the infant or corpse' (2016: 163). The abject is indeterminate and liminal, always on the verge of becoming a whole, subjective, meaning-laden body. It can therefore only be understood upon the body, as affective. It inhabits the space between, as Coates (2016) states, object and subject, just as affect lies in the space between perception and action. The abject therefore is open to multiplicities of being and meaning through its indeterminate status and can fluctuate between different potentialities. For audiences, these abject bodies offer ways to reimagine or reconfigure subjectivity, a particularly important utility in times of trauma and transformation such as the post-war period in Japan and even recently. In fact, as Coates states, 'the idea that Japan must fail, fall, or sink into the abject in order to emerge with a new subjectivity grew in popularity' (2016: 172) during the post-war period.

Coates's (2016) allusions to the fluidity and mutability of subjectivity and meaning, however, point to an issue with her study. She does not discuss in-depth how female characters, actresses and abject bodies have the potential, through their affective, transformative natures, to subvert, falsify and go beyond traditional, hermeneutic understandings. She instead conceptualizes their affectiveness as primarily contributing to the reterritorialization of molar ideas. Overall, there is a lack of distinction between affect and hermeneutic registers within Coates's (2016) work. She conceptualizes a discourse where affective intensities within or outside film space contribute to the realization of and enhance the hermeneutic meanings derived from the texts. Following this line of thought, Coates (2016) argues that repetitive images, characterizations and themes, related to Japan's post-war situation, render affective responses from audiences productive. Affects provide audiences with an energy source or vitality to negotiate the issues represented on-screen into linear, molar understandings. This is certainly a potential outcome within the formulation of assemblages between audiences and such repetitive, affective filmic texts, but it constitutes just one amongst many other potentialities. If the texts considered in this study are so affectively intense, their indeterminacy as a result of this (as affect cannot be understood in language) could lead to a falsification of the hermeneutic tropes, ideologies and representations that Coates (2016) argues they are encoded with. The films, their characters, stars, themes, representations and so on, in their indeterminacy, could be opened up to a myriad of potential meanings and apprehensions at the site of the audience. By neglecting such considerations of the molecular, Coates's (2016) text appears antithetical to the work of Shaviro (2010) which has the opposite issue of disregarding molar regimes which can still inform the reception of affective works of cinema. A balance between considerations of the molar and the molecular, the hermeneutic and the un-representable, is therefore sought in this book.

David Deamer's work, *Deleuze, Japanese Cinema and the Atom Bomb: The Spectre of Impossibility* (2014), the first text dedicated to formulating a direct encounter between Japanese film and Deleuzian frameworks, perhaps comes closest to forming such a balanced, nuanced consideration. Deamer's (2014) book explores Japanese atom bomb cinema, consisting of films from various genres, including documentary and horror, which in various ways address and deal with the atomic events of 1945. Deamer (2014) constitutes this event as a particular breaking point where national, social, cultural, political and economic linearity ceased in Japan and it became suspended and unable to progress. As is discussed in more depth through the course of this book, such events as the Japanese economic crash of the 1990s could similarly be perceived as breaking points, where linear ways of conceptualizing society and people's positionings within them, alone, become insufficient. These types of events, as Deamer (2014) supports (alluding to Shaviro (2010)), lead to the formation of a wide range of interesting, unique films which express them in different ways and tap into both the sensory and cognitive registers of the audience. Thus, such films are composed along both molar and molecular lines and can be understood affectively and fluidly through Deleuzian thought, as well as hermeneutically. Deamer makes the case for scholarly nuance, highlighting that whilst the Deleuzian taxonomy is 'meant to create new terms for talking about new ways of seeing' (Bogue, n.d, cited in Deamer, 2014: 3), it should not preclude 'a rigorous unfolding of the semiotic logic, an enumeration of the signs' (2014: 3). In other words, the molecular thought of Deleuze should not lead to an eradication of molar thought within scholarship. This, as is discussed in the following chapter, is something which Deleuze himself also purported.

2

Theoretical transformations: The perspectives of Gilles Deleuze

To develop thought on Japanese horror cinema and incrementally transform some of the hermeneutic theories most often utilized in relation to it, this chapter mobilizes the perspectives of Gilles Deleuze as well as (in part) his collaborative works with Félix Guattari. What follows is, first of all, an outline of some of the main Deleuzian perspectives that inform the transformations of concepts that take place. Beyond this outline, this chapter explores how Deleuzian thought can be applied to and mutate key concepts related to the horror genre, psychoanalysis, national, transnational and world cinema. Here the theoretical groundwork will be established and prepared for application in Part Two of this book.

As part of this exploration of the Deleuzian taxonomy, it is, however, also pertinent to investigate those scholars (beyond Guattari) who have influenced his work. This is so an understanding of how Deleuze's perspectives were formed can be established. Furthermore, it is important to explore scholars who have been influenced by Deleuze as they may have developed his concepts and extended them in unique and useful ways.

The Deleuzian taxonomy

Initially, it is perhaps useful to explore the nature of Deleuze's philosophies, particularly his perspectives on and attitudes towards cinema, which have been described as 'vitalistic', or emphasizing notions of bodily energies or intensities. Deleuze perceives cinema as experiential or as an event which impacts upon and comes to be embodied, mimetically, by the audience. As Marks usefully summarizes, our experience of cinema is perceived to be one of 'bodily similarity to the audio-visual images we take in'

(2000: XVII), we resonate with, respond to and reflect the affects, movements and fluctuations which we experience on screen. Deleuze understands the cinematic experience as an exchange event, however, between two bodies or machines (as he terms them), the human body and the cinematic apparatus. There is therefore a relationship of reversibility here where the film impacts upon the viewer's body and the viewer can also impact upon the film event.

Whilst it may seem that once the film ends the audience's mimetic engagement also ceases, in fact it continues and we can recognize its ongoing reverberations. Here an interconnection between the film and spaces, bodies and experiences beyond it, within our lived world, is created, transforming the way we receive and interact with them. By acknowledging the film's continuing reverberations beyond its boundaries and by reflecting upon it, we are then able to overlay different layers of thought and experience, manifesting from our experience of the film, onto real world events, and vice-versa. This creates dynamic, rhizomatic interconnections of thought and feeling.

These are fundamentally different perspectives from the theories outlined in the previous chapter which largely fail 'to provide an adequate understanding of how film matters, how it impacts, how it acts as a body in motion, in space and in time, with other material elements of our world' (Kennedy, 2000: 4). The concepts discussed in the previous chapter deal in actuality, that which has manifested as a whole or a complete object, including ideologies of signification, image and representation (molarities or a macro-politics), rather than hidden, always fluctuating and changing, forces within the body (molecularities or a micro-politics). A macro-political or molar exploration of cinema engages with film's visual elements and masters them through languages of signification and representation, as Deleuze and Guattari state, when 'one studies large molar aggregates', one studies 'large social machines – the economic, the political, etc. – and this entails searching for what they mean' (2000: 183) and how they are expressed. Micro-political or molecular perspectives, on the other hand, deal with more immediate, tactile, embodied ideas and intensities which, as they are fluctuating, transformative and multifaceted, cannot recede into cognition and be given a language. Within a micro-political analyses of a body (like cinema), 'one searches for the way in which these machines function ... One then reaches the regions of a productive, molecular, micro-logical, or microphysical unconscious that no longer means or represents anything' (2000).

The fluid, multifaceted and intensive nature of micro-political perspectives is encapsulated within Deleuze and Guattari's concept of the 'body without organs', which, as Powell usefully summarizes, is a body (human or otherwise) composed of 'a cluster of affective forces in process; an intensive anarchist body that consists solely of poles, zones, thresholds and gradients' (in Brown and Martin-Jones, 2012: 178). The body without organs is composed along molecular rather than molar lines, it 'resist[s] using words composed of articulated phonetic units, it utters only gasps and cries that are sheer unarticulated blocks of sound' (Deleuze and Guattari, 2000: 8). In other words, it is beyond a socio-linguistic fixing. This concept was proposed by Deleuze and Guattari to provide an escape from psychoanalytical conceptualizations of subjectivity and, as such, is 'the ultimate residuum of a deterritorialized socius' (Deleuze and Guattari, 2000: 33). They assert that:

> The full body without organs is produced as anti-production, that is to say, it intervenes within the process as such for the sole purpose of rejecting any attempt to impose on it any sort of triangulation implying it was produced by parents. How could this body have been produced by parents, when by its very nature it is such eloquent witness of its own self-production, of its own engendering of itself.
> (Deleuze and Guattari, 2000: 15)

The body without organs is also relational, forming interconnections or assemblages with other matter and bodies surrounding it, 'machines attach themselves to the body without organs as so many points of disjunction, between which an entire network of new syntheses is now woven' (Deleuze and Guattari, 2000: 12). By forming such assemblages, the body without organs can transform itself or become-other. It is not fixed within a static psychoanalytical conceptualization; it continually mutates and alters its positionings. Some cinema can be considered as a body without organs, consisting of these micro-political forces rather than molarities or macro-political forces. Other bodies, like the human body, can also be considered as such.

However, it would be very difficult to conceptualize any body as consisting solely of poles, zones, thresholds and gradients, including cinema, as each body also has nodes of underlying fixity or molarity which lead to the establishment of linear, cognitive understandings within language. All bodies exist in modulation, therefore, where, at times, they perhaps encapsulate more fully the body without organs and at others they may return to their grounded, static nodes, where their existence is more linear than fluid. Supporting this, Deleuze and Guattari argue that the body without organs can never fully escape from systems like psychoanalysis. It exists on the frontier between the molar and the molecular, 'the body without organs is the limit of the socius, its tangent of deterritorialization' (Deleuze and Guattari, 2000: 281). While it seeks alternative modes of being from the molar, the body without organs must maintain some connection with these regimes or risk obliteration or complete reterritorialization into these systems.

Bodies, Deleuze and Guattari argue, are composed of a series of lines and latitudes, the first being what is referred to as a line of segmentarity, which can be explained as a 'stratified, territorialized, organized, signified, attributed' (Deleuze and Guattari, 1987: 9) line, upon which macropolitical elements or molarities, such as those related to subjectivity and identity (e.g. gender, nationality, ethnicity, sexuality and class), exist. This line exists simultaneously with lines of flight, upon which molecular elements, affects, poles, thresholds, zones and the body without organs exist. Lines of flight create 'movement, deterritorialization and destratification' (Deleuze and Guattari, 1987: 3), leading the body to unground itself from molar organization, continually form divergent assemblages with other bodies, and metamorphoses. The body, existing in modulation, fluctuates between deterritorializations and reterritorialization of molar existence and experience. Sometimes it is grounded upon the line of segmentarity, and, at other times, it becomes free of this line and its regimes, existing more fluidly, forming new multiplicities of connection and transforming itself. As Deleuze and Guattari state: 'You may make a rupture, draw a line of flight, yet there is still a danger that you will reencounter organizations that restratify everything, formations that restore power to a signifier, attributions that reconstitute a subject – anything you like, from Oedipal resurgences to fascist concretions' (Deleuze and Guattari, 1987: 9).

Deleuze and Guattari (1987) usefully analogize these ideas of segmentarity, molarity, molecularity and flight by considering the structure of a tree and the rhizome. The tree structure adequately reflects the structures and natures of the regimes upon the line of segmentarity as it is a hierarchy, but also functions according to binary systems. Every new branch, in this binary system, can be essentially tied back to the root which makes all growth possible. As Deleuze and Guattari assert, 'binary logic is the spiritual reality of the root-tree. Even a discipline as "advanced" as linguistics retains the root-tree' (Deleuze and Guattari, 1987: 5). The tree is the model upon which linear, hermeneutic thought (including, for instance, psychoanalytical thought) is based as they chart linear chains of causality (how the root extends into new branches), work with dualistic categories and binary choices, and search for the source of things (the root) or their conclusion.

Conversely the rhizome, whilst also originating in botany, contends these hierarchical, centralizing structures and instead favours a nomadic system of growth which reflects the forces existing upon the line of flight. The rhizome allows for multiplicity rather than binaries (the branches do not tie back to any single root), there is no clear unity between different nodes of the rhizome, no pivotal positioning. It also allows for non-hierarchical interconnections between any number of distinct or even disparate, elements (including human and non-human bodies and bodies of thought). 'Any point of a rhizome can be connected to anything other, and must be', furthermore, 'not every trait in a rhizome is necessarily linked to a linguistic feature: semiotic chains of every nature are connected to very diverse modes of coding (biological, political, economic, etc.) that bring into play not only different regimes of signs but also states of things of differing status' (Deleuze and

Guattari, 1987: 7). Unlike the tree, whose branches have all grown vertically from a single trunk and which all inevitably end, the rhizome has no distinct source from which all development occurs, and no conclusion. The rhizome is heterogeneous, and it is always in the middle, in a state of becoming. Even if the rhizomatic structure were to be broken up, new multiplicities and new connections with other bodies would form from the fragments. As Deleuze and Guattari argue, 'a rhizome may be broken, shattered at a given spot, but it will start up again on one of its old lines, or on new lines (Deleuze and Guattari, 1987: 9).

The rhizome, whilst different to hierarchical, causal structures, can still incorporate bodies composed along these lines within itself, just as the tree structure may have some rhizomatic elements. As Deleuze and Guattari state: 'there are knots of arborescence in rhizomes, and rhizomatic offshoots in roots' (Deleuze and Guattari, 1987: 20) of the tree structure. Thus, these two organizations are not opposed to one another. The first, arborescent, or tree structure 'operates as a transcendent model and tracing, even if it engenders its own escapes; the second operates as an immanent process that overturns the model and outlines a map' (Deleuze and Guattari, 1987), and there can be both stratifying tracings and immanent, fluid mappings informing one body.

Static, hierarchical bodies form nodes or modules within the rhizome, from which, because of the rhizome's principle non-linear, ungrounding nature, strands, taking lines of flight or reaching out and connecting with other nodes, can potentially branch. Thus, when assimilated into the rhizomatic structure, arborescent models or molarities (such as subjectivities and hermeneutic models of thought) may not remain fixed, untransformed and distinct. Within a body then, such as cinema or the human body, if a rhizomatic structure, lines of flight and molecularity are particularly prominent at any given point, any arborescent structures, molarities or lines of segmentarity crossing the body will transform through these more dominant lines' fluid nature. They will become less rigid, more relational and open to multiplicities. The reverse, however, can also occur. If, within the body, the arborescent structure is principally informing its organization then any molecularities crossing the body at this time may become territorialized and understood through molar regimes.

Territorializations along lines of segmentarity or under molar regimes are considered by Deleuze and Guattari as blockages or resistances to molecular or nomadic flows. As they state, 'the prime function incumbent upon the socius has always been to codify the flows of desire, to inscribe them, to record them, to see to it that no flow exists that is not properly damned up, channelled, regulated' (Deleuze and Guattari, 2000: 33). Thus, they are limiting impediments to transformation or the becoming-other of the body and free, fluid thought. This understanding of molarities was founded upon Nietzsche's views that 'language and the judgements we form from language actually falsify life, whether by simplifying the complexity of living processes or by distorting and overlooking the unique character of our experiences' (Kennedy, 2000: 86), turning them into universal characteristics.

Nevertheless, Deleuze and Guattari consider that the outright rejection and eradication of arborescent models and molarities would be problematic. They argue that deterritorializing molarities within a rhizomatic structure can produce more innovative becomings or lines of flight. As they assert through their idea of 'the art of dosages', the fine file is needed rather than the sledgehammer when challenging such molar, overarching ideologies, as:

> You have to keep enough of the organism for it to reform each dawn; and you keep small supplies of significance and subjectification, if only to turn them against their own systems when circumstances demand it ... ; and you have to keep small rations of subjectivity in sufficient quantity to enable you to respond to the dominant reality. Mimic the strata. You don't reach the BwO [Body Without Organs] ... by wildly destratifying.
> (Deleuze and Guattari, 1987: 160)

Thus, if understandings of how all bodies are crossed by lines of segmentarity and sometimes grounded upon molarities were thrown aside in favour of comprehensions of how bodies are composed upon lines of molecularity and flight solely, the full transformative potential of this thought would be lost. To achieve this potential then, molar regimes and their hierarchical structures must be falsified rather than rejected.

A falsification of molar regimes occurs when their linear, binaristic cause and effect structures are opened to the multipotentialities of being and thought, or the 'out-of-field' (Deleuze, 2005: 17), that the rhizome allows for. Thus, highlighting that they are not the only, one-true structure or conceptualization possible. Deleuze defines the out-of-field as 'what is neither seen nor understood, but is nevertheless perfectly present' (Deleuze, 2005). Within a system or set, such as hermeneutic thought, there are elements of the set which are framed and therefore seen. However, there are also other elements beyond the frame, other ways of thinking for instance, that are not seen but are nevertheless connected to the seen elements, and to even wider sets, via threads. The realization of this sort of rhizomatic web of interconnected sets reveals the whole of duration (a different, multi-layered, non-chronological formulation of temporality discussed further in this chapter) and its multipotentialities of being and thought. It 'testifies to a more disturbing presence, one which cannot even be said to exist, but rather to "insist" or "subsist", a more radical elsewhere, outside homogeneous space and time' (Deleuze, 2005: 18).

Particularly when the thread between the framed and unseen elements is very thin, as within the closed system, like molar, hermeneutic thought, it is not content to reinforce the closure of the frame or to eliminate the relation with the outside ... but the finer it is – the further duration [and thus multipotentiality] descends into the system like a spider – the more effectively the out-of-field fulfils its ... function which is that of introducing the transspatial and the spiritual into the system which is never perfectly closed.

(Deleuze, 2005: 19)

That is to say, the out-of-field, the realization of its interconnections, is much more deterritorializing for perceivably closed, demarcated systems, falsifying their adherence to singular thoughts or ways of being and opening them to multiple, different potentialities for becoming-other.

Such interconnections between sets, systems, bodies and thoughts are termed assemblages within Deleuze and Guattari's work. Assemblages are 'complex constellations [or ecologies] of objects, bodies, expressions, qualities, and territories that come together for varying periods of time to ideally create new ways of functioning' (Livesey, in Parr, 2010: 18) or new becomings. Crucially, the concept of assemblage is distinct from 'the negative concept of interpellation, imbrication or suture, via which, according to screen theory, the spectator is passively stitched into the film's reactionary ideology' (Powell, 2005: 4). This entails an engagement which does not lead to the production of new becomings or ways of functioning.

When bodies, subjects, objects or knowledges meld together in an assemblage they can transform and mutate by drifting different intensities and attributes of themselves to each other. These transformative elements are what Deleuze would call 'noble' or 'good', they know how to transform themselves, to metamorphose, 'according to the forces ... [they] encounter ... which forms a constantly larger force with them, always increasing the power to live, always opening new "possibilities"' (Deleuze, 2013: 146). These stand in contrast to 'base' or 'bad' elements, however, which can no longer transform through the assemblage. Base objects, bodies, knowledges and so on, in the assemblage, are no less affective or powerful, but, instead of giving 'the creation of new possibilities in the outpouring of becoming', they attempt to 'dominate in the exhausted becoming of life' (Deleuze, 2013: 147), suffocating emergent potentialities.

One example of melding that Deleuze picks up on, producing noble, transformative elements, is when the human assemblage of mind, brain and body connects with the technology of cinema when we view a film. This creates a machinic assemblage of material movement, force and intensity (Powell, 2007: 210–11) and can open both bodies to a multiplicity of becomings, new thoughts and experiences. As Powell (2005: 65) argues, bodies desire their own extremity and transmutation (becoming) when in assemblages as they become agitated or overloaded with affect or intensity and need to utilize this energy and release it down different lines of flight.

Affects, as already discussed, are pre-cognitive sensations, ungraspable ranges, thresholds and gradients (the micro-politics that Deleuze and Guattari discuss). They are generated within situations freed from their spatio-temporal coordinates and flow through the body (both human and non-human), even drifting to other bodies that form a part of an assemblage. Affects, in recent years, have become more central to cinema and other media products and our understanding of them within theory. As Shaviro argues, corporations and filmmakers 'increasingly commodify and market pure virtualities in the form of events, experiences, moods, memories, hopes and desires' (2010: 45).[1] This is as much the case within Japan as it is within the West.

This affective sensibility has perhaps emerged because of accelerations in the processes of globalization and events like the economic crash of the 1990s, which have rendered many societal, economic, cultural and political processes, flows and transformations difficult to understand or conceptualize within language. Certainly, taking Japan as a specific contextual example, many of the effects of globalization and the economic crash are concrete, palpable and intimate, and are thus susceptible to representation (2010: 37). However, Japanese filmmakers and other media producers, through affect, attempt to make the many invisible forces and transformations which these events have brought about knowable through the body.

Complex social processes are transduced, condensed and rearticulated in film, in the form of 'blocs of affect' (2010: 38), creating an affective map which can be used to navigate and understand, albeit fragmentally, the conditions and transformations of Japanese society. Whilst affects are generated in situations which have been abstracted from spatio-temporal coordinates, they are 'none the less created in a history which produces it as the expressed and the expression of a space or a time, of an epoch or milieu' (Deleuze, 2005: 101). In this sense then, it is important to not lose sight of the specific Japanese contextual perspectives, the molarities, that also inform these renderings of current situations within film and media, that contribute to the generation of affect. In other words, these affective renderings are crossed by both molarities and molecularities, deterritorialized (non-specific) and territorialized (context specific) elements, and it is imperative to acknowledge this balance.

The most successful cinematic works at tapping into micro-political, affective levels and lines of molecularity and flight are the rhizomatic time-image films that Deleuze conceptualized. Within his books, *Cinema 1: The Movement-Image* (2005) and *Cinema 2: The Time-Image* (2013), Deleuze theorized two categories of image in cinema, the movement-image and the time-image, by developing on the work of Henri Bergson. Bergson developed a model of the universe which he theorized as variable, 'a world of universal undulation, universal rippling' (Deleuze, 2005: 61), which, furthermore, is temporally defined as an open, constantly changing and expanding whole, or what he refers to as a 'duration'. Duration is ineffable, a continuity which cannot be comprehended without dividing it, but one which 'cannot be divided without changing qualitatively at each stage of the division' (Bergson, 1954, cited in Deleuze, 2005: 10). Thus, each fragment or phase of duration is experienced uniquely by each of us as they pass. Within abstractions of duration, we experience the open whole indirectly, through images of movement within space (matter [such as the human body] in movement is constituted as an image) that can never fully reveal the open expanding whole of duration. As Deleuze states, 'movement relates the objects between which it is established to the changing whole which it expresses [as an abstraction], and vice versa' (Deleuze, 2005: 11).

Further to this, we have a habit of placing these abstractions of time in linear sequences, creating notions of temporal order, past, present and future. This chronological way of perceiving time has been conceptualized negatively, as a subtraction, insofar as 'there is never anything else or anything more than there is in the thing [the timeline]: on the contrary there is less. We perceive the thing, minus that which does not interest us as a function of our needs' (Deleuze, 2005: 63). Chronological time, like hermeneutic thought, is a closed system, which is nevertheless open to falsification in the face of other ways of conceptualizing time. As suggested, however, perceiving time in this way is essential to our own and society's functioning, for if we were to perceive time as a pure, open whole, we would become suspended, unable to act upon the world or progress. This is because the innumerable potentialities (of pasts, presents and futures) offered to us within the whole of duration would be too confusing and disabling. Thus, coherent, linear, abstracted models of time are needed to minimize difference and multiplicity and produce predictable expectations for the future. Habitual methods of dealing with and understanding a range of different life experiences are developed in-line with these linear, abstracted models of time so that we may act quickly and effectively within the world. This includes the development of hermeneutic bodies of thought, which simplify and act as a shorthand for understanding various facets of our societies and subjectivities, precluding other conceptualizations.

Deleuze perceived that movement-image cinema maps this abstracted, chronological time that Bergson theorized,[2] rendering also these linear ways of perceiving and acting within the world, and more firmly ingraining them within a society's habitus. Deleuze argues that language can 'get hold of' these abstracted sections of duration, 'giving rise to utterances which come to dominate or even replace the images and signs, and which refer in turn to pertinent features of the language system, syntagms and paradigms' (2013: 29), molar or macro-political regimes. Conceptualized as signifying wholes, these abstracted sections of duration present singular truths of time.

Movement, Deleuze argues, has two facets, 'on the one hand it modifies the respective positions of the parts of a set, which are like its sections, each one immobile in itself; on the other it is the mobile section of a whole whose change it expresses' (Deleuze, 2005: 20). Within a film, movement is attributed to shots (through the mobility of the camera itself and montage, or the connecting of shots in the editing process), subjects and objects (or the set) within the frame and this can be recomposed or related to the movement, the constant change and flux, of the whole of duration. Film constantly 'puts bodies, parts, aspects, dimensions, distances and the respective positions of the bodies which make up a set in the image into variation' and it is through this movement or variation 'that it also relates to a fundamentally open whole' (Deleuze, 2005: 24). As other film scholars have also elaborated, movement and progression of, for example, the main protagonist on-screen, is indicative of time within these images, creating an equivalence between character movement and the movement of the world the audience experiences (Martin-Jones, 2011: 46). Through this then, the movement-image is an abstraction of time, of the whole of duration, which it can never fully reveal, only partially or in fragments. The whole of duration is not equivalent to the movements of one character, 'it is we who are internal to time, not the other way around' (Deleuze, 2013: 86). Movement-images thus refute labyrinthine duration, positioning it as other and disparate, claiming there can be only one, true, chronological time.

Movement-image cinema, in particular, is exemplified by the large form action-image (a component of the movement-image), which Deleuze refers to as the SAS form (where 'S' stands for the initial situation, 'A' for action and 'S' for the new situation), that proceed 'from the general situation to the re-established or transformed situation through the intermediary of a duel, of a convergence of actions' (Deleuze, 2005: 32). The duel is essentially the conflict between two ideologically disparate entities that is central to linear narratives. These entities or 'parts' 'must necessarily act and react on each other in order to show how they simultaneously enter into conflict and threaten the unity of the organic set, and how they overcome the conflict or restore the unity' (Deleuze, 2005). The transformed situation, reached through the intermediary of the duel, Deleuze (2005) argues, can be an improvement upon the initial, constituting situation (expressed by Deleuze as the SAS' form), be the same as, or a re-establishment of the initial situation (SAS), or be a worse situation than before (SAS").

The action-image also has another form, the small form or ASA, which moves from an initial action, to the encompassing situation, and towards a new action. Action, within this form, discloses the milieu, or a fragment of it, which triggers a new action. 'From action to action, the situation gradually emerges, varies and finally either becomes clear or retains its mystery' (Deleuze, 2005: 164). Exploring how the small form works, Deleuze utilizes the English 1930s school of documentary film-making as an example (amongst others), which began from the premise that the actions and behaviours of individuals would reveal the nature and character of their situation and their culture.

Despite the refutation of labyrinthine time, as Deleuze highlights, within the movement-image, 'there will always be breaks and ruptures, which show clearly enough that the whole is not here' (Deleuze, 2005: 29). The out-of-field can be realized within the movement-image, falsifying the continuities they espouse and highlighting their subtractive nature. As Deleuze argues, a mental-image can be created, where 'action, and also perception and affection [the three components of the movement-image], are framed in a fabric of relations' (Deleuze, 2005: 205) with thought, and with audiences 'whose reactions must form an integrating part of the film' (Deleuze, 2005: 206). Hitchcock's cinematic texts, such as *The Birds* and *Dial M for Murder* (1954), in particular, demonstrate the mental-image at work. 'He makes relation [or thought] itself the object of an image, which is not merely added to the perception, action and affection images, but frames and transforms them' (Deleuze, 2005: 207), causing them to become unstable or deterritorialized. Within *Rear Window* (1954), for instance, it is images of the protagonist with a broken leg, alongside photographs in his room of a racing car, rather than action or dialogue that expresses the situation of the film. These images provoke the audience to think, bring thought into relationality within the film and question the possibilities of the images. It is not movement here that is the object, but thought, hence why it is a mental-image. These works, Deleuze (2005) argues, rather than bringing a completion of the action-image, heralded its crisis (leading into the time-image), as his inclusion of the viewer in the films he produced, through the mental-image, began to slacken sensory-motor connections and thus the linear progression from perception to action.

The perception-image, affection-image and the action-image make up the key components of the movement-image. A film is never made up solely of one of these images, but a combination or montage of them, however, one type of image is always dominant within a film. Hence why the action-image is both considered by Deleuze as a component of and a type of movement-image cinema.

In the perception-image, emblematic within the long-shot, the characters, the camera and the audience fluctuate between 'total, objective perception[3] which is indistinguishable from the thing [being perceived], to a subjective perception' (2005: 66), where we, the audience, or, for example, a character (a central and privileged image), subtracts from the thing only the facets of it which are of interest.[4]

In the action-image, of which the medium shot is characteristic, a reaction to what is perceived occurs, producing an end or a result. The universe is incurved and organized around the perceived, 'which simultaneously causes the virtual action of things on us and our possible action on things' (2005: 67).

In-between these two images lies the affection-image, of which the close-up of the face[5] is representative. This is an indeterminate stage, abstracted from spatio-temporal coordinates, where it is impossible to discern an encompassing milieu or a temporality within which these images can be placed. Here then, within the affection-image, many different potentialities of further perception, action or reaction are possible. This is where the whole of duration can be determined, in this interval, which therefore establishes the subsequent realization of a singular action or outcome within the movement-image as a subtraction. As Deleuze discusses, 'it is not sufficient to think that perception – thanks to distance – retains or reflects what interests us by letting pass what is indifferent to us' (2005), these excesses are expressed within the affection-image, marking the 'coincidence of the subject and object in a pure quality' (2005: 68), and opening us to multipotentiality, duration and the falsity of singular realizations.

The operation of the affection-image is very different to those of the perception and action-images, movement within the affection-image does not function to translate perception into action, but functions to express. It is therefore an interruption in the sensory-motor continuum. Albeit, this is often only a brief, perhaps even unnoticeable, interruption and opening onto duration within the movement-image which, instead, makes use of the affection-image to establish a relation between the perception-image and action-image. As Deleuze argues, affects can become 'forces' which are 'actualised in particular states of things, determinate space-times, geographical and historical milieu, collective agents or individual people. It is here that the action-image is born and developed' (2005: 100). Affect, within the movement-image and its progression, is likely to become a power or energy used to reach a realization of certain molar actions, outcomes and understandings. What would happen if this interval were prolonged, however, as it is within some of Hitchcock's works, through the mental-image (although action and re-establishment of an encompassing milieu is eventually realized through the characters within his films), and affects, qualities or powers were considered for themselves without reference to their actualization? As Deleuze states, 'affects would need to form singular ambiguous combinations which were always recreated ... and movement in its turn would need to go beyond the states of things, to trace lines of flight, just enough to open up in space a dimension of another order favourable to these compositions of affects' (2005: 104).

The 'favourable order' that Deleuze (2005) refers to here is duration and there is a specific type of cinema which can achieve an opening onto this dimension; the time-image. This is a very different formulation of cinema than the movement-image which emerged in light of the crisis of the action-image in the post-war period. People, nevertheless, continued to make movement-image cinema, particularly large and small form action-images, as 'the greatest commercial successes always take that route', however, 'the soul of cinema no longer does' (2005: 210).

Whereas the movement-image expresses a subjective abstraction of duration, the time-image expresses a direct image of the whole of time, a crystal-image, as it is perceived within the interval. The crystal-image captures how 'time has to split itself in two at each moment of present and past ... it has to split the present in two heterogeneous directions, one of which is launched towards the future, whilst the other falls into the past' (Deleuze, 2013: 84). There are therefore two types of time-image or crystal-image (a third, however, is explored shortly). One which presents myriad sheets or possibilities of the past which characters and audiences can slip into and between, and the other which presents peaks of the present, where a multitude of different potentialities of being and living within the present are given, which are plausible and possible in themselves but incompossible together (Deleuze, 2013: 106).

Within both types, however, time is out of joint, it is, as Deleuze states, 'off the hinges assigned to it by behaviour in the world, but also by movements of world' (2013: 41), which create abstractions of it and singular truths. The crystal-image creates a coalescence of the actual, the real, the virtual and the imaginary, and it thus presents 'a radical plurality of durations, coexisting cacophonously at different rhythms' (Lim, 2009: 13); a heterogeneity. Through the crystal of the time-image, the characters and the audience can explore the non-chronological whole of time, its multiple potentialities 'in which all possible pasts, presents and futures (including those that are physically impossible) ... coexist simultaneously' (Brown, in Brown and Martin-Jones, 2012: 101). These multipotentialities ensure that actions are not pre-given, thus breaking down established orders and allowing becoming-others, new realities or 'the bursting forth of life' (Deleuze, 2013: 95) to occur.

Molar orders are deterritorialized in the time-image, it is often a Deleuzian body without organs, the camera and the characters cannot perceive and act according to such linearities (deriving action from, and contributing to, an encompassing milieu) and nor can the audience understand the film and its action through the ideologies of these regimes. As Deleuze states, at the crisis of the action-image and emergence of the time-image, 'we hardly believe any longer that a global situation can give rise to an action which is capable of modifying it – no more than we believe that an action can force a situation to disclose itself, even partially' (2005: 211). It is the power of the false which replaces the formation or disclosure of milieus and singular truths within the time-image, 'because it poses the simultaneity of [diverse] incompossible presents, or the co-existence of not-necessarily true pasts' (Deleuze, 2013: 136). These all have the potential to be actualized as the singular encompassing situation but cannot achieve this indefinitely as they are falsified as the one true conceptualization through the emergence of and their intermingling with other potentialities. As Deleuze states, 'there is no more truth in one life than in the other; there is only becoming, and becoming is the power of the false of life, the will to power' (Deleuze, 2013: 146).

Whilst the two types of time-image identified lead to becoming, becoming in itself, Deleuze argues, also constitutes a third type of time-image within cinema, which expresses duration. Becoming is not simply an intermediary between events, between the before and after of a transformation of an event, it is a characteristic of the perpetual production of events which is without a clear end-point. Without a conclusion, the series of becomings is non-linear, each event, each mutation within a becoming, is simultaneously a start-point, mid-point and end-point. Furthermore, the before and the after are brought together in a becoming and it creates its own sense of a crystal-image. It embodies a disjunction, a forking between a past, in which forces have had some transformative impact, and a future, in which new forces are propelled forward and will form new mutations and events. Like the other two types of time-image then, becoming, 'shatter[s] the empirical continuation of time, the chronological succession' (Deleuze, 2013: 160).

All time-images render what Deleuze terms 'any-spaces-whatever' which are not spaces that are 'universal, in all times, in all places', but singular areas which have lost their 'homogeneity, that is the principle of ... [their] metric relations or the connection of ... [their] own parts, so that the linkages can be made in an infinite number of ways' (2005: 113). Any-spaces-whatever are detached spaces, freed from spatio-temporal coordinates and from molar groundings which may fill them and cause them to be territorialized, understandable spaces. Just as the face, in the close-up, according to Deleuze, is indeterminate, these spaces are too. As indeterminate, these spaces are pure loci of the possible, their parts and orientations are not determined in advance and they are thus multipotential and open onto duration. The any-space-whatever constitutes the second type of affection-image that can manifest within cinema. However, Deleuze argues that perhaps the any-space-whatever is more subtle than the close-up, 'more suitable for extracting the birth, the advance and the spread of affect' (2005). This is something which would need to be explored on a case by case basis, according to each film, as different films may place more emphasis on certain types of the affection-image.

There are, Deleuze argues, two types of any-space-whatever that manifest within the time-image: disconnected spaces and empty spaces. Highlighting the distinction between the two types, Deleuze (2013) discusses the film *Bakushū (Early Summer)* (1951) by Ozu Yasujirō. Emblematic of a disconnected any-space-whatever is a scene where 'the heroine goes forward on tiptoe to surprise someone in a restaurant, the camera drawing back in order to keep her in the centre of the frame; then the camera goes forward to a corridor, but this corridor is no longer in the restaurant, it is in the house of the heroine who has already returned home' (Deleuze, 2013: 16). In this scene, connections between the spaces and their individual parts are not established, nor are their molar orders, as part of a subjective point of view. They are disconnected from such understandings. As for empty spaces, Deleuze discusses the still images of this film, 'without characters or movement ... interiors emptied of their occupants, deserted exteriors, landscapes in nature' (Deleuze, 2013). Unlike the disconnected spaces, these empty spaces are devoid of all sensory-motor links as well as any molar, subjective groundings, they therefore produce different pure optical and sound situations, different affects, and, perhaps, even more direct relations with duration and thought.

As affection-images, the affects generated through the any-space-whatever, can be placed in intensive series. One way in which this is achieved is through the formation of assemblages between any-spaces-whatever, creating what Deleuze (2005) calls 'an amorphous set'. These are 'a collection of locations or positions which coexist independently of the temporal order which moves from one part to the other, independently of the connections and orientations which the vanished characters and situations gave to them' (2005: 123). Thus, an amorphous set can be conceived between the spaces of the restaurant and the home in *Bakushū* (*Early Summer*), as well as with the empty spaces it renders. Amorphous sets like this generate a spectrum of affective qualities in their interconnections, which they transmit to each other and to other bodies that become part of the assemblage. This includes the bodies of audiences and characters, who, in assemblage with any-spaces-whatever, become suspended in time, unable to turn perception into action and experience everything as affect or bodily intensity. They become, as is discussed in-depth shortly, 'seers'. As such, they can perceive the crystal of time, the whole of duration and the multipotentialities of becoming that it offers.

Amorphous sets can extend beyond the space of the film to incorporate, for instance, ungrounded, a-temporal environs depicted within other media or those of the real world. Deleuze argues that, particularly after the Second World War, there has been a proliferation of any-spaces-whatever, both in cinema and, exterior to it, in the real world. The war and its consequences, the unsteadiness of the 'American Dream', the new consciousness of minorities and the crisis of Hollywood and its classic genres, are all examples of contributory factors to the creation of any-spaces-whatever within and external to film that Deleuze cites. This post-war period can be described as a break where conceptions of time altered and where the time-image superseded the movement-image, as:

'The post-war period has greatly increased the situations we no longer know how to react to, in spaces which we no longer know how to describe. These were "any spaces whatever", deserted but inhabited, disused warehouses, waste ground, cities in the course of demolition or reconstruction. And in these any-spaces-whatever a new race of characters was stirring, kind of mutant: they saw rather than acted, they were seers.'

(Deleuze, 2013: XI)

The term 'seer' was utilized by Deleuze to conceptualize those people, or characters within film, inhabiting 'the interval between perception and action that is prolonged when they become uncertain as to how to act' (Martin-Jones, 2011: 72). Instead of becoming active, the person or character becomes a contemplative witness, standing still within the flow of time, perceiving its multipotentialities or its crystalline nature, and experiencing the environment affectively, as pure optical and sound situations. As Deleuze states, discussing a character within film:

He shifts, runs and becomes animated in vain, the situation he is in outstrips his motor capacities on all sides, and makes him see and hear what is no longer subject to the rules of a response or an action. He records rather than reacts. He is prey to a vision, pursued by it or pursuing it, rather than engaged in action.

(2013: 3)

Characters (and audiences, potentially, through them), within these pure optical and sound situations, also become ungrounded from their subjectivities. The multipotentialities of being that they are opened to in duration falsifies their grounding and exposes them as embodying 'one virtuality among others' (2013: 73). Within the pure optical and sound situation then, characters and audiences are free to try a multitude of different subjectivities and ways of being.

The pure optical and sound situation is fundamental to the time-image, being that it is established within the any-space-whatever, replaces the sensory-motor links of the action-image which tend to disappear, and forms direct relations with duration or the crystal of time. Within the pure optical and sound image (the depiction of these pure optical and sound situations), 'there is a new breed of signs, opsigns and sonsigns' (2013: 6), as well as tactisigns, which inform the construction of the image and the experience the audience has of the film. Opsigns are movements or fluctuations of light and colour on-screen which create affective resonances, whereas sonsigns indicate sounds which have an affective dimension. Tactisigns, on the other hand, indicate the tactile or haptic dimensions of visual elements of film where audiences are given the sensation of touching the film and being touched by it. The affective forces that these signs generate within the pure optical and sound image are particularly important as they ensure that the image 'escape[s] from a world of clichés' (2013: 23), from re-establishing the molar regimes, paradigms and significations that movement-images continually re-produce. It is through the generation of interstitial, affective states that these pure optical and sound images and situations open onto duration and the multipotentialities of thought, being and becoming that it expresses.

Beyond opsigns, sonsigns and tactisigns, time-image cinema employs several other different cinematic and editing techniques to express a direct image of time, create any-spaces-whatever, and centralize an affective, embodied experience. Deleuze, for instance, discusses how 'depth of field' within cinema can help create an affective time-image. Exploring *Citizen Kane* (1941), Deleuze argues that Welles, creating a depth of field, 'deforms space and time simultaneously; dilating and contracting them in turn, he dominates or gets deep inside a situation' (2013: 115). High- and low-angle shots, bands of shadow from and to which characters emerge and recede and having the background in direct contact with the foreground, all work, within *Citizen Kane,* to create an affective depth of field, a deformation of space and therefore time. Within the suicide scene for instance, 'Kane bursts in through the door at the back, tiny, while Susan is dying in the shadow in mid-shot and the large mirror is seen in close-up' (Deleuze, 2013: 113).

Further techniques also include montage, which, in the time-image takes on a new function, 'instead of composing movement-images in such a way that an indirect image of time emerges from them, it decomposes the relations in a direct time-image in such a way that all the possible movements emerge from it' (ibid.: 135). Within the montage of the time-image, we no longer ask how images are linked, forming a progressive narrative, but what do the images show? (Deleuze, 2013: 42), how do they create an affective, bodily impact?

As well as this, time-image films may have multiple, perhaps disparate, rhizomatic narrative strands, allowing for alternative experiences of time, producing stories which are so dense they expand into space as much as they move forward in time (Marks, 2002, cited in Wada-Marciano, in Choi and Wada-Marciano, 2009: 29). This challenges conceptualizations of causal, linear time, creating an a-temporal narrative experience, where past, present and future become indiscernible and it is unclear within what time-frame events of the film are taking place. Through this a-temporality, the regimes normally associated with the movement-image structure, namely molar ideologies, are also ungrounded. As Moussavi argues, employing a non-linear storyline with multiple perspectives creates a multi-layered, assemblage of interweaving concepts and forms, thus allowing characters and audiences to 'blur the lines of culturally concrete definitions' (in Khorana, 2013: 23).

Whilst the post-war period constitutes a break within linear time, producing these pure optical and sound situations, time-images and seers, one must consider the contexts and subtleties of this break. For whom does this constitute a break? Do certain molar thoughts, regimes or understandings of the break mix with molecular, affective renderings of it? Within *Cinema 2: The Time-Image,* Deleuze primarily discusses time-image cinema from North America and Europe and therefore situates the post-war break within a Western context. Thus, approaching Asian cinema using Deleuzian concepts perhaps requires care as this could constitute an application of Western-centric thought onto a disparate, Eastern body of work. Highlighting the dangers of this, scholars, such as Standish (2006), 'have challenged the historical interpretation of 1945 as a total break in the Japanese historical trajectory, arguing that many aspects of the Japanese social structure not only survived the Allied occupation, but were strengthened by SCAP (Supreme Commander for the Allied Powers, the title given to General Douglas MacArthur who led the occupation of Japan) policy' (Coates, 2016: 18).

Nevertheless, Deleuze does discuss the pre- and post-war time-image cinema of Ozu, highlighting that the post-war break arguably applies in the Japanese context too. A pertinent issue perhaps then, taking Deleuze's viewpoint forward, is that Eastern countries, especially Japan (as part of the Axis powers), had very different experiences of the war and post-war from European nations and America, thus the break may be constructed and felt very differently in these places.[6] Neglecting to take into account such differences would directly contradict the methodology and the spirit of the study of world cinemas, as it has been conceptualized in the previous chapter. World cinema studies, in this book, is understood as being able to 'acknowledge precisely the aesthetic and cultural differences apparent in films from around the world, even while often exploring their formal and generic similarities and their circulation in the same spheres internationally' (Martin-Jones, 2011: 2). Nevertheless, Deleuzian thought is transformative and fluid and is flexible enough to account for different contexts, allowing for considerations of differences within time-image cinemas and their renderings.

In this regard, Deleuze's commentary of Ozu's pre- and post-war time-image cinema is very insightful. He observes within Ozu's films that 'the visual image of what a character is, and the sound image of what he says' are the only elements of importance and this is a result of him placing particular stock in the physical and moral appearance of the actors he chose and his 'establishment of any dialogue whatever, apparently without a precise subject-matter' (Deleuze, 2013: 14). This creates a pure optical and sound situation, typical of time-images, or, under Japanese terminology and sensibilities, creates a sense of 'mono no aware' (translated as 'the pathos of things') (Standish, 2012: 6). This term describes an ephemeral situation, where everything (people, places and things) is impermanent, transient and always in flux and is thus experienced by the spectator 'in the realm of bodily sensation' (Charney, 1995, cited in Standish, 2012: 6) or affect.

The fact that Deleuze identifies the time-image within the pre-war work of Ozu is particularly significant as it highlights how his thought is not restricted to the boundaries of the immediate post-war period and to Europe and the West. Deleuze's consideration of this work suggests that it was not his intention to formulate an irrefutable, single point of origin for all time-image cinema. It is possible therefore that this post-war breaking point can be interpreted as an example amongst others, utilized to explore and explain the time-image. Following this then, there are perhaps several different breaking points throughout history and in different locations and contexts, occurring after or during particularly tumultuous events which spark the production of a-temporal, time-image films. In terms of Ozu's pre-war time-images, these may have formed in response to a disjuncture in conceptions of time which occurred during the Meiji restoration (1868–1912) when an age of Westernization and modernization was ushered in. This caused a traumatic mutation within society and a disconnection between the past, present and future. Although, as Deleuze suggests, perhaps the pre-war time-images of Ozu were produced independently from any breaking point, with the post-war period simply helping to confirm his thinking (2013: 15).

This book asserts that the Japanese economic crash of the 1990s, along with other disruptive events and processes (including globalization), converging and forming relationalities with each other during the decade, has created another breaking point and suspension of linearity within Japan. This has then led to the production of new time-image films which express these situations (and not the post-war situation as in Deleuze's considerations of the time-image film), including many of the Japanese horror films of the late 1990s and early 2000s.

The contexts of this particular breaking point are explored in more depth in the following section as we now look towards transforming some specific ideologies and theories related to national, transnational and world cinema (as they apply to Japanese horror of the late 1990s and early 2000s), through the taxonomy of Deleuze.

Theoretical transformations: National, transnational and world cinema

National concepts are constructed upon and contain underlying notions of homogenized, abstracted time. As Lim, a scholar inspired by Deleuzian thought on cinema and time, argues, the imagined unity of nationality 'also crucially presumes a temporal unity. The fiction of a homogenous national culture is founded on the ascendancy of homogenous time' (2009: 34). In other words, we formulate concepts of national fellowship and shared experience based on the idea that our position in national time is the same.

This type of synchronized time, particularly at a national level, has come to seem increasingly natural and incontrovertible and has been integral to maintaining productive, progressive, successful societies (as Anderson (2006) and Gellner (2009) consider especially). The idea of the progression of the nation, in particular, is inseparable from conceptualizations of linear time, fostering notions of the timelessness of nations, their mythic, 'golden age' pasts, and ideologies of how much the nation has evolved and where it will progress to in the future. This in turn has led to dichotomous comparisons between nations based on notions of time, namely the primitive society versus the modern, highly developed society. Within such dichotomies, those who are defined as primitive others are temporally excluded, or seen as anachronistic, belonging to an incompatible time. As Iwabuchi (2002) highlights within his work on Japanese cultural landscapes and globalization, in the past, it was often conceived that Japan occupied a different, more modern temporality than Hong Kong and Taiwan, in particular.

These ideologies about national time can be successfully perpetuated within movement-image cinema as it has the ability to 'only show one "true" time, and marginalizes, expels or eradicates all others from the frame' (Martin-Jones, 2006: 24). Like nations reject all other concepts or forms of nationality and national time, the movement-image rejects the idea of multiple potentialities or multiple co-existing times. Furthermore, like concepts of national time, the movement-image measures the progression of time through movement. The narrative of the progression or evolution of the nation and the large form action-image can be conceptualized as sharing the same fundamental structure, where an initial situation is altered or challenged through action and then comes to form a new, yet still commensurate, situation of the nation.

Significantly, however, due to a number of recent coincident events (discussed in detail shortly) occurring within Japan specifically, a break in linear, national time has occurred. This is where the linear progression of nation, through time, is disrupted and the irrefutability of one true national time becomes increasingly problematic. Like the movement-image's conception of progression and one true time can be suspended and falsified through the revelation of the existence of multiple, potential times, so too can the ideologies of 'one "correct" narrative of national [time and] identity' (Martin-Jones, 2006: 4) be similarly falsified. Namely, through the revelation of the existence of other potential routes that the national narrative could travel down. Due to this break in linear time, much as Deleuze observed in the West's post-war context, there has been an increase in the formation of any-space-whatevers within Japanese society, situations within which people no longer know how to act or react. Coincident with this, a new time-image cinema has emerged in Japan, particularly within the horror genre, to express this multifaceted break and the fragmentary, suspended situations it has fostered. These time-images express 'the difficulty of narrating national identity at a time of historical crisis or transformation' (Martin-Jones, 2006: 1). Furthermore, as Coates expands, time-images also present a means for audiences 'to work through issues, hypothesize futures, and allow the affected consciousness not only to make sense, or meaning, of contemporary circumstances, but also to imaginatively inhabit potential futures, or even pasts' (2016: 8).

The bursting of the economic bubble in Japan, occurring in 1990, is the principle event, constitutive of this particular break with linear time, although there are other, interlinking disruptions, which occurred throughout the 1990s. There are also, arguably, other breaks with linear time that can be conceptualized as occurring throughout Japan's history (including, for instance, the events of the Second World War and the subsequent allied occupation). However, it is this particular break, from 1990, which is important to this book, due to its proximity to and relations with the time-image cinema under consideration here.

Before the bubble burst, Japan experienced a significant period of growth which peaked in the 1980s, seeing Japan become the second biggest economy after the United States. This growth was sparked by American Cold War policy, from which 'Japan was perhaps the greatest beneficiary' (Iwabuchi, 2015: 49). During this time Japan relied upon the United States for security and thus could concentrate spending in other sectors, prioritizing expenditure to foster economic growth and trade for its exports. Through this growth, the end of economic struggle and suffering, a re-establishment of national linearity and a continuity with the past were achieved. The war period, as well as the time of the post-war occupation, 'could now be seen in a more positive light, as the necessary passage from militarist imperialism to economic nationalism' (Gibbs, 2012: 112). At the helm of this great period of economic growth were the 'salarymen', corporation employees who worked tirelessly for the good of their company and the nation.

The bubble economy was, however, built on 'the unstable foundations of a highly favourable trade surplus, land speculation and unsecured bank loans' (Iles, 2008: 22) and by 1990 the stock market spiralled unstoppably into decline. A prolonged economic recession, dubbed the *Heisei* recession, began, lasting, many have now conceptualized, twenty years (up until 2010). The economic crisis caused a deep, nihilistic societal malaise to form and brought 'scandal to Japanese politicians and corporate leaders, disaster to banks and businesses …, unemployment and homelessness to countless thousands of Japanese' (Iles, 2008). There was also a 'decisive structural breakdown' corresponding to 'changes in such Japanese institutions as state bureaucracy, corporate organization, the education system, and family relationships' (Iwabuchi, 2015: 50). Through this structural breakdown, individual people, companies and the Japanese state itself did not know how to react to the situation, how to reinstate national continuity and linear progression. As Iida notes, commenting upon the state, 'Japanese politicians and bureaucrats of the 1990s have been incapable and unwilling to demonstrate leadership in the internal restructuring necessary to integrate

Japan into the globalized economy' (2002: 216). Furthermore, for individual people, particularly the salarymen, previous, nationalistic discourses of working hard for one's company, community and family were no longer possible courses, due to the mass redundancies that were made.

Contributing to and exacerbating the economic crisis was a shift that occurred within the leading sector of the international economy, which went from producing 'high value-added industrial goods, such as automobiles and computer hardware, to information technology software and technology networks' (2002: 214). This shift facilitated Japan's transition towards a more flexible economy, one based on service rather than manufacturing, and the immateriality of information, communication and affect (Allison, 2009: 91). These shifts can be seen within other countries around the world also, including the West, as Shaviro (2010) discusses extensively. However, exploring Japan specifically, this flexible economy led to a state of socio-economic precariousness amongst young people entering the job market especially. Trends in irregular, part-time employment emerged and without steady employment, the youth were 'getting stuck in time without the means to become adults' (Allison, 2009: 90), they were futureless members of, what was dubbed, 'the lost generation'. Japanese youth, here, through the economic crisis, experienced a specific ungrounding from linear, developmental progression, inhabiting an any-space-whatever where they existed in a liminal state between child and adulthood.

This suspended, precarious state was (and still is today) something which older generations blame the young themselves for. In particular, they are criticized by older generations for floating 'from job to job in a pattern called "freeta"', for lacking 'skills or employment altogether in a pattern called NEET (not in education, employment or training)', for 'marry[ing] later or not at all' and for 'over-spend[ing] time and money on pleasurable things such as brand name goods and the internet' (Allison, 2009: 97). Informing the particular any-space-whatever that many Japanese youths inhabited (and still do)[7] is pre-recession ideologies about development, life stages and ways of being. These have been held, largely, by older generations who have (in times of greater economic development) more successfully implemented, carried out and fulfilled this linear path. Older generations within Japan perceive the ideal, linear narrative of life as progressing through childhood, education and into employment, where one dedicates themselves to the company they work for and thus, to the furthering of the national economy. Furthermore, young Japanese people should, ideally, leave the parental home, get married and have children.

However, now that many of these stages are delayed or even impossible for young Japanese people to achieve (without work they cannot leave the parental home, cannot get married, etc.), this milieu has been deterritorialized and can only be reterritorialized once again if the youth manage to meet these ideals (or at least partially). Whilst this narrative is positioned by older generations and the state (which increasingly acknowledges the problems with youth unemployment and, for instance, the aging population and the childbirth crisis, in its policies) as the ideal, it is important to acknowledge that youth, perceived to be within this suspended state, may not recognize this milieu as informative of their lives and their ambitions. Many have potentially found alternative, non-conformist ways of being and subjectivities which re-establish linearity and progression for them. This is most evident within the youth sub-cultures that have emerged in these contexts, for instance, amongst the *otaku*[8] and the *kogyaru* (or *kogal*).[9]

New forms of subjectivity and ways of being beyond these traditional ideals, for Japanese people more generally (but for young people especially), were generated through the prevalent and expanding consumer culture during the 1980s and into the 1990s. This consumer culture has been understood by commentators as embodying the attributes of 'lightness, fragmentation, and stylistic sophistication freed from the burden of representing meaning and content' (Iida, 2002: 7). Consumer products and commercial images from this period were absent of grounded, cultural meaning, they were 'free-floating signifiers delinked from their original meanings and/or historical referents' which could 'arbitrarily attach themselves to almost any meaning/referent regardless of their original attachments' (Iida, 2002: 207). During the 1980s, these molecular artefacts were perceived positively, as allowing for affirmative, revitalizing becoming-others of identity and experimentations with different forms of subjectivity.

However, in the 1990s, this consumer culture came to be perceived as a more malign force which broke down subjectivity and made it expressly more difficult for people to form stable senses of identity.[10] Commercial penetration into the realms of subjectivity, during the 1990s, advanced far beyond what had been seen within the previous decade, encompassing such things as the body and sexuality. This was due to the expansion of the high-tech information-based economy, the instatement of a more flexible, immaterial model, which caused subjectivity to become 'a preferred area for profit extraction' (Iida, 2002: 8). The disruptions to the formation of individuals' subjectivities, created because of these developments, directly coincided then with the economic crash, the break with linear time it instigated and the mutations that the economy underwent as a result. This consumer culture, in the 1990s, became a contributory factor to the break in linear, national time, overall, that Japan was experiencing. It produced, alongside the economic crash, its own, unique forms of suspension related to identity formation.

The difficulty in forming stable senses of identity and finding meaning within a heavily consumeristic society has led to a number of reactionary responses. Amongst the youth subcultures mentioned previously, for instance, in various ways they have adopted a survival strategy of 'incorporating the high-tech media and commercialized images of the self in the construction of their identities' (Iida, 2002: 226). They become fluid, relational subjects, forming different assemblages with the consumeristic world around them. *Otaku*, for instance, are renowned for partaking in such activities as creating online personas or avatars to communicate and play with others in online games and 'cosplay', dressing-up and playing the roles of their favourite anime and manga characters. These activities allow *otaku* to appropriate and construct senses of identity for themselves.

However, many cultural commentators have noted the dangers of living in such artificial realities. Substituting familial and communal forms of sociality and identity building for technologically mediated, virtual forms, can have significant psychological consequences it seems (as is explored further in the *Kairo* (*Pulse*) case study). The *otaku*, for instance, are commonly perceived as sexually frustrated young males, obsessed with violent and pornographic media, who 'no longer effectively relate to real world people (especially women) ... [and] harbour dangerous, sexual proclivities and fetishes' (Schodt, 1996, cited in Iida, 2002: 228).

Amongst the *kogyaru*, many young girls appropriate commodified, sexualized images of femininity into constructions of their identity, some of which are liberatory and allow them to transcend normative laws regarding femininity. Responding to, for instance, constructions within the consumer culture of women's sexuality and bodies as objects, some *kogyaru* have been known to partake in *enjo kōsai*, or, compensated dating. This is a practice where young girls meet, spend time with and even engage in sexual activity with older, usually middle-aged, men (*oyaji*) in exchange for money, which they use to buy luxury goods. This practice, whilst perhaps allowing these young girls to 'momentarily free themselves from their everyday context and the governance of self-consciousness and social morality' (Iida, 2002: 232), has, nonetheless, caused significant moral outrage within Japan. Many commentators, in light of this trend, have attacked, once again, the immoral consumer culture of the 1990s which has caused significant deterritorializations in conceptualizations of the body and sexuality. It has displaced ideas of the body and sexuality as sacred and manufactures different ways in which people can continually modify and consume their bodies and erase themselves.

In part response to such moral outrage at the state of the consumer culture, but mainly in reaction to the wider break with linear time, caused by the economic bubble bursting, many individuals, scholars and intellectuals have looked towards the nation. They have returned to traditional cultural values and moral codes to try and reinstate linearity, groundings and unity amongst the Japanese people. Invoking the ideas of *Nihonjinron* and *Nihonbunkaron* from the past, as well as the notion of *kokutai* (literally translated as the 'national body'), of a 'timeless Japanese cultural essence often linked to the emperor as the symbol of Japanese unity' (Iida, 2002: 5), these groups aimed to build a more hopeful vision of national society for the future.

They varyingly aimed to re-bond Japanese people to the superstructure of the nation state, instil a sense of national pride and foster new communal bonds, based upon traditional ideals and cultural values.

These nationalistic discourses were spurred on by increasing tensions between the USA and Japan, caused by such events as the Persian Gulf War in 1990[11] and the controversial exhibition of the Enola Gay (the aircraft which dropped the atomic bomb on Hiroshima in 1945) at the Smithsonian Museum in Washington to mark the fiftieth anniversary of the end of the Second World War. These tensions gave impetus to historical revisionists who sought to re-establish connections with the Second World War and a continuity with the imperial past. Many, such as the *Jiyū-shugi Shikan Kenkyūkai* (The Liberal view of History Group), 'strongly objected to the government's apologies for Japanese war atrocities in Asia and the compensation of ex-comfort women, contesting what they described as the excessively negative view of [our] own history' (Iida, 2002: 245) which had been constructed by the USA during the occupation.

Nationalistic sentiments, however, particularly the controversial revisionist ideas, did not find popularity amongst everyone in Japan and largely, despite endorsements from conservative sects of the Japanese state, failed to reinstate a linear, encompassing milieu or provide resolutions to the issues of the time. This failure was evidenced by the growing number of violent acts that Japanese society witnessed during the course of the 1990s. Some of the most shocking incidents of violence were perpetrated by the *Aum Shinrikyō* cult, led by Asahara Shōkō, most notably, the sarin gas attack on the Tokyo subway system in 1995, which killed thirteen people and injured many more.[12]

This attack was to be 'the opening salvo in the cult's attempt to take control of Tokyo, the first phase of its self-declared rescue mission to purify world-wide spiritual decay and to inaugurate a new era under the leadership of a core of "psychically-gifted" human beings' (Iida, 2002: 239). The cult predicted that, following their initial attacks and take-over of Tokyo, a worldwide nuclear war would ensue which, at its end, would leave only a few, gifted people alive to lead the world into this new era. These gifted people would consist of those who had followed the cult's teachings, taken part in its religious exercises and achieved a sort of enlightenment, a transcendence of the earthly self. Such a transcendence, the cult believed, could be achieved through the aid of technology and technological assemblage (linking, as will be discussed in the *Kairo* (*Pulse*) case study, to posthuman and transhuman ideas), thus the group funded its own research labs, where it, incidentally, also developed a range of chemical weapons.

The cult, its leadership and disciples, was largely made up of young adults, people aged between twenty and thirty-five, many of whom were university graduates. It extensively utilized images, symbols and narratives borrowed from popular culture, perhaps explaining, to an extent, its appeal amongst young people. However, typically, as Iida notes, 'the students who joined Aum ... were later to explain their motivations for joining the cult in terms of satisfying an emotional lack, and giving themselves a second chance to "mature" in a protected space away from the "real world" in which they felt they had failed' (2002: 242). Young Japanese people were joining *Aum* due to the difficulties they faced in Japan at the time, the suspensions between childhood and adulthood they experienced, the inability to find employment, purpose and meaning in life and to form close familial and communal bonds with people around them. As Nishio argued, 'contemporary life in Japan, particularly for young people, lacks a defining frame in which identity might be healthily constructed, and is so awash in infinite freedoms, ambiguities, and a lack of moral guidelines that ... [they] are haunted by the desire to fill their lives with meaning' (1995, cited in Iida, 2002: 243). The *Aum Shinrikyō* cult provided its disciples with a sense of meaning, purpose and unity. It reinstated, for them, a sense of linear time and progression, something which traditional cultural values and nationalistic discourses, had, so far, failed to achieve.

For the majority of Japanese people who did not buy into the cult, *Aum Shinrikyō* and its violent acts served to embed them further within an any-space-whatever, a state of suspension. Their actions were reflective of a Japanese society that was increasingly becoming unrecognizable and many no longer knew how to act within this landscape. Such acts of violence then further constitute and inform the break with linear time Japan was experiencing in the 1990s.

Contributing to this break and exacerbating its effects further was 'the rapid development of globalization, in which transborder flows and connections among capital, people, and media accelerated at an unprecedented scale and speed' (Iwabuchi, 2015: 50). Whilst one might perceive that these developments generated new opportunities for economic expansion and growth and thus offered the potential for a re-establishment of national, economic (and through this, social) continuity and progression, in fact, they also contributed to the extension of the break in different ways. They further deterritorialized milieus ungrounded through the economic crash. As Iwabuchi discusses, 'Japanese discourses on globalization have most notably revolved around the necessity for Japan to readjust itself to the new US led global economic order' (Iwabuchi, 2015), thus Japan can be perceived as quite passive and less confident in its approach to globalization. Instead of fostering a specifically Japanese economic policy on globalization, potentially re-establishing the milieu of nation at the levels of economy, politics and society, it largely follows and adapts to the American model (although the discourses of nation branding contest this). This has perhaps led, as Iwabuchi (Iwabuchi, 2015) suggests, to the pessimistic views that, in general, Japanese people have of globalization. Citing a survey conducted by *Dentsu* in 2001, Iwabuchi highlights how people in the UK, United States,

France and Germany have optimistic views of globalization whereas, in Japan, people tend to stress the negative effects of globalization, such as a 'widening economic gap and employment insecurity' (2015). Thus, globalization here appears to have deepened the state of suspension and crisis that the Japanese economy, society and its people have been trapped within.

Contributing further to this state of suspension is the greater interconnectedness between nations and cultures that globalization fosters. These processes have made it apparent that the times, and along with it, the narratives, of other nations and cultures, rather than incompatible or irreducibly different, are relational. Nations like Japan continually form diverse assemblages with other cultures, the out-of-field, drifting ideologies, peoples, cultural products and intensities to each other. Societies all over the world, including Japan, are now more multi-cultural spaces which ungrounds the linear, homogenous view of nationality and national time.

However, as discussed previously, this has not prevented scholars and intellectuals especially, from developing new, nationalistic discourses which try to re-instate a homogenous view of nationality and national time. Furthermore, as noted previously, the discourses of nation-branding within, for instance, 'J-Cool' cultural products, may also, similarly, reterritorialize visions of a unified, homogenous Japanese society.

This highlights therefore, the nuanced way in which Japan and the Japanese people have experienced this multifaceted break, as both deterritorializing and reterritorializing, molar and molecular. Within the time-image cinema expressive of this break, despite being particularly effective at mapping deterritorialized, affective flows, we find both representations grounded upon molar thought and molecular, ungrounded renderings.

Such molarities and molecularities, within the time-image cinema analysed in this book, as well as being connected to national, transnational and global issues and thought, are also tied to the horror genre specifically. It is to a consideration then, of how Deleuzian thought can form assemblages with the horror genre and incrementally transform understandings of it that this chapter now turns.

Transforming thought: The horror genre and psychoanalysis

The concept of genre appears, like other forms of molar thought, to be opposed to the Deleuzian taxonomy. As Herzog comments, the 'overly determined codes and conventions of the genre film seem hopelessly colonized by the forces of causality and commercialism' (in Brown and Martin-Jones 2012: 137). Concepts of genre impose a unity upon often diverse texts and are part of the regimes of language and the line of segmentarity. Genre codes and conventions therefore are perhaps most noticeable within movement-image cinema as it allows for and, in fact, fundamentally encourages the repetition of codes, conventions, clichés, experiences and sensations. They create habitual viewing experiences which can then be understood through habitual, hermeneutic thought.[13]

However, there is innovation within a wide range of genres particularly as, like the boundaries of the national, they have become increasingly leaky and hybrid. This hybridization demonstrates the potential for genre codes and conventions to cross boundaries, form relationalities and mutate, becoming more fluid than previously thought. Furthermore, as Hand and McRoy argue, the horror genre specifically, as it has its origins in oral culture and folktales, where stories were told, transformed or variegated and then retold, inherently presents the idea that a 'multiplicity of potential interpretations is possible' (2007: 2) and that there is no more truth in one iteration of a tale than another. Thus, genre, and the horror genre in particular, as bodies, are crossed by both molar and molecular elements, lines of segmentarity as well as flight, which allow for transformation and hybridization.

Providing further evidence of this, many horror genre codes and conventions, in particular, are designed to produce intense affective experiences for the audience. This generation of affect serves to disrupt and suspend the narrative flow and the instatement of molar, linear understandings of the action on-screen, giving rise to lines of flight and transformation. Scholars such as Powell (2005), Ndalianis (2012) and Reyes (2012, 2016), in particular, have studied the affective and sensorial powers of horror film, avoiding discussions of plot, theme and symbolic content. Powell (2005), for instance, utilizing a Deleuzian approach (rather than a phenomenological one as in Ndalianis (2012)), analyses the horror cinema of Dario Argento, amongst others, who utilizes a variety of sonsigns, opsigns (a colour-force, as she terms it) and tactisigns to affect and move us. Such elements within Argento's films, Powell argues, 'exceed the symbolic properties of both languages and image' (2005: 11).

Reyes (2012), on the other hand, drawing upon Deleuzian thought as well as the works of Shaviro (1993, 2010) and Massumi (2002) on affect, specifically focuses upon post-millennium torture-horror cinema, such as *Saw* (2004) and *Hostel* (2005). He argues that psychoanalytical and cognitivist theories of horror cinema, although very fruitful, cannot adequately account for how this sub-genre, in particular, effects or makes itself felt upon the body of the audience. Reyes (2012) positions post-millennium torture-horror films as quite unique in their generation of affect. As he states: 'the corporeal nightmares propounded by torture-horror exceed the supernatural "body horror" of previous decades, and their emphasis on torture, as opposed to the relatively diligent killings of the slasher subgenre, point towards the need to contextualize and explore the intricacies of a more direct and affective process of film consumption' (2012: 244).

Both Reyes (2012) and Powell (2005) highlight the dominance of, in particular, psychoanalytical thought within horror cinema scholarship to date and suggest alternative, Deleuzian inspired, affective ways of exploring horror film. Both of these scholars, however, aligning with Deleuze and Guattari's 'art of dosages' (1987) idea, suggest that psychoanalytical thought (and other ideas also, such as cognitivist concepts) should not be entirely rejected in favour of affective models. We should not lose touch with 'our formative socio-political contexts, familial experiences or psycho-sexual fantasies' (Powell, 2005: 205), and nor do we have to, as Deleuzian thought 'affords space for a hybrid response that mixes philosophical thought with cultural awareness and psycho-sexual frames' (Powell, 2005).

As has already been explored briefly in the previous chapter, combining Deleuzian thought with psychoanalytical concepts can produce significant developments in thought, releasing molar interpretations and opening them onto duration or multiplicity. One of the most significant ways in which Deleuzian (and Guattarian) perspectives can introduce transformations to psychoanalytical thought is through opening up notions of subjectivity to multiplicity. This is a particular topic of discussion within Deleuze and Guattari's *Anti-Oedipus* (2000), one which warrants a more detailed exploration here. Particularly in relation to notions of female subjectivity, as it is this specific type of identity which manifests prolifically within the case studied films.

In psychoanalysis, just like within conceptualizations of the national subject, the character on-screen and the audience member watching a film are perceived as already fully formed and static, refuting any multiplicities of being or becoming-others. Both bodies of thought perceive the subject as such as both have a hermeneutic core. Through the any-space-whatever of the time-image, however, these static subjects can be opened to a multiplicity of potential becomings or ways of being, a 'non-decidability of the body' (Deleuze, 2013: 210). Within the stasis that the time-image produces, subjectivity is forever coming into being, perpetually flowing and transforming. This effect of the any-space-whatever may have particularly interesting implications for the abject or monstrous beings of horror films who are already, by nature, more fluid entities. As scholars such as Coates (2016) argue, the abject being is already conceptualized as liminal, transgressing the boundaries of subjecthood.

As one of the first and primary things to be abjected, the female therefore has a particular connection with notions of subjective transgression and liminality within psychoanalytical thought. Interestingly, Deleuzian and Guattarian perspectives also emphasize the fluidity and becoming-other of the female figure in an idea termed becoming-woman. Combining such thought on the abject female, becoming-woman and the any-space-whatever, particularly at the site of time-image cinema, has the potential to produce some interesting transformations and extensions to thought on the female subject.

Within Deleuze and Guattari's concept of becoming-woman, the female body is reconceived as a series of molecular flows rather than a series molar affiliations, 'a woman's body achieves a strange nomadism which makes it cross ages, situations and places' (Deleuze, 2013: 202). This nomadism is akin to how Taylor-Jones (in Hipkins and Plain, 2007) conceptualized two Japanese actresses (Hara Setsuko and Tanaka Kinuyo). The notion of becoming-woman then perceives identity as not adhering to the rigid gender subjectivities conceptualized by the over-arching regimes of psychoanalysis, it is more akin to the body without organs.

The bodies of women, as nomadic, molecular entities, therefore form relationalities with a wide variety of other bodies. As Kennedy (discussing this concept) argues, 'woman cannot merely be described as part of a binary [man vs. woman], but as part of an assemblage of processes connecting and forming in new alignments within culture, across the social, the libidinal, the material, the psychological, the biological, and personal spaces' (2000: 94–5). Here, the dichotomous nature of psychoanalytical thought is challenged. In particular, Lacan's idea of the mirror phase where the infant initially becomes aware of ideas of separation such as inside outside, self and other, man and woman, wholeness and lack, is falsified through the concept of becoming-woman. It is replaced by a perception that all bodies are relational rather than opposed, demarcated and disparate.

Deleuze and Guattari's utilization of the term 'woman' within this concept, as a molar, linguistic indicator, has been considered as a blockage by some scholars, however, as it places the idea in danger of returning to essentialist, dichotomous categorizations. It implies, perhaps, that man is the norm, the locus of logical, rational thought, culture and law and the woman is destratifying, chaotic and fluid. However, what is forgotten within such criticism is the fact that, whilst the figure of becoming-woman has distinct, molar attributes which situate her as female and part of the patriarchal milieu, these are combined with molecularities and transgressive features which unground and challenge the milieu. In, according to the 'art of dosages', a much more profound way than if no territorialization were present within the body.

Powell, perceiving the notion of becoming-woman differently, sees it as 'an inspirational model for all becomings' (2007: 99), not just those of women. It is a particular idea to look towards to apprehend the process of becoming and to understand how deterritorializations of molar subjectivity can occur (as well as reterritorializations).

These notions of subjectivity and becoming-woman are explored further in relation to the film *Ju-On: The Grudge*. This is the case study that now follows, where, rather than an intonation of a polemic, as was the purpose of this chapter, the methodologies established are utilized to cut new pathways of thought on the film.

PART TWO

Case studies

3

The 'any-space-whatever', 'becoming-woman' and *Ju-On: The Grudge* (2002)

Shimizu Takashi's *Ju-On: The Grudge*, the film selected for this first case study, tells the tale of an accursed, suburban house, situated in Tokyo. The house is haunted by two spirits, the *onryō,* Kayako (Fuji Takako) and her son, Toshio (Ozeki Yuya), who were brutally murdered by the patriarch of their family, Takeo (Matsuyama Takashi). All who enter the house are condemned to be pursued, tormented and eventually killed by the spirits. In the film we witness six main characters enter the home, alongside a number of other periphery characters, and we experience their encounters with the spirits in a multilayered, a-temporal rhizomatic narrative.

Of particular interest in this chapter are the characters Rika (Okina Megumi), a care worker who enters the house to tend to an elderly resident, and the *onryō*, Kayako. These two characters can arguably be conceptualized as hybrid, mutating beings who encapsulate the concept of becoming-woman. They deterritorialize and mutate psychoanalytical ideologies, patriarchal concepts and gendered cinematic motifs (the molarities) that also inform them. These characters especially (although there are others discussed in this chapter, such as Toshio, who can be similarly conceptualized as ungrounded), cannot be defined and understood wholly by one ideology, concept or motif such as the monstrous-female, victim or the final girl. Rather, they mutate these notions by hybridizing their roles and subjectivities. Such transformations into and hybridizations with different forms of subjectivity can be difficult to grasp under singular hermeneutic concepts. Thus, to know these characters in a different way, we can turn towards forming bodily assemblages with them, capturing and apprehending their mutations, behaviours, actions and communications affectively upon our bodies. This may, in turn, facilitate our own (the audiences') deterritorializations and becoming-others, instilling within us a fluidity and mutability of being.

It is not only with such characters, however, that audiences form potentially transformative assemblages. The any-space-whatevers of the film, freed from molar groundings or spatio-temporal coordinates (such as the national), similarly have the potential to deterritorialize the audience as well as the characters. Within this film, the any-space-whatevers, opening on to duration, allow us to split ourselves between many different existential layers of past, present and future and thus open us to multipotentialities of being.

The any-space-whatevers of *Ju-On: The Grudge* also create assemblages or relationalities with spaces beyond the screen, with external, social and cultural environments surrounding the film. They map the deterritorialized, transformed and (potentially, at points) reterritorialized environments of Japanese society.

Exactly how *Ju-On: The Grudge* achieves these renderings of space and character and such affective, transformative functions is mapped out in this chapter, beginning with its conceptualizations of space and the a-temporality associated with its any-space-whatevers.

Assemblages and any-spaces-whatever

An analysis of the a-temporality of *Ju-On: The Grudge* is a unique research project in that it cuts into different levels other than the molar. Such an analysis does not require the pursuing of easily mappable elements of Japanese horror films onto Western hermeneutic models, the degradation of facets of Japanese horror as simply different or alien, and the ignoring of problematic elements. Instead, the methodologies employed here are much less restrictive and more relational, allowing for the consideration of multiple potentialities of understanding. In the following passages, the ways in which, through a-temporality, various spaces within the film and external to it are ungrounded from normative understandings, creating multipotential, rather than static, singular conceptualizations, is explored. Additionally, the ways in which both audiences and characters form assemblages with these any-space-whatevers and the potential outcomes of these are discussed.

From the outset we are presented with multiple, potential ways of understanding the film and its spaces through a complex, a-temporal sequence which allows an almost incomprehensible glimpse of the violent and frenzied murder of Kayako and her son at the hands of Takeo. This sequence also 'anticipates the film's larger organizational logic, a tangled and non-linear narrative' (McRoy, in McRoy, 2005: 179) which, previously, has not been analysed in any great detail by any scholar in relation to the

Deleuzian taxonomy. However, due to its significance to the film as a whole, the a-temporal complexity of *Ju-On: The Grudge* has been usefully explained by some scholars, such as Wada-Marciano (in Choi and Wada-Marciano, 2009) Kinnia (2009) and McRoy (in McRoy, 2005), in other ways, relating it to certain traditions, discourses and even structural attributes of media formats.

Wada-Marciano (in Choi and Wada-Marciano, 2009) interestingly argues that the a-temporality of the film is a microcosm of a larger media and societal shift towards digitalization within Japan and the rest of the world. The structure of the film, which is separated into a number of distinct, yet interlinked 'episodes', each telling the tale of a different character as they encounter the accursed house, resembles the '"chapter" format of the DVD' (in Choi and Wada-Marciano, 2009: 21). Wada-Marciano (in Choi and Wada-Marciano, 2009) suggests here that each episode could be watched independently from the rest of the film or in a different order to the one suggested by the film's full running sequence. This would make it a particularly apt product for the digital age where audiences pick up, leave and return to film texts in more fragmentary viewing patterns. This is certainly one potential way in which the a-temporality of the film could be interpreted, as responding to the new formal, structural capabilities that the DVD format allowed for and to the new viewing patterns of audiences. This film then, under Wada-Marciano's (in Choi and Wada-Marciano, 2009) idea, renders the contemporary contexts and logics of today's digitalized, globalized societies, commenting upon these discourses and helping us to understand them cognitively and, perhaps, apprehend them experientially. However, the idea that this film may allow us to apprehend these processes through experiencing them within its space is not explored by Wada-Marciano (in Choi and Wada-Marciano, 2009). Her study could, however, be expanded in this way, producing, like Shaviro (2010), an account of how the film affectively maps these discourses of digitalization and changing viewership habits. Wada-Marciano's (in Choi and Wada-Marciano, 2009) work therefore is a useful gateway into thinking about *Ju-On: The Grudge* more complexly and in more multifaceted, nuanced ways.

Adding to this complexity of understanding, Kinnia argues that this a-temporality has been derived from *mugen Noh* or fantasy *Noh* plays which depict 'dreams ... gods, ghosts, demons or spirits' and have a 'non-linear narrative style through the manipulation of time and space' (2009: 206). This is another potential interpretation of *Ju-On: The Grudge* which could be realized, placing it within a linear, historical progression of the arts.

Similarly, McRoy argues that the a-temporality of *Ju-On: The Grudge* resembles 'the horror manga' (in McRoy, 2005: 179) through its episodic format and its rhizomatic narrative strands, which, as within manga novels with their various 'spin-off' series and arcs, have the potential to expand, create depth and diverge from the main narrative thread.[1] One could imagine many different ways in which individual episodes within *Ju-On: The Grudge* could be extended, revealing more details about the backgrounds of characters, for instance.

Rather than discuss these separate insights as distinct and incompatible with each other, we should consider them as forming an assemblage. This therefore allows the filmic space to become relational, negotiable and indeterminate rather than strictly categorized. We, the audience, can be opened to multiple ways in which the a-temporality of the film can be understood. These scholars present to us different avenues for thought on how we may navigate the filmic space of *Ju-On: The Grudge*, however, at various points in the film these multiplicities of understanding will collide, fuse and fluctuate between becoming adequate and insufficient. This is very much reflective of the way in which audiences in Japan and other societies navigate and comprehend increasingly complex, fragmentary, multifaceted spaces external to the film. Thus, this assemblage of various conceptualizations of how we may understand the a-temporality of the film can be said to form extended relationalities with the way audiences understand and navigate their external worlds.

Returning to a consideration of the a-temporal, opening montage specifically, Kinnia (2009), unlike the other aforementioned scholars, highlights how we can position this particular element of the film within a tradition of Japanese media. Japanese arts and cultural products have had a particularly long, well-established relationship with montage (something which Eisenstein also discussed himself).[2] It has often, within this cultural context, been utilized for rendering particularly tumultuous, transformative periods of history. As Silverberg discusses (2009), during the period between 1920s and 1940s, which saw such tumultuous events as the Great Kantō earthquake in 1923, a growth in trade with the West, the emergence of a reinvigorated consumer culture, and the rise of fascism, montage was appropriated as a dominant way of representing Japanese society. This was so that mass media forms (the press, radio, theatre, cinema, literature and manga) could juxtapose various dimensions of identity available to Japanese people for appropriation. Thus, the multifaceted, fragmentary flows, processes and constructs of today, perhaps expressed in this opening montage of *Ju-On: The Grudge,* can be placed within this historical, national context. The opening sequence is perhaps exemplary of a recurring discourse of dealing with and negotiating tumultuous, transformative periods through popular forms and through montage specifically.

However, placing montage within such a national discourse, although a potentiality of interpretation, perhaps detracts somewhat from the complexities of what it achieves in its assemblage with the audience. The montage has the potential to position audiences in an indeterminate state where they are not able to comprehend the actions on-screen or able to attribute molar, hermeneutic ideas to it. Thus, it may be in some cases (as with *Ju-On: The Grudge*), difficult to perceive montage as allowing for a negotiation of complex, societal discourses and transformations and contributing to a reinstatement of linear, progressive nationality. This does not mean, however, that the forces, ideas and contexts rendered within such montages are unknowable to the audience. Montages can be exemplary devices for tapping into alternative, affective registers, allowing the audience to apprehend these conditions upon the body. They can create pure optical and sound situations which suspend the sensory-motor schema and facilitate affective engagements with film. They therefore make the impacts of, and the ways in which forces such as economic recession, globalization and technologization work, knowable to audiences through the body.

When engaging with cinema in this bodily, affective way audiences perhaps (according to Shaviro (2010)) become trained to traverse multifaceted, mutable environments external to the film which, like montage, can unground molarities and suspend the subject in a state of indetermination. Within the suspended state audiences can become a body without organs or an 'any-person-whoever' (Brown, in Brown and Martin-Jones, 2012: 99), who have had their molar, subjective groundings disrupted and have become 'a more fluid, mobile and detached subjectivity, in sync with the speeded-up, informational circuits' (Allison, 2009: 105) of affect and immateriality. However, this is not a constant state as people can become reterritorialized or aligned with molar conceptions of subjectivity again as they are traversing these spaces and forming different assemblages. Although briefly touched upon within this section, these mutable, fluid becomings are explored in more detail within the next section of this chapter, with a particular focus on the ungrounding of gendered subjectivities.

More pertinent to this section, spaces, similarly bombarded by such forces as economic recession and globalization, have experienced their own suspensions. They have been, at times, deterritorialized from their positions as, for instance, nationally or culturally encoded spaces. They become, at points, any-space-whatevers, which suspend and unground subjects who encounter them from molar understanding as they do not know how to react to these spaces. One must not forget, however, how these spaces are characterized by tension, where reterritorializations of molar conceptions of space are always possible, and, in fact, such spaces fluctuate between different states of molarity and molecularity, reterritorialization and deterritorialization.

Ju-On: The Grudge can be said to render such ungrounded spaces. Within the opening montage scene, a space conventionally used in cinema to establish settings and time-frames that the rest of the film will take place in, there appear to be no explicit anchoring points which position it within a specific national, cultural environment or timeline. This a-temporal montage begins by depicting a series of eclectic images from deserted streets, the cursed house, blood-stained walls, to extreme close-ups of Takeo biting his nails whilst piecing together a photograph from the fragments that litter the table and floor. Takeo, within the scene, is also shown brandishing a box-cutter, juxtaposed with extreme close-ups of Kayako's lifeless hands, mouth and eyes. We also see a shot of Toshio clambering into a closet to take refuge as his cat is being killed. These scenes are all accompanied by an eerie piano score and extra-diegetic sounds of a cat hissing, slashing, stabbing and the retraction of the box-cutter.

However, considering the nuance and tension imbued within these film spaces, this scene does have some sense of temporality and grounded

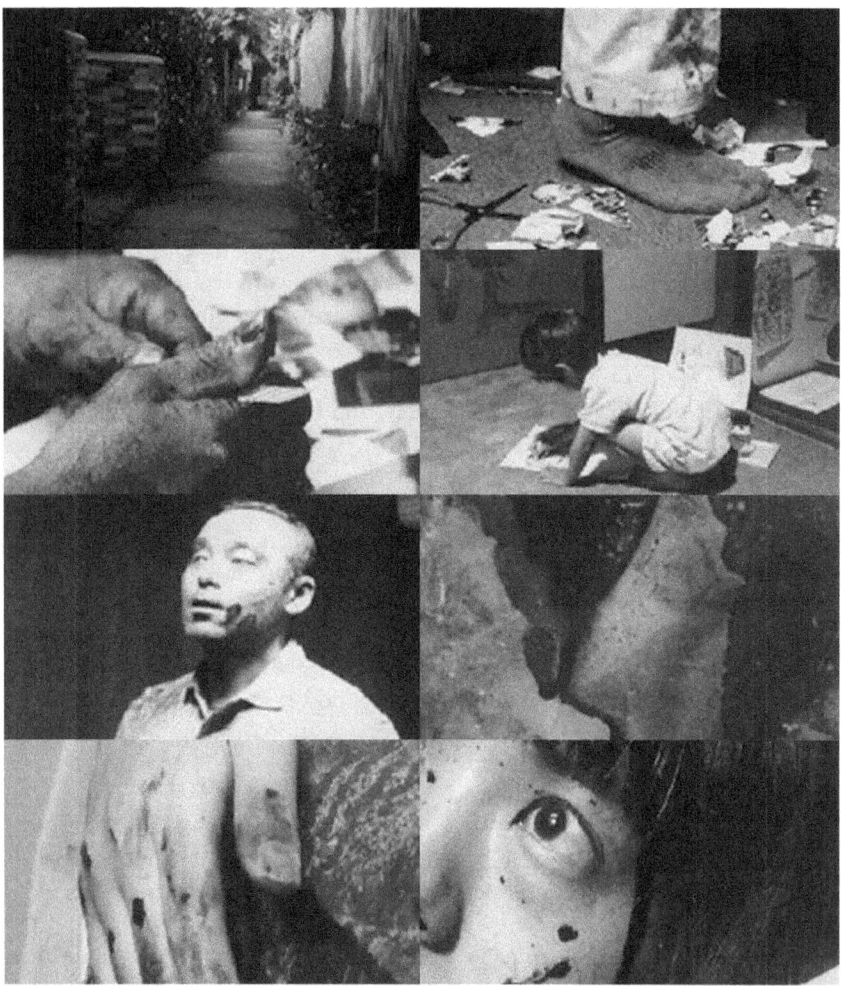

FIGURE 1 *The opening montage, a collection of stills,* Ju-On: The Grudge *(Shimizu, 2002).*

context, as its black-and-white palette and a series of shots of text explaining the background of the story just after the opening credits, 'alerts the audience that this murder took place in the past' (Blouin, 2011: 183). This perhaps negates the creation of an any-space-whatever as the audience is then provided with some sense of linearity unto which further molar understandings can be built.

Through such grounding elements within this scene, the space of the home and its setting can be interpreted as a container for the curse, a symbol for female anger at the past abuses of patriarchal society and domestic violence. Furthermore, the surrounding streets, walls and fences can be interpreted as iconographic boundaries for the reach of the curse which, as we are told in the opening scene, frequents the places most often visited by the spirit in life. This makes these structures symbols for the confinement of the feminine in the home under the oppressive forces of patriarchy. Alternatively, through its encasement within a home, the curse can be interpreted as symbolic of Japanese malaise at the loss of (through processes such as globalization and the economic crash) traditional Japanese culture and community bonds, where the home was the centre of the family with the *ryōsaikenbo* at its heart. Thus, we can perceive more than one molar interpretation that can be formulated here, ensuring that one singular understanding cannot be unproblematically territorialized.

The house and the surrounding streets, by invoking such hermeneutic perspectives, can aid a pronounced deterritorialization and transformation of their regimes. As Deleuze and Guattari (1987) argue within their 'art of dosages' analogy, images which provide some grounding force, some inclination of the hermeneutic, which, when taken to with a fine file rather than a sledgehammer, produce a much more profound deterritorialization, or transition into molecularity, than if molar regimes were non-existent within an interpretation of the film. These molar understandings of the space of the home become falsified through the potentialities of other interpretations, producing a much more profound ungrounding of their static truths.

There is also the potential here then, for the formation of a deterritorializing any-space-whatever. As well as acting as boundaries or casing in the hermeneutic sense, the walled street and the structure of the house can also be seen to act as boundaries or gateways into the a-temporality of the space, which does not follow the normative, linear, human experiences of time, space and subjectivity. This is not to say that other, uninfected, surrounding areas of the house are not also any-space-whatevers. In fact the closing scene, depicting a much wider area with more deserted, littered streets, missing person posters and deathly silent roads, alludes to the fact that time seems to have been suspended here too and the people inhabiting these spaces, if there are any at all, are similarly unable to continue linearly through time. However, this house is a particular hotspot, a black hole which draws people to it, ungrounding them and allowing them to become affectively charged and fluid in order to become-other.[3] The house is an anomaly or a particularly concentrated, powerful any-space-whatever that, whilst not following natural laws, still has a specific shape, structure, size and logic of its own which is linked to violent transition.

The bodies, spaces and regimes this cursed house interrupts are perhaps much broader than those, based upon interpretations of the diegesis, suggested previously. It is a vacuum that could potentially unground and challenge any subjective, static positioning that comes into contact with it (not just gendered and national ideologies and positionings). In fact, the audience, in an assemblage with *Ju-On: The Grudge* have the potential to become ungrounded from their wide-ranging, subjective positionings in the a-temporal space of the house. Rather than just distanced witnesses to these a-temporal spaces, the audience is, at some points within the film (particularly within the opening montage), immersed into the filmic assemblage as a direct participant. This further confuses the film's temporality and the montage's perceived place within the past by giving it an immediacy and a sense of 'presentness' for the audience. This immediacy leads to our own (as the audience) ungroundings of subjectivity as the affective forces of the film become more intense and impactful upon our bodies. At one point within the montage it appears that Takeo's bloodied, shaking hands, rising up from the bottom of the frame may be our own, infusing our own bodies with the intensity of feeling that these hands are reacting to. Furthermore, towards

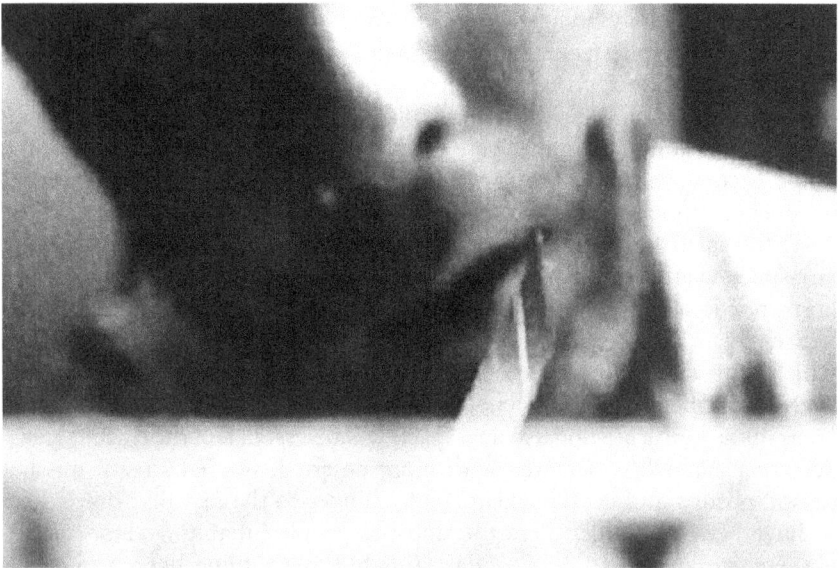

FIGURE 2 *Becoming Kayako: Takeo threatens us with a box-cutter,* Ju-On: The Grudge *(Shimizu, 2002).*

the end of the montage we become Kayako, seemingly dead, yet we see a blurry extreme close-up of Takeo coming towards us with a box-cutter, filling us with tension.

These scenes have the effect of schizophrenizing us as both audience member and direct participant, opening us to new affective forces, multifarious becomings and mutations. We can become ungrounded from our own personal subjective positionings within such an immersion in the film. Considering a reterritorialization of these scenes, however, we may simply become Takeo or become Kayako, taking on their subjective, molar positionings and their ensuing ungroundings which may not necessarily resonate personally with us. This schizophrenization involving Takeo perhaps places us within the position of the monster, allowing us to feel emotions of revulsion at the actions we have seemingly committed and confusion and fear because of our frantic behaviour. Conversely, we may feel an adrenaline-filled thrill at our violent acts and demonstration of power. Through Kayako, we may become territorialized within the position of victim, terrified and subjugated by the actions of Takeo. In addition, as we still retain some consciousness, despite the fact that, in a previous mid-shot of Kayako, we can clearly see that she is dead, we may also gain a thrilling, satisfactory feeling of vengeful intent. However, as these schizophrenizations, when in assemblage with the film and the scene, are very fleeting (lasting for no more than a few seconds in this montage), one could question whether these complex molar positionings are realistically inferred, registered and embodied simultaneously as the audience is watching. Perhaps many of these hermeneutic interpretations are created (or 'become') after the event, after the audience has disconnected from their assemblage with the film and are given time to realize these becomings. Within the immanent moment of the film it seems nothing (thought, comprehension and concepts) but affective intensity and bodies can exist.

We are never more so bombarded sensually and affectively than within this opening montage scene and this one brief moment of immersion may seem short lived. However, once we are plunged into this affective, immersive, a-temporal discourse we are perhaps primed to receive other scenes of the film in such an immersive way. In other words, the audience transfers the affects accumulated within this opening scene to future scenes, melding them with the affects produced in the montage and diversifying the quality of the affective experience throughout the whole film. Deleuze also refers to this discourse of affect in his discussion of the affection-image. He explores films such as *La Passion de Jeanne d'Arc* (*The Passion of Joan of Arc*) (1928) where the affection-image dominates, but highlights how, within some films, such images do not need to be predominate as they 'flow' 'so well that they permeate all other shots in advance' (Deleuze, 2005: 111). The opening scene in *Ju-On: The Grudge* then affectively permeates other subsequent shots and sequences within the film.

The opening scene is so affectively violent as it ungrounds our expectations of cinema and the usage of linear, movement-images that we are used to. Instead these are superseded by time-images which open us to multipotentialities of progression and becoming for the film. As discussed, this a-temporality is perhaps problematized by some sense of linear logic, of a positioning within the past. However, it is through these time-images that any molar interpretations formed become falsified and never quite fully explanatory of the scene on their own without supplementation from other, once separate hermeneutic ideas. Thus, linear regimes of time which could have been the primary, territorializing force, informing our understanding of the film, persist within this time-image, but only liminally and fragmentarily. It can be conceptualized, however, that such hermeneutic regimes were perhaps the primary, informative forces within a time prior to the violent murder of Kayako and Toshio, and exist as remnants after this event, one which is distinctly associated with the time-image and its deterritorializing effects.

The montage scene then renders a breaking point in linear time, which, considering its reterritorializing facets, has taken place in the past. This scene could be interpreted therefore as a recollection-image. Within these recollection-images, Kayako, Toshio, Takeo and, by association, the audience, in the process of interminably becoming-other, due to their sensory-motor link being severed (their linearity disrupted), slip between different layers of the past, exploring 'the myriad layers in which they exist as many past selves' (Martin-Jones, 2006: 62). Therefore, the film, rather than, in a sequential manner, beginning with a depiction of the breaking-point of linear time in the present, may begin in the thick of this indeterminate state. The audience (through their schizophrenization) and the characters slip into the layer of the past when the murder took place, which, unlike a linear, molar flashback, becomes our own and the character's imminent present. The flashback, as Deleuze argues, 'is a conventional extrinsic device: it is generically indicated by a dissolve-link ... It is like a sign with the words: "watch out! Recollection". It can, therefore, indicate, by convention, a causality which is psychological [or in the mind], but still analogous to a sensory-motor determinism' (2013: 49), allowing for the progression of a linear narrative. Within this recollection-image on the other hand, indiscernibility and suspension between different layers of time, past and present, the actual and the virtual, is created. This produces the affective pure optical and sound situation inherent to the any-space-whatever, the indeterminate, crude and brutal state where the sensory-motor schema breaks down and the space, its flows and transformations, can only be apprehended upon the body.

However, Deleuze argues that the recollection-image may not 'give us the proper equivalent of the optical-sound image' (2013: 56). To achieve this, the film and its characters would have to be in a state of not being able to remember, as the act of remembering or recollecting can be perceived as acting as a link between perception and action, re-establishing sensory-motor continuity. It is in this state of not being able to remember, Deleuze (2013) argues, that connections with virtuality, with duration, are made. Therefore, there are molar, grounding elements of the montage scene within *Ju-On: The Grudge*. This recollection-image can be perceived to create a linear continuity where violence experienced by Kayako and Toshio, in a layer of the past, directly leads to their actions within the present and their future actions, specifically, their violence against those who enter the house.

It is not only, however, within the montage scene that the film slips to different temporal layers. This further confuses, not just the characters', but our own temporal positionings as audience members and perhaps confuses the act of remembering, as, within some of these scenes, it is unclear who is the active character in this sense. These scenes then, heighten a suspension within an any-space-whatever, ungrounded from molar dictates.

Within a scene involving the ex-detective Tōyama Yūji (Tanaka Yoji), who returns to the cursed house to burn it to the ground, having been tormented for years by the spirits, we experience a particularly interesting temporal slippage. Yūji opens one of the doors in the house to see his own daughter, Izumi (Uehara Misa), merely a child in what he perceives as his present, now grown into a young adolescent, exploring the cursed house with her school friends. Izumi also sees her father, her past, at this same moment and both stare at each other for some time.

FIGURE 3 *Izumi and Yūji stare at each other across a temporal void,* Ju-On: The Grudge *(Shimizu, 2002)*.

However, neither communicate as both become suspended in the face of such a-temporality, not knowing how to act or move forward. Here we see a collision between a number of layers of time and existentiality which Izumi and Yūji come to lie between, confusing what we perceive to be the present. Izumi simultaneously exists on a layer of time she perceives as the present and a layer of the past where her father appears to her as a virtual being. However, from Yūji's perspective, he inhabits the present rather than the past, Izumi is the virtual being, and the layer of time she originates from is an image of the future. Here then, the act of remembering is confused: who, Yūji or Izumi, is actively thinking, remembering here? Thus, this scene is perhaps closer to producing a pure optical and sound image than the montage scene. Within this scene, the cursed house is the site of this particularly intense a-temporal, affective void where past, present and future intermingle, suspending both ourselves and the characters.

Despite no schizophrenization of the audience occurring within this scene, they are still in assemblage with the filmic body, intermingling with it and receiving and transmitting affects. Within this assemblage, rather than becoming fully immersed in the filmic body, audiences 'straddle that threshold between here and there' (Barker, 2009: 72) inhabiting both their own individual bodies in a separate existential plane (of the theatre for instance) and the body of the film itself. Thus, even before audiences encounter the ungrounded cursed house, they are interstitial. Forming assemblages with the cursed house then exacerbates the state of suspension between different layers, making it more difficult to reterritorialize molar understandings (not that this is impossible, however) and bringing them closer to becoming malleable, transformative beings.

Such an intermingling of layers of time occurs once again when Izumi, terrorized by Kayako and her deceased friends in her own home, witnesses her father, long dead, sitting on the floor in her family's shrine room.

This exemplifies another recollection-image which facilitates a dynamic, affective return to the past, that is much more physical, and embodied than any linear flashback. However, it could be argued that both of these scenes involving Izumi and Yūji are quite repetitive as in each scene a layer of the past or future (depending upon whose perspective, Yūji's or Izumi's, you take) is traversed and each time the same person is inhabiting this layer. Why can more diverse layers not be traversed to when there are a multiplicity of temporalities and existentialities that exist? Why cannot Izumi, for instance, travel to other layers of time when other people have fallen foul of the curse, people like her classmates whom she left behind to perish in the house? Whilst these recollection-images may not be as varying as they have the potential to be, the affective, embodied responses these slippages into different layers of time induce, for both characters and audience members, still vary in quality and it therefore becomes difficult to argue for a repetitiveness. Further

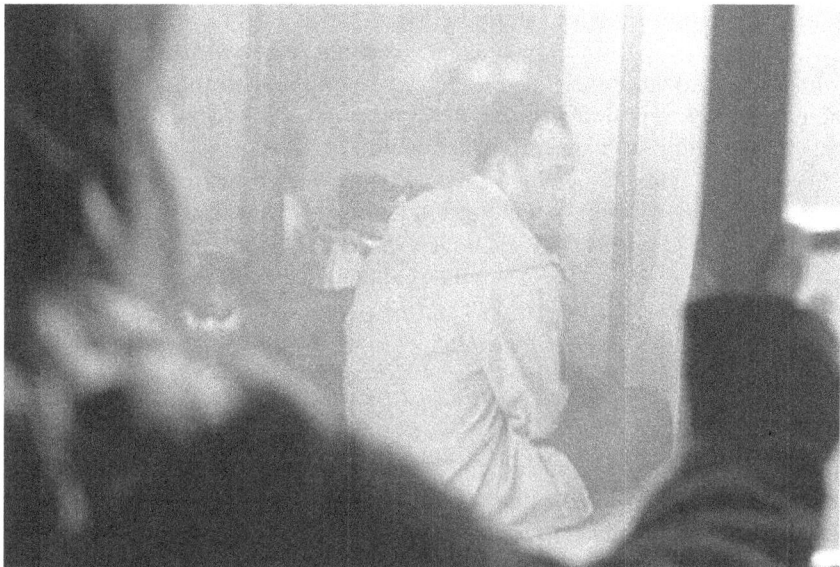

FIGURE 4 *Izumi sees her deceased father in her home's shrine room,* Ju-On: The Grudge *(Shimizu, 2002).*

challenging this repetitiveness, the second recollection-image scene is quite significant in terms of its rendering of overlaps between layers of time and existentiality, opening us to new relational thoughts on further collisions. Its significance lies in the fact that the slippage between layers of time, whilst previously only occurring at the site of the cursed house, here occurs at another, separate location. This attests to the ability of the a-temporal void of the house to expand its reach, to capture environments which surround it in its gravitational pull, deterritorializing or knocking out of sync the linear conceptions of time and space within them so that they too become affective, disconnected any-space-whatevers.

Thus, we can imagine that much wider ranging environments than this, not even just those within the boundaries of Japan, but within America, Britain, China, Korea etc., can potentially be pulled into the a-temporal void whose epicentre lies in the cursed house (creating a larger amorphous set). Here they become relational spaces, ungrounded from their national, cultural boundaries, intermingling and colliding with other environments, one amongst many disconnected spaces that have been knocked out of sync and can be apprehended upon the body. Indeed, international spaces have become such when we consider that the film and its sequels have travelled transnationally, infecting other nations and audiences with their affective, deterritorializing forces. In relation to this, the force of the house and the curse upon it has also infected horror film producers from other nations with its intense affective, aesthetic forces, inspiring them to not merely remake these films but to imagine new becomings, new potentialities for the curse in their own filmic versions. For instance, the Korean film *Gabal* (*The Wig*) (2005), inspired by *Ju-On: The Grudge's* imagery of the *Onryō*, creates a new imagining of a vengeful spirit which has possessed a wig given to a leukaemia patient, cursing the wearer. These spaces, however, which become intermingled within the a-temporal void of the house, are not completely deterritorialized and they bring their own national, cultural molar regimes into the assemblage. This is reflected within *Gabal* (*The Wig*) which brings distinct Korean inflections to the tale of the vengeful spirit.

Special consideration should also be given to the American remakes of *Ju-On: The Grudge* and its sequels in relation to the idea of the becomings-other of the curse, the expansion of it and the a-temporal voids that house it. The first and second American iterations of the *Ju-On: The Grudge* mythos (*The Grudge* and *The Grudge 2* (2006)) were directed by Shimizu Takashi and thus the becomings-other of the original film were perhaps not so radical in these instances, particularly when one considers that *The Grudge* keeps its Tokyo setting from the original Japanese film. Although, within *The Grudge*, different characters from the original, such as Karen Davis (Sarah Michelle-Geller) and Doug (Jason Behr), two Americans who have moved to Japan, fall victim to the curse. Therefore, new strands of narrative are formed within this remake which, when considered relationally and in an assemblage with the original film, become part of a rhizomatic web of narratives of those inflicted by the curse. Thus, we can perhaps imagine *The Grudge* as a sequel, a spin-off, rather than a remake, as it does much to add new realizations of the *Ju-On: The Grudge* mythos rather than just simply re-create and copy it faithfully.[4]

In the case of *The Grudge 2* and *The Grudge 3* (2009) (directed by British filmmaker, Toby Wilkins) the effect of the cursed house is visualized as expanding into other territories as its force reaches Chicago, creating an a-temporal void within an apartment block after a cursed girl moves there. This void may interestingly allow Kayako and Toshio to not only traverse time, again travelling between different layers of the past, but also space, flitting between existential planes in Japan and Chicago. This movement between spaces means, in itself, a collision of temporal layers and the creation of a-temporality, as both Japan and the USA exist within different time-zones. Thus, the boundaries between Japan and the USA become less clearly demarcated and more relational and intermingled at the site of this film. The space-time compression that occurs here between these two geographically distant voids aptly reflects the use of digital media today, in particular the web. In many of our social interactions on the web we have the ability to instantaneously interact and communicate with people on the other side of the world to us. Like Kayako and Toshio, within these interactions we split ourselves across different time-zones and spaces, existing on the plane we are communicating from and also upon the plane of the other body we are communicating with.[5]

Further eroding the boundaries between Japan and the USA and contributing new realizations of the *Ju-On: The Grudge* mythos is Pesce's 2020 film, *The Grudge*. Alluding, again, to the space-time compression which characterizes contemporary experiences and interactions today, Pesce's film envisions the curse being imported to the USA (Pennsylvania specifically) in 2004 via an American woman, Fiona Landers (Tara Westwood), who visited the iconic house in Japan in her capacity as a social worker. The very beginning of the film is the only point at which we see Kayako, who torments Fiona as she flees the house. After bringing the curse to Pennsylvania, Fiona eventually succumbs to it, killing her family along with herself and becoming, like Kayako, a vengeful spirit, condemning all those whom enter her house. We see many of her victims throughout the course of the film, flitting between the years 2004 and 2006. Fiona's family home thus becomes a new a-temporal void, perhaps connected to the house in Tokyo and the apartment block in Chicago, creating another node in the rhizomatic web of the curse's connections.

Considering the American remakes as alternative versions within the web of the original Japanese productions, rather than apart from them (as has often been the case in other scholarly works), the spaces and people infected by these a-temporal regimes increase and diversify. Within this web we could also consider any transmedia products that build upon the *Ju-On: The Grudge* franchise. In particular, the *Ju-On: The Grudge* mangas, the recent Netflix series (*Ju-On: Origins,* 2020–) and even the innumerable works of fan-art and fan-fiction, could be considered as expanding the reach of the curse transnationally. Multiple texts centred around one main filmic text that are integrated closely become a 'transmediated story, which unfolds across multiple media platforms, with each new text making a distinctive and valuable [and most notably, affective] contribution to the whole' (Booth, 2010: 33–4).[6] As well as new imaginings and becomings for the central text, these transmedia texts bring new, affective qualities to the experience of the franchise as a whole.

Whilst perhaps not in the case of works inspired by *Ju-On: The Grudge* (like *Gabal (The Wig)*) which fragment and transform elements of the franchise more prolifically, the characters Kayako and Toshio are constants throughout the various film series' and transmedia products. Thus, we can view them as particularly useful, primed characters who traverse the rhizomatic web of transmediated and transcultural products. They exist as many selves, encoded (sometimes partially) with many different molarities and many variations of affective quality within the many different nodes that constitutes the rhizome of the *Ju-On: The Grudge* franchise. It is here, if we perceive the wider duration of the original film, in this broader external reality, that Kayako and Toshio, really demonstrate their powers of becoming and their traversal of space. Spaces which continued to diversify and expand, not only as extra-filmic products surfaced, but also as the original film travelled the globe and infected other cultures. These are figures then that can perhaps be appropriated transnationally within film culture to explore tumultuous societal shifts and the deterritorializations and reterritorializations that societies perpetually undergo.

This is precisely what the following section explores, predominantly focusing upon Kayako (although Toshio and others are discussed briefly) as she is the main antagonist of the film. Kayako can be understood under the Deleuzian concept of becoming-woman, a fluid transformative being, able to traverse the any-space-whatevers of the film. She can mutate into other forms and new economies of identity and by doing so inspires within us our own becoming-others and transformative states. As Lewis argues:

> By embodying such paradoxes, of incorporating seemingly discordant fragments, these beings call in to question the categories according to which a culture defines the boundaries between normal and pathological ... by virtue of inhabiting the "borderlands" they promise liberation from the very strictures of binary definition. Their hybridity challenges our ontological hygiene.
>
> (in McRoy, 2005: 120)

Subjective fluidities: Becoming-woman

Ju-On: The Grudge depicts a wide range of female characters who each have their own distinct experiences of the curse and the deterritorializing any-space-whatever of the house. The emphasis on the representation of women in this film perhaps makes reference to a specific experience or interpretation of ungrounding and societal transformation occurring in Japan. Namely, 'how changing gender roles in Japan have recently created instability in the dominant narrative of national identity' (Martin-Jones, 2006: 195), contributing to a 'stuttering' or a breaking point within conceptions of linear Japanese national time and space. The idea of disruptive, mutating gender roles is explicitly linked to the wider break of the economic crash of 1990, as following this, many men, consigned to unemployment, directed their malaise towards women who were now competing with them for a limited number of jobs (competing with them, also, to end their suspension) when their traditional role should be in the home (a role that the men also felt they could not appropriate). This is an interesting argument as it is possible that the film does render such a specific, gendered dislocation. By placing the blame for such disruption on women, particularly the monstrous Kayako, linearity and progress can perhaps be reinstated as the figure of woman can be abjected and rejected, re-establishing the dominance and power of the patriarchal order.

Such a linear discourse, however, does not play out within *Ju-On: The Grudge*, Kayako is not (as one would conventionally expect) destroyed at the end of the film, thus, the milieu, the patriarchal order, cannot be said to be reterritorialized here. Instead, the film fuses gendered, molar ideologies with molecularity, creating a perpetual status of the encompassing milieu never being able to fully reconstitute the situation. Molar, gendered thoughts here inform and influence the state of molecularity, the film positions gender as the most transformative, fluid element of Japanese society, breaking free from and disrupting the normative order. However, these molarities can never stabilize the situation, arrest the transformations occurring and place them back within the patriarchal milieu.

To explain further, the structure and narrative of the film does not return to, in any sense, the one correct narrative of Japanese national gender discourses and roles, using the labyrinthine structure 'to strengthen its claim to legitimacy as the dominant narrative form' (Martin-Jones, 2006: 5). In such a scenario, all other labyrinthine possibilities for gendered ways of being would be refuted, positing the reinstatement of the subordinate role of women to men in society as the only workable, viable option for existence and progress. Instead, the film remains within an indeterminate state with multiple, viable conceptualizations of gender on display. For women, this film is then perhaps an empowering rendering or mapping, creating a fluid and performative identity for them with a 'labyrinthine ability to unground the repetition of the same on which identity is based' (Martin-Jones, 2006: 198). The film is perhaps then a 'subversive celebration of the new-found power of this re-emergent section of society' (Martin-Jones, 2006: 203), the power of women to dislocate and suspend the repetition of the same and classical, patriarchal time. Of course, the reverse could be argued, however (emphasizing the pessimism of Deleuzian thought as Culp (2016) does); that, rather than empowering, women too (like men) are confused, disrupted and trapped within an indeterminate space between perception and action, because of the new roles they have sought to appropriate.[7] Regardless, the characters, especially Kayako and Rika, can be understood in conjunction with Deleuze's ideas of becoming-woman or,[8] similarly (in the case of male characters perhaps), in relation to body without organs. The characters are potentially more fluid, relational, transforming and unfixed beings, rather than clearly defined, gendered, subjective beings, who stand for or signify a molar regime. However, these bodies are also crossed by molarities or lines of segmentarity in some way.

Within the concept of becoming-woman it is implied that 'actual women might be potentially closer to becoming-woman [and the body without organs] than men' (Powell, 2007: 99) and that men may have to imitate the behaviours and encapsulate the ideologies of women in order to become-other.

As Rio also highlights, the woman is often aligned with bodily expressivity and as such is a particularly productive site 'for the emergence of the affective-performative' (2008: 31), for deterritorialization and becoming. As briefly discussed already, the usage of the term 'woman' by Deleuze has been disparaged by other scholars as it incites molar ideologies of women when its aim, seemingly, is to produce ideas of the molecularity of being. Rather than simply dismissing this concept and its molar implications however, grounded, encoded women and the molecularity and fluidity that they simultaneously demonstrate under this concept, can be interpreted as inspirational models for all becomings, the becomings of men and women alike.

Perhaps one of the most informative characters, within *Ju-On: The Grudge*, to analyse in relation to this concept is Kayako, who has often been conceptualized as the archetypal monstrous-female by Japanese horror cinema scholars. An abject, threatening being who challenges the normative roles of women and dismantles the patriarchal order. One of the more obvious ways in which the film territorializes Kayako into this psychoanalytical ideology is during scenes when reference to or representation of Kayako's sexuality is made. In particular, depictions of blood on her skin during the montage scene and a scene in which she crawls down the stairs to confront Rika can be said to depict Kayako's sexuality by signifying menstrual blood.[9]

However, what is perhaps more significant is the prolific presence of Toshio within the film who is a constant reminder of Kayako's sexuality and her reproductive functions and organs, the most abject of all things 'for it contained a new life form which passed from inside to outside bringing with it traces of its contamination – blood, afterbirth, faeces' (Creed, 1993: 49). The predominance of this representation of Kayako as a mother has led to further theorizations of her as a monstrous, nightmare mother who subverts the traditional, national ideology of the *ryōsaikenbo*. Many scholars have highlighted how the film contains signs of the neglect of Toshio, a clear indication of the demise of the *ryōsaikenbo*, including obvious aesthetic indications such as cuts and bruises on his legs, and representations of some disturbed behaviour and actions, including a lack of speech and allusions to him scavenging food whilst his parents are absent.

These depictions have subsequently been linked to wider contextual issues in Japan by scholars like Balmain (2008), especially the crisis in birth rates, a perceived lack of interest of women in having children and the rise of women in the workplace who therefore have no time to care for children. However, whilst scholars like Balmain (2008) position the concept of the nightmare mother as culturally and nationally specific to Japan, it is actually a hybridized, transnational concept, speaking to audiences both in Japan and in the West. In particular, it draws upon Freud's theorizations of the mother who wishes to keep the male child from entering the symbolic order and desires the child's regression back to the womb, as the child is an extension of herself which allows her to be part of the symbolic order.

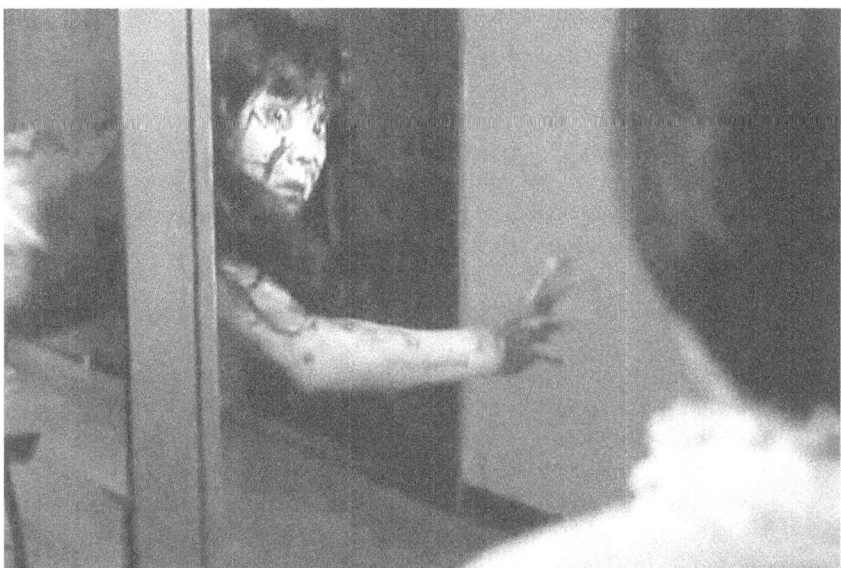

FIGURE 5 *Kayako covered in blood, signifying her abject femininity,* Ju-On: The Grudge *(Shimizu, 2002).*

Thus, Toshio can be theorized as such a child, unable to separate himself from his mother, an idea that has great credence when one considers that Toshio never ages, he remains in a perpetual state of childhood and is thus unable to take his place in the symbolic order. Furthermore, Toshio is often confined within the cursed house, the domain of his mother, which becomes 'an abject rendering of the maternal womb' (2008: 132) a container which controls, limits and unifies the two as one entity.

On an aside, however, this is perhaps an oversimplification of Toshio's character, particularly when we consider how Toshio is able to break free from his confinement in the home and haunt Rika in various locations. Toshio is also rarely depicted alongside Kayako, each are always featured on-screen separately which, again, highlighting a separateness, an individuality and a freedom of action, perhaps challenges the idea of Toshio as the eternal foetus. Toshio, as a distinct being from Kayako, is also able to become-other, and perpetually transform to suit differing situations and environments. However, following Powell's (2007) comments, highlighted previously, about the concept of becoming-woman, perhaps Toshio is such a fluid being because of his proximity to femininity and the woman, he is an extension of Kayako and is thus also emblematic of the figure of becoming-woman.

Toshio, however, can be said to often become-animal (a more fluid concept, like becoming-woman, where the psychoanalytical restrictions imposed upon desire are ungrounded), or, more specifically, become a cat. Within a segment depicting the deaths of two characters, Katsuya (Tsuda Kanji) and Kazumi Tokunaga (Matsuda Shuri), who have moved to the cursed house with their elderly mother, Sachie (Isomura Chikako), Toshio appears alongside a catatonic Kazumi lying on a bed, making cat-like noises and violently hissing at Katsuya as he attempts to save his wife. Toshio is also depicted as assimilating many of the mannerisms of a cat, he moves swiftly and is often unseen as he slams doors and litters the floor. Furthermore, we are often presented with the image of a black cat within the film. For instance, in an early scene, depicting Rika's initial exploration of the cursed house, she enters one bedroom, presumably once Toshio's, and hears scratching coming from a sealed closet. Opening this closet, a black cat is revealed, resting on some pillows. The cat then moves towards Rika and the camera, switching to a shot of Rika from behind, then pans around again to reveal Toshio sat in the corner of the closet, holding it.

The becoming-animal of Toshio can be considered alongside Japanese folklore, as, within traditional tales and subsequently horror cinema, there has been a trend of *bakeneko mono* or monster cat tales, a variation of the *Kaidan* (ghost) and *onryō* (vengeful spirit) tales. These *bakeneko mono* draw upon the belief that 'if a cat's owner is killed and it licks their blood, the creature will become a cat monster or kaibyō (also known as a bakeneko) that could possess people and control malevolent spirits' (Balmain, 2008: 65), as well as shapeshift from cat to human forms. There are some significant parallels between *Ju-On: The Grudge* and the *bakeneko* film, *Kaibyō Otama-ga-ike (The Ghost Cat of Otama Pond)* (1960), where a young couple, lost in the woods, come across an abandoned house and seek shelter within it. There, the female character, Keiko (Kitazawa Noriko), is cursed as she catches sight of the ghostly form of an old woman, a transformative *bakeneko*, and, like Kazumi, she falls into a catatonic state. Thus, *Ju-On: The Grudge* can be said to pay homage to and ground itself partially within this historical, folkloric and filmic trend.

However, such an interpretation of Toshio can be problematic. Often, within these tales, it is women that turn into *bakeneko*, 'suggesting a causal link between femininity, shape-shifting and death' (Balmain, 2008: 73). For instance, within *Yabu no naka no Kuroneko (Kuroneko)* (1968) two seductive women, taking on the mannerisms of a cat, entrance and entrap their prey, draining them of blood. Thus, these films and tales have often been interpreted as, once again, a comment on male anxieties, centred around, during the 1960s, female emancipation and sexual liberation (which were, as in the West and other countries during this time, prominent movements in Japan). However, once again, considering the previous comments of Powell (2007), if we think of Toshio as close to becoming-woman through his connections with Kayako and his inability to enter the symbolic order, such an interpretation ceases to be incongruent with these traditions. This does little, however, to transform the alignment of femininity with notions of mutation, malleability and chaos. Toshio, if understood as male, however, appropriating these so-called feminine properties, poses the potential to mutate these molar notions.

Considering these different interpretations of Toshio, which can never be unproblematically accepted as encapsulating the singular truth of his character, one of the other ways in which to apprehend him then is upon the body. Within such an apprehension we register the two entities of Kayako and Toshio as distinct, with differing affective qualities (one scene particularly exemplifies this, which will be examined later). However, both Kayako and Toshio are intimately connected in an assemblage at the site of the cursed home, both forming part of a complex rhizomatic web of beings, subjectivities, forces and affects, which grows when others come into contact with this void.

Returning to a deeper consideration of Kayako and the concept of becoming-woman, similarly her character cannot be defined wholly by a singular archetype like the monstrous-feminine. At various points in the film Kayako, like Toshio, appears as a victim figure, brutalized and murdered by her husband. Furthermore, Kayako often appears as an invisible force or else a dark, shadowy, ill-defined mass where, due to the lack of identifying features, no such paradigm like the monstrous-feminine can be unproblematically applied. In the face of such hybridity and multiplicity, singular molar ideologies and concepts become somewhat inadequate in trying to form an understanding of Kayako. Thus, as before, a useful way in which audiences can apprehend her or know her at some level is through engaging with her through the body, registering her actions and transformations (and the mutations she potentially induces in ourselves, as audiences, when we form a bodily assemblage with her) in an affective manner. How does Kayako then, specifically demonstrate such a fluidity and intensity within *Ju-On: The Grudge*? And how do we, the audience, apprehend this? To address such questions, below, Kayako's transformations, her malleability of being and the affective forces produced are mapped out.

Upon her initial mutation into a malevolent spirit (captured within the opening montage depicting the break with linear time), Kayako becomes a perpetually transforming figure, with the ability to also change the objects, environments and people around her. The first encounter we have with the affective, becoming-woman Kayako is within the first scenes depicting Rika, where, claiming the life of Sachie, whom Rika is caring for, she is at first invisible, yet her presence is palpably felt through the eerie, foreboding undertone of music, creating an affective reaction, a chill up the spine. She then mutates into a dark, ebbing, shadowy figure leaning over Sachie, only her eyes a discernibly different colour, the rest existing as pure intensity. This shadowy Kayako, in one shot, appears to have grown from the shadows of the room itself and beyond, the lower half of her body extending through

FIGURE 6 *Kayako's shadowy force engulfs a security guard in Hitomi's building,* Ju-On: The Grudge *(Shimizu, 2002).*

the *shōji* doors, highlighting her malleability and flexibility to mutate or become-other, her ability to create an infinite multitude of assemblages with her environment and manipulate it. This shadowy form is one we see her appropriate only once more when she stalks Katsuya's sister, Hitomi (Itō Misaki), in her office block. Taking on this dark shape, we witness on a CCTV camera, Kayako leaking from the shadows of the washroom to engulf an investigating security guard.

Soon after, as we see when watching the CCTV footage back within a scene involving the ex-detective Tōyama Yūji, she eventually takes on a much more recognizable and distinct form of a female figure. Walking into the corridor, she gradually engulfs the security camera image in the same darkness, revealing at the last second, a pair of wide, staring eyes.

This scene is particularly a-temporal and affective, highlighting Kayako's ability to transgress normative laws of time and space. The audience, and even the character of Yūji himself, are unsure as to whether, following the capture and presumed death or disappearance of the security guard, Kayako, at the time of this recorded incident or in Yūji's present moment, has possessed or manipulated the footage. This leads to ungroundings of linear, logical temporality and existentiality. It is clear through this scene that Kayako can transform and open herself (as well as the audience) to further multitudes of becoming.

FIGURE 7 *Kayako in a more discernible form,* Ju-On: The Grudge *(Shimizu, 2002).*

Kayako, in her much more emblematic, recognizable form, with her ghostly, white face, dark, shadowed eyes, long black hair and white funeral gown, is first seen in the third episode, telling the tale of the Tokunaga family. Here, she appears only briefly at a window overlooking the landing of the house. A fleeting vision which appears quite late within the film, considering that this is the main aesthetic associated with the character. This form does recur throughout the film, particularly towards the end, however, its use is not as prolific as would be expected, perhaps as it is arguably not the most affective and transformative becoming of Kayako. This could be attributed to the numerous moments within the film where Kayako is unseen. Whilst her presence is not always visually portrayed within the film, we register it affectively, at the level of the body. This element of the film is achieved through the depiction of fleeting shadows (opsigns), the appropriation of some of the 'slasher-stalker' camera techniques such as high-angled shots looking down on characters and shots showing the back of characters, giving the impression the character is being followed, and through extra-diegetic scores (sonsigns) of eerie, discordant music. These elements of the film, which target other parts of our sensorium as well as our vision, create a much broader range of qualities of affect which are potentially more intense than the affects generated when we finally come to witness the full visual appearance of Kayako.

Within the third episode, Kayako's presence is felt at the level of the body throughout, except for the brief moment of visual recognition at the very end.

We are first introduced to the unseen presence of Kayako when Katsuya returns home from work to find his wife in a catatonic state on a bed, the ghostly form of Toshio standing next to her. Once Kayako's force enters the room, the tone, tempo and composition of the music (sonsign) change from one of slight playfulness associated with the child Toshio, to one much more sinister, drawn out and foreboding. We, the audience, feel this change in presence and a sense of greater imperilment at an affective, bodily level through these sonsigns which create a different intensity and quality of affective resonance. We are also made aware of Kayako's presence through our assemblage with the body of Kazumi, her catatonia resembling our own suspension in the film viewing process, an indeterminate, affective state. As Kazumi's body arches painfully in response to Kayako's entrance, her voice resembling the death rattle of Kayako's, we become similarly shocked and pained by the affective charge of Kayako. These intensities disengage us from static, molar notions of subjectivity, and, unable to be explained by them, push us towards bodily engagements with these sequences.

Furthermore, within this episode we are bombarded by more affective forces as we also connect with Katsuya and engage with his sudden descent into a dark, sinister state. This can be considered a becoming-other as he takes on many of the same psychotic mannerisms and expressions of Kayako's murderous husband, Takeo. This differing accumulation of affect begins with a sudden, deep release of air from his lungs, reflecting our own

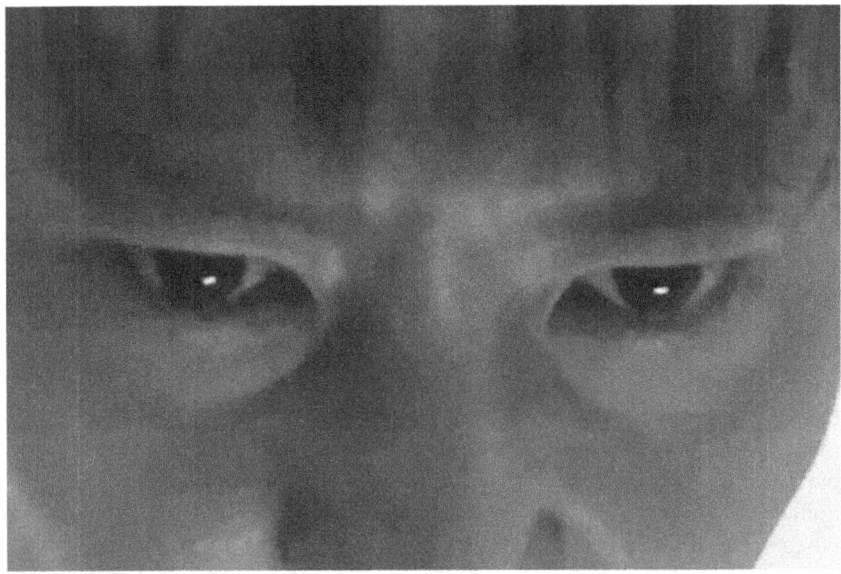

FIGURE 8 *Extreme close-up of Katsuya's face,* Ju-On: The Grudge *(Shimizu, 2002).*

release of affective tension when we disengage with Kazumi's charged body. In an affection-image (the close-up), a dark shadow then appears at his forehead, his eyes turn to slits, he begins the violent biting of his nails which creates a puncturing sound and he starts murmuring aggressively about the paternity of his (non-existent) son. As with Kazumi, the audience, in assemblage with the character of Katsuya, becomes-other with him, a surge of affect is felt, heightened by the use of extreme close-ups on his face, as we too feel Kayako manipulating and mutating us along with him.

These images of Katsuya, the dark shadow which descends upon his face, the sonsign of the biting of his nails, and of his deep, laboured exhalation, produce eclectic affective forces which impact our sensorium.

By rendering these affective forces traceable to the malevolent Kayako, it is clear she has mastered the state of being affective and forming bodily assemblages with the world and the people she encounters. Thus, by forming assemblages with Kayako, this film attempts to enable audiences to realize their potentiality for becoming affective and transformative. Whilst we do not always witness Kayako visually, and thus we may not realize this potentiality through her changing form specifically, we become-other through registering the sonsigns associated with her presence upon our bodies and also through our engagements with the living characters (e.g. Katsuya, Kazumi, Rika and Izumi), who are, like ourselves, transformed by her power. We are aware of her presence, her affective, transformative power through these characters, and we too perhaps become-women or deterritorialized any-persons-whoever who have the ability to traverse the world in a bodily, affective manner.

Finally, one of the most profound demonstrations of Kayako's fluidity, her becoming-woman or becoming-other, occurs within the final scenes of the film. Within these scenes, Rika rushes to the aid of her friend Mariko (Shibata Kayoko) who has been lured to the house by Toshio. As we see what appears to be an illusion of Mariko, screaming and kicking her legs as she is dragged into the attic, only for her to completely disappear without trace, it can be inferred that we have once again slipped to another layer of time where Mariko was captured, a transcendence once again instigated by the affective, mutable forces of Kayako.

Rather than Kayako instigating the recollection-image, or the playing out of the potentiality of Mariko being dragged into the attic, however, perhaps this time it is the affective forces of Rika, firmly trapped within the any-space-whatever of the cursed house and losing her conception of linear time and sensory-motor capacity, who has forced this becoming or slippage. Prior to this, it may even be so that Kayako fabricated the phone call Mariko makes to Rika, transforming herself to match Mariko's voice and appearance, just as she did at another stage in the film. When tormenting Hitomi, Kayako transformed herself into her brother, Katsuya,[10] and stood at her door, tricking her into opening it.

FIGURE 9 *Kayako becomes Katsuya*, Ju-On: The Grudge *(Shimizu, 2002)*.

Nevertheless, this is not the most significant becoming under consideration here. In fact, multiple, significant becomings occur within a sequence shortly following the events involving Mariko. Rika searches around the dark attic for Mariko, until a point of view shot shows Kayako, in her most recognizable *onryō* form, swiftly crawling towards her. Rika flees down the stairs, passing by a mirror on the wall. Here, all urgency to escape the house is lost as the reflection caught in the mirror was not that of her own, but that of Kayako's. This scene can be considered as demonstrating a becoming-other of both Kayako and Rika, yet for now it is considered on the part of Kayako. Affective tension, accumulated from the rapid, frenzied scene of Rika's escape from the attic, accompanied by a fast tempo score, is dissipated, particularly through a sonsign where the music fades out into a wispy echo and then silence. However, affective tension soon begins to accumulate again when Rika is stopped in her tracks and begins inspecting the mirror. An eerie, graduating score accompanies a quick zoom-in on Rika's reflected face until, her face filling the frame, a conventional flashback occurs, depicting a quick succession of images presenting various characters Rika has encountered, some of them holding their faces in their hands, their fingers framing their eyes.

These flashback images differ significantly from the recollection-images described previously as, rather than inter-mingling with an assumed present and becoming experiential, flashbacks such as this occur within the mind.

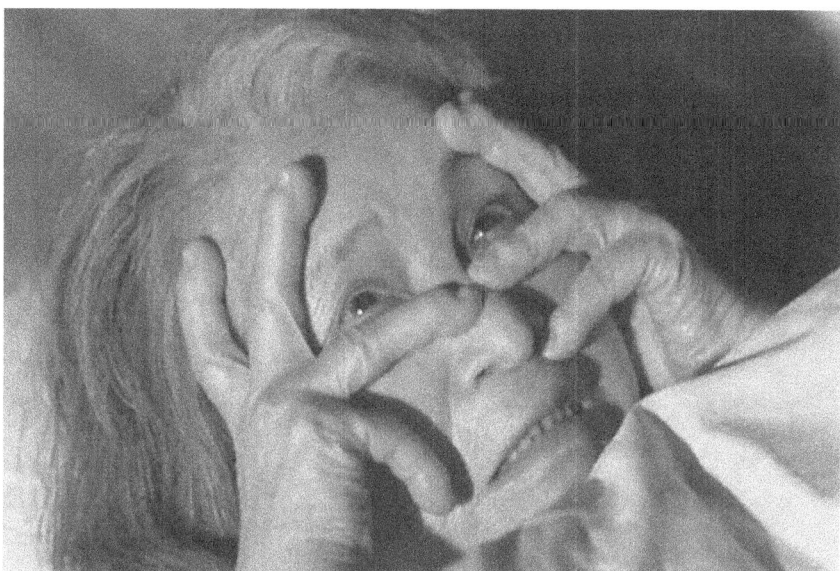

FIGURE 10 *One of the flashback images, Sachie holds her hands to her face,* Ju-On: The Grudge *(Shimizu, 2002).*

In this instance, Rika's mind, as the camera zooms into her face to signify this. They are therefore an objective mechanism pertinent to the formation of linear, progressive thought on past events. Thus, this sequence perhaps disrupts the accumulation of affect, disrupts our bodily engagement with the film as we become more distanced and objective through it. Here we can reterritorialize ourselves and the characters of Rika and Kayako into more linear, static positionings. For instance, because of the re-establishment of linearity through the flashback, Rika arguably becomes the 'final girl' of Carol Clover's (1992) conception, the privileged female character able to reach out and understand the mind of the monster.

However, the flashback's transition through the causal chain to the desired outcome is relatively short. Rika recalls these images so that she too frames her eyes with her fingers, channelling her vision to see more clearly the uncanny, invisible things occurring around her. Whilst our bodily engagement may be disrupted it is soon restored. While still looking in the mirror, Rika covers her face and peers through the gaps in her fingers, potentially mimicking the actions of the audience, too afraid to look but at the same time too enthralled to look away. Upon doing this, a side-portrait shot of Rika transitions into a quick, disorientating room spin, accompanied by a high pitched score, which signals a 'becoming-other'. Rika's reflection then becomes Kayako and Kayako becomes Rika's reflected image.

FIGURE 11 *Kayako becomes Rika's reflected image,* Ju-On: The Grudge *(Shimizu, 2002).*

Seemingly, she becomes our own reflection too as a point-of-view shot immerses us once again into the filmic space and we stare into the mirror at our transformed reflection.

The audience return to a bodily assemblage with the film and inhabit the confusing, a-temporal any-space-whatever of the house, enabling them to become transformative, fluid beings, ungrounded from their static positionings.

Further intensifying these becoming-others, in subsequent shots, Kayako demonstrates her ability to mutate, infect and become with other bodies, by seemingly fusing herself to the body of Rika, her hand and head bursting from her blouse.

This fusion is discussed further in relation to the becoming-other specific to Rika; however, this scene aptly reflects the bodily assemblage we, the audience, form with the film and the character of Kayako. They fuse with our skin, meld with our bodies and open us to new existentialities.

Following Kayako's melding with Rika, the audience might experience a reterritorialized becoming of Kayako's character. Pulling away from the mirror, Rika and ourselves see and hear the door leading to the attic passage open, and crawling down the stairs, we see Kayako, blood spattered across her body and clothing, in a much more pitiful form than we have ever witnessed her previously. Kayako's blood spattered skin (symbolizing her sexuality in a previous interpretation discussed) is here symbolic of

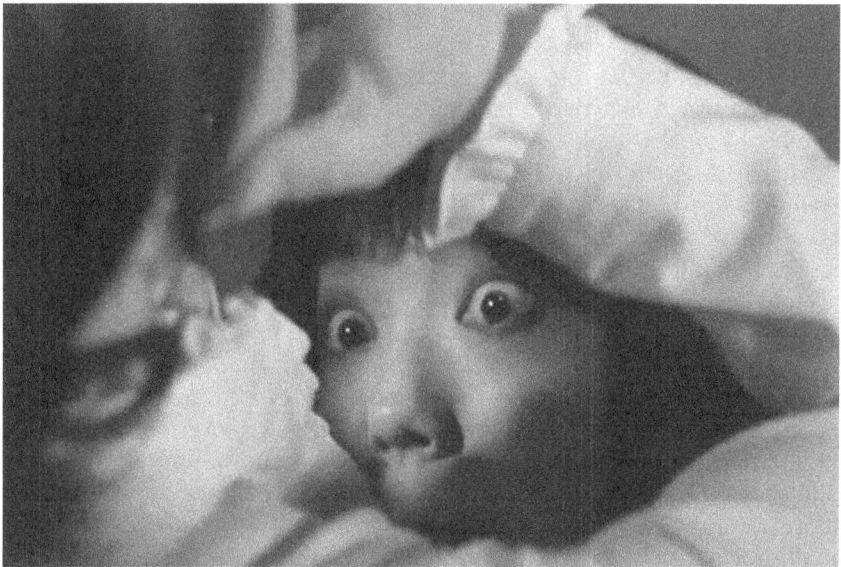

FIGURE 12 *Kayako bursts from Rika's blouse,* Ju-On: The Grudge *(Shimizu, 2002).*

her victimization and metonymic of wider issues of domestic violence in Japan. Kayako thus becomes more personable to Rika, and by association ourselves. Rika recognizes within her their similarity in experience as both are victims of a patriarchal society which undermines all women. However, these hermeneutic interpretations are not the only ways in which this scene can be received by audiences. In fact, as we have been primed to do so within subsequent scenes, we perhaps engage with these sequences through our bodies and register their impact as affect.

The sonsigns of this scene, in particular, heighten the bodily intensity felt. A foreboding, echoing, slow-tempo score accompanies Kayako's traversal on all fours down the stairs, building up affective tension. This is intensified by our captivation and immobility at the scene, reflective of Rika's entrapment at the bottom of the stairs. However, this score is a misleading affective mechanism which, rather than ending in a culmination and release of affective tension through, as would be expected, a frenzied attack on Rika, serves to facilitate a sharp, deterritorializing contrast of affects. When Kayako reaches the bottom of the stairs, whilst the music retains its slow, foreboding tempo in the background, we also hear the incomprehensible, yet pleading and painful whimpers of Kayako, accompanied by an image of her limp, gesturing, hand reaching towards Rika. The blending of affects at this point illustrates a point of hybridization for Kayako. The differing affective qualities blending together opens Kayako to more diverse becomings, a hybridity of molar positionings we can associate with her, allowing her to become or feel more human-like and less threatening or incomprehensible. We can imagine Kayako here in such human positions as being able to experience pain. We are also then opened perhaps to a number of more complex imaginings of her, questioning how she may have existed as different past, human selves (the independent, career woman, the traditional mother to Toshio, the victim of patriarchal abuse) and exploring how she may become or exist as different future selves (will she become even more human-like in appearance, able to blend in with those living humans around her?).

Answering this, Rika, putting her hands to her eyes in horror at Kayako reaching the bottom of the stairs, triggers a further transformation of Kayako. This time she becomes even more humanized, more feminine in appearance, as her blood-spattered skin becomes no more, her complexion becomes less ghostly white, and she becomes beautiful and alluring. The audience is then transported once again to different layers of the past, or more accurately, different potentialities of the past. We experience Kayako in this form in familiar scenes, including when she appears under the covers of Hitomi's bed in her apartment, when she follows Yūji to the bottom of her stairs and corners two detectives who were working with him, when she watches Rika sleep and when she touches the back of her head while she is showering.

FIGURE 13 *Kayako watching Rika in a much more human-like form,* Ju-On: The Grudge *(Shimizu, 2002)*.

Her appearance within these potentialities, her transformation, changes the meaning of these scenes significantly from the last time we experienced them. In another layer of time these acts were threatening and malevolent, here they appear less so, with a more sympathetic, pleading edge. This serves once again to position Kayako as a relational, anomalous[11] being who cannot be understood under one genome of subjectivity. She is 'always at the frontier, on the border of a band or a multiplicity; ... [she] is part of the latter, but ... [she] is already making ... [a] pass into another multiplicity' (Deleuze and Parnet, 2002, cited in Powell, in Brown and Martin-Jones, 2012: 181).

This raises questions about whether Kayako's becomings are restricted between the two poles of monster and victim. Can she never attain a becoming beyond a degree or mixture of these two molarities? Perhaps not, meaning she is arguably not the most successful, inspirational becoming-woman or transformative any-person-whoever that we could potentially encounter. Nevertheless, perhaps Kayako's becomings-other are opened to further possibilities that diverge from variations of these molarities through the bodily assemblage she forms with Rika, who is a particularly interesting character in relation to the notion of becoming-woman.

Within previous scholarship Rika has been considered under the concept of 'the final girl', a character who largely deviates from her traditional gendered role, function and subjectivity as we see her taking on the traditionally masculine role of rescuer, exercising 'the active investigating gaze normally reserved for males and punished in females' (Clover, 1992: 48). She sets herself apart from others of her sex (particularly Mariko) due to a perceivable psychic ability which enables her to be more resourceful within the film, able to feel the presence of spirits, communicate with them and dig deeper into the layers of experience of these ghosts. Furthermore, as in other final girl films, Rika shares a bond with Kayako. When she encounters Kayako she 'not only sees a monster, she sees a monster that offers a distorted reflection of her own image' (Williams, in Jancovich, 2002: 64). Both are constructed as biological freaks by patriarchy and Rika recognizes her and Kayako's similar, objectified status within patriarchal structures of seeing, the monster as one of the many mirrors patriarchy holds up to the woman (Williams, in Jancovich, 2002.). Their gendered bond is cemented further when Takeo subjects Rika to the same violence Kayako was in life. It is unclear, however, whether this is the actions of Takeo himself or if Kayako has manifested into Takeo. If so, this would unground the hermeneutic interpretation of Rika and her feminine, oppressed position as it would not be the violence of the male, but the violence of Kayako, that is carried out upon Rika. Furthermore, if it is so that Kayako transforms into Takeo, a mutation instigated by her bodily encounter with Rika, she can be said to demonstrate a fluidity of being which deviates from the polarities of victim and monstrous-feminine discussed previously. Here, she transforms her gender altogether and opens herself to innumerable other becomings which do not have to lie along the lines of female victim or monster.

Ungrounding the positioning of Rika within the final girl paradigm, it is difficult to argue that Rika, as the main character in the film, is 'regendered' or given masculine qualities and interests so that she 'is not so feminine as to disturb structures of male competence and sexuality' (Clover, in Jancovich, 2002: 83). Whilst Rika, at the beginning of the film, appears to dress in very baggy, masculine clothes, wears no makeup, has lank, un-styled hair and seems to have little interest in the opposite sex, she also has many feminine traits. These include working in the care sector (a traditionally feminine occupation), she has a female friend, Mariko, and thus does not set herself too apart from others of her sex, and finally, towards the end of the film, when meeting with Mariko, Rika is wearing a dress, make-up and has styled her hair. Thus, Rika can be considered as not simply holding the position of the final girl in a traditional sense, or the classical victim role, in fact she hybridizes her roles and her subjectivity much like Kayako. Rika, and in fact many of the characters within the film, are not limited to set paradigms and linear functions, they become-other, hybrid and transformative, especially when they encounter the a-temporal, any-spaces-whatever of the home. Rika may, through this encounter, as is implied in her death, become Kayako, a malleable, transformative spirit able to traverse different layers of time, mutate her form and knock other spaces and beings out of their temporal sync.

Many would consider the transformation of Rika into a more traditional figure of femininity at the end of the film (by wearing a dress and make-up) as damning, causing her to be firmly reterritorialized into the traditionally ascribed role of victim. In image she becomes an iconic passive, repressed, female victim at the hands of a violent patriarch.

However, rather than becoming the final, all-encompassing milieu which defines Rika at the very end of her life, as though we have finally learnt the singular truth of her character to bring the film to a satisfactory conclusion, we can consider this scene through the notion of becoming-woman. Her transformation into someone much more perceivably feminine perhaps brings her closer to the nomadic regimes of becoming (something which men must also do to achieve such a state). It is upon her feminization that she is allowed to mutate into a new existentiality and become like Kayako, a becoming-woman, closer to the body without organs. This becoming-woman, becoming more feminine, is a catalyst for Rika to diverge, spread and realize a much wider multitude of potentialities of subjectivity and being. Along with her, the audience is, through their break in bodily assemblage with Rika, free to develop new bodily assemblages, diverge down a wider multitude of paths, explore numerous subjectivities and hybridize themselves further.

FIGURE 14 *Rika in more traditional, feminine dress,* Ju-On: The Grudge *(Shimizu, 2002).*

Much like the audience in this case, this book now breaks away from Rika, Kayako and *Ju-On: The Grudge* and forms new assemblages. The following case study explores and maps out Takashi Miike's film *Audition.* Far from a clean break, however, a connection is maintained to some of the transformations in thought that have occurred in this chapter and they drift into the mapping of *Audition*, mutating as they do so.

4

Auteurship, adaptation and the molecularity of *Audition* (1999)

Audition, directed by Miike Takashi, is an adaptation derived from a short novel of the same name by Murakami Ryū. Whilst there are some significant differences between the two texts, both tell the story of Aoyama Shigeharu (Ishibashi Ryō), a widower who lives with his teenage son, Shigehiko (Sawaki Tetsu). Shigeharu is prompted by his son to find a new partner and, working within the film industry, he and his colleague, Yoshikawa Yasuhisa (Kunimura Jun), formulate a plan to hold auditions for the position of his new wife, under the guise that the women are auditioning for a lead part in a new film. Shigeharu is captivated by one auditionee, Yamazaki Asami (Shiina Eihi), whose respectful, traditional, demeanour along with her background in ballet, appeals to him. Asami hides a dark, twisted facet of her identity, however, as is revealed over the course of the film. She has tortured and killed numerous people, mainly men, who have sought to exploit her and other women and it soon becomes apparent that Shigeharu is her next target.

Whilst there are numerous, hermeneutic-based studies on *Audition*, this is a horror film deserving of more developed exploration due to its critically acclaimed, often controversial style of a-temporal, surreal, affective violence which firmly cemented Miike's status as a Japanese auteur. *Audition,* in comparison to *Ju-On: The Grudge,* is unique in that, due to its status as a body horror film, it creates interstitial states and experiences through depictions of bodily disintegration, reducing bodies to a series of parts which can be interchanged with those of others. These depictions not only challenge our perceptions of bodily integrity and wholeness but also open us, through affective forces, to wider realizations of how the characters on-screen, and how ourselves as audiences, could potentially experience various subjective deterritorializations. As Linda Williams observes, body genres, such as porn and graphic horror, and the 'perverse pleasures that they afford are distinguished by an apparent lack of proper aesthetic distance, a sense of over-involvement in sensation and emotion' (1995, cited in Stadler, 2010: 687). They immerse the spectators' body into an affective, indeterminate relationship with the film space, into the actions on-screen, which trigger 'involuntary mimicry in response to the image of a character caught in the grip of intense affect' (1995, cited in Stadler, 2010: 686). The film, through its various depictions of bodily disintegration as well as (like *Ju-On: The Grudge*) its renderings of any-space-whatevers and time-images, provides a more a-temporal, affective experience than the novel from which it is derived. This opens characters and audiences through them to multiple potentialities of thought. In particular, the fluidity of female bodies (including Asami's) and Shigeharu's bodily disintegration in the film ungrounds these characters from static, molar categorizations of subjectivity, inspiring and opening audiences to multiple imaginings of how the characters (and themselves) have hybrid, polynomial and transformative personae.

However, that is not to say that the film is not crossed by molarities, nor that the novel is not crossed by molecularities. In fact, if one considers the spaces of the film and novel as relational, or forming an assemblage with one another, the potentialities for these texts to become more complex or become-other, either more adherent to lines of molecularity or segmentarity, expands. To consider these two texts as forming an assemblage, however, would mean that some incremental transformations to thought established within the field of adaptation studies would have to take place via the Deleuzian taxonomy. Developing upon the works of Stam and Raengo (2005) and Hodgkins (2013) in particular (who have already made Deleuzian-inspired developments within the field), if the spaces of texts are reconceptualized as relational, then languages of copy, loss and perversion, pervading adaptation studies in the past, can be replaced with ideas of transformational energies, movements and becomings. By considering, in this case, adapted texts like the film as becomings of the novel, it is possible to analyse the creative and affective work that they conduct without hierarchical or judgemental notions. The film can be considered to transform the novel, realize different potentialities of it and produce new qualities and intensities of affect.

By considering the *Audition* novel and film as relational, one must also explore the assemblages that are formed between the two authors of the texts, Miike and Murakami. This chapter therefore maps the ways in which Miike and Murakami creatively intertwine through their assemblages with the tale of *Audition,* each bringing different themes, concepts, ideas, aesthetics, structures and affective qualities to the experience of it. This chapter argues that Murakami may be an auteur whose narratives are more linear and grounded upon lines of segmentarity. On the other hand, Miike's narrative structures are more eclectic and a-temporal, allowing for greater affective, bodily responses from audiences and openings onto multipotentiality. However, as their bodies are relational, their styles of storytelling can be mutated through their intermingling with each other.

Through this exploration of the assemblages between Miike and Murakami, a Deleuzian transformation of concepts about the auteur of cinema takes place. In particular, the idea 'that some directors may express an individual vision, a worldview, over a series of films with stylistic and thematic consistency' (Grant, 2008: 1) can become ungrounded. Rather than discussing in rigid, linguistic terms how Miike's consistent, distinctive, style may manifest itself within this particular film space, constituting part of a catalogue of acclaimed works, the auteur can be reconceptualized as a fluid, relational body with ever-mutating ways of being and ways of creatively producing media and film spaces. The auteur mutates their style each time they undertake filmmaking as they form relationalities with other, alternative bodies to their previous projects, including other, different auteurs or authors, studios, personnel, bodies of thought, issues and social, cultural, political contexts. How such assemblages, flows and transformations can be mapped out in relation to Miike specifically is now explored in greater detail, before analyses of the novel, film and concepts of adaptation take place.

Auteurship and industrial assemblages

Considering the narrative of *Audition*, it is perhaps no wonder that Miike Takashi has been conceptualized as an auteur specializing in extreme, violent themes and aesthetics. He is famed for his 'outrageous, violently over-the-top flights of fancy' within the horror and the *yakuza* (Japanese gangster) genres, which are often uniquely coupled with 'tender, complex dramas of multi-character interaction' (Desjardins, 2005: 189). Influencing these ideas about Miike's style, particularly here in the West, was the involvement of the distributor, Tartan Asia Extreme, in his productions. A relatively large number of Miike's films reached UK and Western shores through this label which extensively promoted (in an Orientalist manner) the mythos that Japanese horror cinema is 'very violent, stylistic and highly transgressive' (Taylor-Jones, 2013: 197).

Adhering to Desjardins' (2005) conceptualization of Miike's style, *Audition*, particularly in its second half, is exceptionally violent and grotesque. This is coupled with, as depicted in the first half of the film especially, a complex melodrama involving the tragic stories of the widowed Shigeharu and the abused Asami, who attempt to start a relationship with each other. However, as will be revealed in the analysis of the film, this understanding of Miike's style is perhaps too formulaic, limiting our understanding of his films which are much more complex than this suggests. So, how can we transform this conceptualization to form new understandings? This is explored specifically within this section of the chapter.

Beginning to explore how to transform the concept of Miike as auteur, it is informative to consider the discernible split existing within *Audition*'s narrative between the first and second halves. In an alternative conceptualization of these halves (straight away highlighting the limits of Desjardins' (2005) ideas), the first half can be characterized by movement-images and linearity whereas the second half can be characterized by time-images, a-temporality and the proliferation of any-space-whatevers.

Considering the linearity of the first half of the film in more depth, it displays the generic conventions of a romantic drama rather than a horror. However, rather than as emblematic of a consistent style of Miike's, this element of the story may have been inspired by the auteur Ozu Yasujirō who, like Miike, worked for the Shōchiku studio in Japan and was famed himself for his tragic, romantic, drama films, including *Tōkyō Monogatari (Tokyo Story)* (1953). Thus, here (and potentially within some of his other films) Miike has formed an industrial assemblage with Ozu and, rather than developing a completely distinct, separate artistic style, he arguably appropriates and mutates the melodramatic style of Ozu. Giving further credence to this, the linear, movement-image segment within *Audition*, on occasion, presents long, drawn out, static shots, usually zoomed out significantly from the benign actions that are taking place within them, a particular feature of Ozu's works also.

Furthermore, as within Ozu's work, a sad, slow melancholic score is used to highlight the emotion of the sequences and to aid the transition of scenes and time. For instance, during the first scene of *Audition*, depicting Shigeharu's wife, Ryoko's (Matsuda Miyuki), death in a hospital bed, a melancholic score begins to play. After Shigehiko has entered the room, the scene fades out, leaving the music to play over the top of a new scene, a long, static shot of Shigeharu and his young son walking up a city street (see

FIGURE 15 *Left: A long, drawn out, static shot of Shigeharu and his son,* Audition *(Miike, 1999). Right: A similar static, long shot from Ozu's* Tōkyō Monogatari *(Tokyo Story) (1953); Miike's possible inspiration.*

Figure 15). As the music fades, we are presented with a caption signalling that we have travelled seven years ahead of that moment. Although very subtle, it appears that Miike, in his industrial assemblage with his studio, has assimilated some of the conventions of Ozu's classical drama cinema. This perhaps gives viewers a false sense of security and makes the transition from such linear, benign movement to the a-temporal, fast-paced violence of the latter half of the film all the more affectively impactful, shocking the body with the extreme polarities of pace, tone, linearity and affect.

This idea of an industrial assemblage is an important facet to consider within the mappings of all films. Considerations of these sorts of production contexts, Yoshimoto (2000: 55) (drawing upon Sarris (1962) argues, have often been neglected within auteur studies to-date. They may be especially significant points of exploration within this case study as, Shōchiku, a node in itself with many artists, directors and films attached to it, has the potential to shape, form and alter Miike's films when he is in assemblage or cooperating with them. Shōchiku's repertoire of films, from the likes of Ozu, Mizoguchi Kenji and Kurosawa Akira, has the potential to transmit aesthetic, thematic and structural ideas and affective forces to other films in close proximity to them at the site of the studio. Furthermore, the studio's assemblage with different personnel and executives who have different agendas and ideologies about what types of film (genre), what messages and ideas they want to portray in their studio's texts, also significantly shapes the affective, aesthetic and thematic layers of a film. Even the less senior personnel within the studio, cameramen (and women), art directors, composers and so on, whom Miike selects to work on his films, all have input into shaping and forming a film affectively, tactilely, audibly and visually.

Another notable person who formed an industrial assemblage with Miike and thus complexified the construction of his filmic works, was the director, Imamura Shōhei, who trained Miike and 'who belonged to the politically motivated Japanese New Wave' movement (Taylor-Jones, 2013: 204).[1]

However, rather than, as one might expect, influencing him to produce social critique films, Desser (cited in Taylor-Jones, 2013: 204) argues that Miike rejects this element of Imamura's work. Producing becoming-others of his politically charged, social critique cinema, Miike instead imagines 'what would happen at the collapse of the social system' (cited in Taylor-Jones, 2013), the destruction of Japanese society. As Standish argues, 'in Miike's films there is no redemptive humanism [as in many social critique films] because his films form part of a postmodern sensibility', he 'portrays a world in which there is indeed no salvation, but on the other hand, nothing to be saved' (2006: 338). There is a distinct destructiveness and nihilism within many of Miike's films which draws upon deterritorializing events like the economic crash in Japan and the rise in violent crime. However, perhaps influenced by his assemblage with Imamura, this is not an aimless destructiveness, as through it his films 'interrogate the boundaries of social normative behaviour and scenarios' (Taylor-Jones, 2013: 205) and address the social and sexual taboos of contemporary society, which, in itself is a form of social critique.

As Taylor-Jones (2013) highlights, bodies are often the site of these interrogations within Miike's films. In *Koroshiya 1* (*Ichi the Killer*) (2001), *Audition* and *Jūsan-nin no Shikaku* (*13 Assassins*) (2010) for example, they are pushed to the most extreme thresholds of pain through torture and violent dismemberment. In *Gokudō Sengokushi: Fudō* (*Fudoh: The New Generation*) (1996) also, normative gender boundaries are subverted through the body of the transsexual character, Mika (Nomoto Miho), who alternates 'his/her gender alignment' continually, and 'engages in sex with both male and female partners' (Taylor-Jones, 2013: 206). The emphasis upon the body within Miike's films is discussed in further detail later within this section.

External to these studio-based, industrial assemblages, Miike has formed an interesting relationship with the director Quentin Tarantino, who has helped perpetuate a vision of Miike as a Japanese auteur, the 'godfather' of Japanese ultra-violent cinema, particularly amongst Western audiences, giving a transnational reach to his works. Many Western and non-Western fans of Tarantino who see that he has endorsed Miike will be more likely to purchase and view his works in their own regions. However, this assemblage is not just a one way flow from Tarantino to Miike, as Tarantino has stated in various interviews, promotional materials and at red carpet events that Miike's distinctive filmmaking style, within *Audition* especially (which gets a special mention in an interview that Tarantino did with *Sky Movies* in 2011) and in such films as *Koroshiya 1* (*Ichi the Killer*), has inspired him and influenced his own filmmaking within such productions as *Kill Bill Volume 1* (2003) and *Django Unchained* (2012).[2] Miike can be seen, in this industrial, auteurial assemblage, to influence, not only Tarantino's violent aesthetics, but also the Oriental mise-en-scène of many of his films. For example, the use of Japanese settings, complete with *shōji* doors, tatami mats, decorative wall scrolls and sushi in *Kill Bill Volume 1*. Whilst Tarantino's endorsement has increased interest in Miike's films amongst audiences in the West, through this he has perhaps been tied (along with a number of other Japanese directors and films he cites as influences) even more tightly to his national identity and to the stereotypically Orientalist iconographies that express 'Japaneseness' within Tarantino's works. More so, perhaps, than if his films were to be considered as entirely separate from Tarantino's work.

All auteurs are 'imbued with a notion of cultural and national identity' (Taylor-Jones, 2013: 3–4). They are perceived to both be informed by and inform (through their art) the ideologies of the national and cultural within their native country. Even if the auteur has a transnational appeal, as in Miike's case, transcending national, cultural particularity, 'the extent that history and cultural tradition cannot but play a significant role in the formation of a "personal vision", [means that] what is supposedly transcended sneaks back into the auteurs' works' (Yoshimoto, 2000: 12). Having a personal vision of the world, which comes to be expressed in cinematic works, is one of the key, defining criteria of an auteur, along with being able to 'transcend time and place' and having a 'consistency and coherence of statement' (Staiger, 1985, cited in Yoshimoto, 2000: 12) across films. The imprinting of the auteur's vision and their individuated expressions within film may be either conscious or unconscious. Wollen, for instance, conceptualizes a structure that can be deciphered within the works of auteurs, that 'underlies the film and shapes it, gives it a certain pattern of energy cathexis' and from which 'an unconscious, unintended meaning can be decoded in the film, usually to the surprise of the individual involved' (1969, in Braudy and Cohen, 2004: 577).

Nevertheless, this grounding of Miike into the position of a distinctly Japanese auteur (through Tarantino's works or otherwise) is often at odds with expressions of identity in his filmic works. Whilst elements of Japanese culture and identity can of course be discerned within Miike's films, one must not prioritize a perception of these over other facets which express how Miike, born to Korean parents, has often felt 'unable to fully belong to a society or wider social grouping' (Taylor-Jones, 2013: 207) like the national. Miike, perhaps in reflection of conceptualizations of his own identity, often depicts, within his works, rootless, foreign and racially heterogeneous characters, as well as characters that move abroad, away from Japan. For instance, *Gokudō Kuroshakai* (*Rainy Dog*) (1997) depicts a Japanese assassin who is stranded in Taipei, Taiwan, and *Hyōryū Gai* (*The City of Lost Souls*) (2000) depicts a Japanese-Brazilian character, attempting to leave Japan for Australia, much to the consternation of a Chinese mafia boss. Even *Audition*, in its representation of Asami, depicts an alienated character unable to stabilize their identity, drifting from place to place in search of prospective victims.

There are, however, within some of Miike's films, sudden instances of hope for reterritorialization and the establishment of grounded, fulfilling identities and connections with other people. At the end of *Audition* for instance, Asami and Shigeharu establish a connection, Asami commenting upon how she feels Shigeharu was the only one to try and understand her and Shigeharu wishing Asami to find happiness. This contrasts with the prevalent sense of nihilism within many of Miike's works, a trait which has come to be most prominently associated with him as an auteur. As Taylor-Jones argues, 'these sudden examples of hope and happiness, compared to the notion of his work as focusing on destruction and nihilism, prove how the work of Miike is almost impossible to categorise' (2013: 209).

Returning to considerations of Miike's nationally territorializing assemblage with Tarantino, if Tarantino's films (most notably *Kill Bill Volume 1*) are considered as 'becomings' of Miike's works, the final products being a result of specific relations they have formed with Miike (assimilating, primarily, his connections with Japanese culture and identity), then there is no reason that such nationalistic, Orientalist conceptions of him as an auteur cannot be deterritorialized in different imaginings or becomings of his work. Here we may perceive that Miike's films have opened audiences, like Tarantino, to other potentialities for the ways in which his style, his ultra-violent depictions, can be mutated and applied to different scenarios, narrative structures and themes. Tarantino then, in his assemblage with Miike, has imagined elements of his films on different (American) temporal and spatial layers and hybridized distinctive facets of them with different cultural and pop-cultural concepts and discourses.

This opening up to multipotentiality that Miike's works induce, points to a way in which we can reconceptualize the figure of the auteur. Specifically, under Deleuzian thought, Miike, as an auteur, can be considered, not as an individual, a whole being with consistent, static ideologies, modes of thought and ways of interacting with media and film, but as a relational being, who has his own transformative, fluid capacities and powers. Each time Miike comes into contact with the medium of film he shapes and moulds the technology and the media through his power, allowing it to become. However, none of his films are the same, presenting the same themes and ideologies in different ways, and each time he encounters film it becomes something other, something fundamentally and affectively different (which may account for his 'uncategorizable' nature). This is reflective of the relationship that audiences have with film, each time they encounter, for instance, *Audition*, they experience different levels and different qualities of affect and bodily resonance.

This relational way of understanding the auteur, despite being inspired by Deleuzian thought, is quite different to how he treats the concept within his *Cinema* books. Deleuze considers the film texts themselves, not the director, as relational, blocs of affect, creating linkages between other bodies, works and with thought. As Deamer, discussing the topic of Deleuze and the auteur, describes:

> A filmic bloc of sensation may be an image, a sequence, a film or a series of films. An image from this film can link to an image from that film, and so on. A filmic bloc of sensation may be a series of movies, independent of director, that conform to one sign of the cineosis [e.g. affection-images]. A filmic bloc of sensation may be a theme explored by an author that traverses any number of signs and images.
>
> (2014: 189)

As suggested here, viewing film texts as relational and the auteur as simply a function of them (an idea discussed in more detail later) can still allow for accounts of 'the artist's relationship with the public, [with the contexts of production,] for the relation between different works by the same artist, or even for a possible affinity between artists' (2014). These are all important considerations which auteurism brings to a filmic analysis. However, within this Deleuzian reconceptualization of the role of the auteur, the problematic way in which films, perceived not to fit with understandings of the director's distinctive style, can be annulled or disregarded as simply degenerative, is negated. Yet, if we go beyond this conceptualization of texts and consider the auteur as a relational, fluid body, instead of simply a function within the filmic assemblage, we can open films up to alternative understandings and other nuances of thought. Films can be opened to new conceptualizations of assemblage and becoming that are, perhaps, formed only through the relational body of the auteur, related to, for instance, the director's subjectivity, the cult of personality and the different, multimedia performances directors might partake in beyond film production (including conducting interviews and acting in films, for instance).

The Deleuzian concept of auteur as function, which relates to the work of Foucault, is arguably not nuanced enough, not fully accounting for the important, influential, conditioning, subjective voice of the director. The auteur as function or, the author-function, bears no resemblance to traditional, conventional conceptualizations of the auteur, the director is not 'a fixed, consolidated entity, from which the work issues and to which it in turn conforms' (Goodwin, 1994, cited in Yoshimoto, 2000: 60). The auteur is not in control of the text under this concept, they simply function as a unifying construction, neutralizing 'the contradictions that are found in a series of texts' (Yoshimoto, 2000: 58), bonding them together under their image (oeuvre). As Goodwin explains, 'conventional belief ... treats the author as an autonomous unified voice, while concepts of the author-function indicate a plurality of voices and subjective relations within a cultural text even while produced by an individual' (1994, cited in Yoshimoto, 2000: 60). In other words, the author-function, unlike traditional perceptions of the auteur, understands the film text as an intersection of multiple insights or intertexts. The auteur is not the sole authoritative voice within the film text, therefore meaning is polynomial and informed by a number of different bodies and concepts. Nonetheless, it is also possible to conceptualize a stronger position for the auteur (through understanding them as a relational body) within the filmic assemblage without reterritorializing the restrictive idea that films are borne solely from the auteur's connections with context, thought, other texts and other bodies.

To further understand how such a conceptualization of the relational auteur might be formed and function, the work of Shaviro (2010) and his Deleuzian influenced discourses on stars and star personas is informative. Although Shaviro (2010) only marginally explores the fluidities of film and entertainment stars, like Justin Timberlake and Dwayne Johnson, his work here has some particularly interesting ideas which could be expanded further and in new directions. Shaviro argues that certain media stars are affectively charged or 'particularly dense nodes of intensity and interaction ... upon which, or within which, many powerful feelings converge' (2010: 10). Such contemporary celebrity icons strive for an 'idealized stillness, solidity and perfection of form ... Yet at the same time, they are fluid and mobile, always displacing themselves' (2010) or becoming-other within different situations, performances and mediations. These figures are immanent to audiences and perpetuate an affective, bodily closeness; however, 'we are never able to grasp them more than partially' (2010: 8) and they are therefore simultaneously distant. Because of the contrast between fluidity and motionlessness that characterizes such celebrities, Shaviro argues that they are emblematic of contemporary, Western, globalized societies with their 'media flows, financial flows, and modulations of control' (2010: 10). He also posits that we, the audience, read these celebrity icons as part of complex assemblages, where performances in different films, programmes, concerts and music videos we experience, interconnect and blend to create complex, hybridized thoughts, feelings and affects associated with the stars. Shaviro says for instance, within his case study of *Southland Tales* (2006), discussing Dwayne Johnson, Seann William Scott, Justin Timberlake and Sarah Michelle Geller's performances, that 'the violent contrast between the character in the diegesis, and the well-known persona of the celebrity who is playing that character, leads to a kind of cognitive dissonance' (2010: 89).

Expanding upon yet diverging from Shaviro's (2010) lines of thought on the celebrity icon, this book proposes that the figure of the auteur, traditionally synonymous with a sense of a static, distinct style of filmmaking, can and should also be reconceptualized as fluid and mobile. However, this is perhaps not, *pace* Shaviro (2010), linked so explicitly to fluctuations and molecularities that have emerged within societal and economic processes. Within each performance of their directorial skill, the sense of their form, being and character that we garner from their work mutates as they make assemblages with different industrial bodies, personnel, concepts, thoughts, themes, modes of filmmaking and materials each time they produce a creative work.

Developing upon Shaviro (2010), this book also conceptualizes that the auteur can be received by the audience as part of an assemblage, where all of their works (filmic and otherwise) interconnect to create hybrid, multifaceted thoughts, feelings and affects about the director, their style, character and their works collectively, which cannot be easily reduced or generalized. It is not simply a 'cognitive dissonance' that is created within the assemblage we form with the auteur and their various works, but more multifaceted and nuanced than this. At points, audiences will be able to territorialize their experience and understanding of the auteur into grounded, hermeneutic thought, thinking of them as a more static being and linking them to such ideologies as the national or cultural. On other occasions, however, the audience may experience the auteur, their various works and style, as more enigmatic.

Certain subjective, characteristic, stylistic, thematic and aesthetic consistencies can be identified when a catalogue of works are considered in assemblage with the auteur body. However, these recurrent elements are not limiting as they are never exactly the same from product to product. They become-other in each case, dealt with differently, taking on a different tone and, most significantly, different affective qualities when they form interconnections and assemblages with different filmic becomings of theme, colour, texture, form, sound and narrative. Thus, it follows that each experience of these consistencies in an auteur's body of work is different for the audience.

One of the consistencies within Miike's works, as suggested by scholars like Ko (2004), includes, as part of his recurrent foray into ultra-violent, body-horror films, the destruction of bodily integrity at the site of characters and a celebration of the energies or affects released by their fragmentation. This important aesthetic and affective element of *Audition* is discussed in more detail in due course. Beyond *Audition*, however, the loss of bodily integrity and the revelling in forces that this exudes occur within *Koroshiya 1 (Ichi the Killer)* with its graphic scenes of violence, maiming and torture, and *Visitor Q* (2001), a similarly violent film with numerous scenes depicting dismemberment. Each of these films celebrates in the affective forces that such violence creates. Miike is, therefore, an affective, malleable auteur working with and manipulating the medium of film and its mechanics to create profound affective resonances which differ each time we encounter his films.

Notably, there are exceptions to this aesthetic and thematic consistency within Miike's work, including his film, *Chūgoku no Chōjin (The Bird People in China)* (1998), which, although depicting elements of the *Yakuza* underworld, refrains from depicting sex, violence and a disintegration of bodily integrity. It is instead a spiritual tale of two characters finding themselves within the idyllic Chinese countryside. Such divergences from these consistencies challenge the applicability of a static conceptualization of Miike's style as an auteur and highlight the relevance of a more molecular, less rigid understanding of him as a virtual, affective director.

As a fluid, relational being, Miike can also be considered to form a dynamic assemblage with Murakami Ryū, the author of the *Audition* novel (amongst others). The relationalities between these two auteurs are particularly interesting as both often explore societal taboos and a nihilistic destruction of social structures within their works. Both also often focus upon a disaffected youth culture in the midst of such societal breakdown. Many of the violent and disturbing scenarios described by Murakami in his books, such as *Kagirinaku tōmei ni chikai burū (Almost Transparent Blue)* (1976) and *Coin Locker Babies* (1980), would 'not look out of place in Miike's films' (Taylor-Jones, 2013: 204). These relationalities in terms of perspective and style are perhaps what drew Miike towards producing an adaption of *Audition*. Murakami's expressions, descriptions and themes within the novel have profoundly impacted Miike's envisioning and creative, affective realization of the film. We can discern many similarities between these two forms, some of which are discussed within this chapter. This, therefore, problematizes *Audition* as a discernible, pure, auteurist work of Miike's as some of the content is not original to him and is borne out of the film's assemblage with Murakami's novel.

However, because such a source material exists, we can perhaps more clearly discern ways in which Miike has uniquely transformed the novel and infused it with his own unique style and affective power. Thus, *Audition* perhaps more plainly reveals the nature of the creative and affective force of Miike (or some sense of it) within the multifaceted filmic assemblage, than any non-adapted text could.

Despite their similarities, fundamentally, we may say that Miike and Murakami are interested in developing different things within their respective texts. Murakami wishes to establish a truth of character within the novel, exploring their psychologies and their thoughts, whereas Miike sets out to dismantle such notions of psychology and motivation and seeks to affectively map characters, spaces, objects, temporalities and the assemblages that they form. However, can these creative elements, that can be more clearly identified within *Audition* as stemming from Miike's assemblage, really be unproblematically applied to understandings of other filmic texts of Miike's and upheld as emblematic of an auteurist style? Arguably not because, as already mentioned, each time Miike forms an assemblage with filmic material, it becomes something fundamentally different. Even the becomings of these potential 'consistencies' will never be the same from film to film.

Further complexifying the process of discerning what could be considered as part of Miike's unique style, as a fluid, relational being, Miike, at the site of his work on *Audition,* can also be considered to form assemblages with Murakami's other novels. Some of these other books have inevitably influenced the development of the *Audition* novel, and therefore Miike's relational connection with the novel means he also forms assemblages with the texts it has been shaped by. Thus, who is to say that a certain creative or affective element of the film belongs to Miike solely, what if it is shaped by a previous novel within Murakami's repertoire? What if it is a hybrid element, formed out of a relation between another novel and Miike's creative, affective force? Such categorizations and distinctions between different creative and affective elements, based upon who has influenced or created them, would be too difficult to make. Furthermore, such distinctions may have very little academic worth, contributing little to our knowledge of Miike, Murakami and their works. This is a point that, whilst being addressed here through the notion of the relational auteur, the author-function (through its views of the relationality of the text) also responds to. However, as previously alluded to, it is also important at times to have an outlet through which to consider the subjective voice of the auteur within the assemblage, how they personally reflect on, or render particular issues and themes within a film or novel.

On a final note, the potential assemblages that Miike forms with the other novels of Murakami also highlight how audiences too may form these dynamic relations, allowing these novels to feed into their experiences of *Audition*. For instance, perhaps having read Murakami's *Kagirinaku tōmei ni chikai burū* (*Almost Transparent Blue*),[3] audiences may bring some of their experiences of and reactions to the sex, drugs and violence described, to their experience of these elements within the novel and the film of *Audition*. This transforms the way in which they receive them affectively and qualitatively and the way in which they understand them. In particular, the presence of drug-induced hallucinations within this book may facilitate a reterritorialization of understanding in relation to the dream-like sequences in the latter half of the *Audition* film, providing a reasoning for the depiction of such things and placing it within a recurring thematic.

Whilst this describes a territorializing effect that such an assemblage could facilitate, deterritorializations are just as likely, not least because an assemblage with the other novels opens *Audition* to a plethora of other potentialities and lines of flight. Taking another example to illustrate this, audiences can perhaps imagine the events of *In the Miso Soup* (1997)[4] occurring at the same time as the events of *Audition*. They can even imagine the two durations becoming tangled and intertwined, for instance, perhaps some of the American patrons that the protagonist, Kenji, guides around the sex clubs of Tokyo become Asami's victims as they conform to her profile of targets. Or, perhaps Asami has a kinship with Frank, the serial killer of this particular story, taking inspiration from his acts of sadistic violence (or vice versa), maybe even joining him to wreak havoc across Tokyo.

In the same vein, Miike's other works may form a part of the assemblage and inform audience experiences of *Audition,* similarly grounding elements of understanding or else opening them up to more potentials and imaginings. *Koroshiya 1* (*Ichi the Killer*), for instance, perhaps opens audiences up to more experiences and narratives of the seedy underworld of prostitutes and gangs that they are briefly introduced to in *Audition,* when, most notably, it is discovered that the bar owner Asami presumably killed was involved with drugs and some unsavoury men. We might imagine Asami traversing these spaces depicted in *Koroshiya 1* (*Ichi the Killer*), gathering intelligence on or scouting out her next victims. Such lines of flight could occur through any such assemblages, made up of vastly different combinations of Miike's filmic works. Through forming assemblages with these other films and bringing these to the experience of *Audition*, audiences broaden its potentialities to become-other and bring a much vaster array of enriching qualities and affects to the event.

Whilst the assemblages that the *Audition* franchise may form with wider, media ecologies are beyond full consideration within this chapter, the types of textual, structural, thematic and affective exchanges that take place between texts and the auteurs that create them are a central concern of the ensuing sections. Considering this then, a mapping of these aspects of the novel takes place in the following section.

Audition the novel: Adaptation and transmedia relations

An analysis exploring the relationalities between the novel and film versions of *Audition*, must not fail to address the scholarly field of adaptation studies, which has informed much of the knowledge produced to date on such transmedia relationships. What follows then is a contextualization of *Audition* within adaptation studies scholarship. However, rather than simply applying established notions from this field to the study of *Audition*, this chapter discusses how such ideas can be re-considered through Deleuzian thought. These reconsiderations take their cue from the works of Stam and Raengo (2005) and Hodgkins (2013) in particular, who also note the potential of the Deleuzian taxonomy to instigate incremental changes to thought on adaptation.

Adaptation studies has developed a wide range of concepts related to the discourse of, in particular, novels being adapted into films. Early scholars, such as George Bluestone, viewed the novel and the cinema as categorically different representational modes, asserting that they 'are essentially incompatible art forms, and consequently any mingling of the two is to be met with healthy scepticism, if not antagonism' (1957, cited in Hodgkins, 2013: 6). Under this line of thought, novels and cinema are conceptualized as incompatible forms because the novel is a temporal medium, 'capable of presenting multiple tenses (past, present and future)', whereas film, 'with its images existing in a kind of perpetual present' (Hodgkins, 2013: 6), is spatial. This idea, a binary distinction between the two media forms, is entirely at odds with the Deleuzian conceptualizations of cinema, which highlight how films can operate on different temporal layers (e.g. through recollection-images) and open onto the whole of duration.

The view that the two mediums are distinct and incommensurable has led to many studies in the field which consider the differences in methods of communication between them, most of which, however, do not take as aggressive a view as Bluestone. Furthermore, despite Bluestone's rejection of the method, these views of the differences between mediums have fed into fidelity-based studies and commentaries within the field. These studies involve conducting comparative analyses in order to ascertain how accurately a novel's narrative content has been transposed into a film. Within such studies, as Stam and Raengo describe, rather than considering filmic adaptations in a traditional Darwinian sense of the term, where mutations and transformations that occur are considered to be helping 'their source novel "survive"' (2005: 3), often they are considered in very critical, derogatory terms. Adapted texts, under notions of fidelity, are often thought to pervert, simplify and 'vampirize their sources' (2005). Such views of adaptations fundamentally derive from 'Marshall McLuhan's "rear view mirror logic" ... [which] assumes that older arts are necessarily better arts' (Hodgkins, 2013: 9).

Nevertheless, many adaptation scholars have since diverged from the perspectives of the likes of Bluestone and fidelity-based studies, perceiving that such strict, binaristic understandings cannot allow analyses to develop more complex conceptualizations of how novels and films interconnect and communicate with each other. Providing a particular counterpoint to these ideas was the influential work of Bazin, who conceptualized the adaptation process as a 'dialectic between cinema and literature', putting into play a 'productive interaction of different kinds of ... "aesthetic biologies"' (1967, cited in Corrigan, in Leitch, 2017: 30). This conceptualization anticipates perspectives that have become much more prominent within adaptation studies today, namely, non-hierarchical, relational understandings of adaptation and, interlinking with this, Deleuzian-inspired conceptualizations, which explicitly mobilize his taxonomy.

Further anticipating contemporary ideas, related, in particular, to the shift towards intertextuality, Bazin also argued that 'adaptations should be considered as extended and multiple variations on core myths, stories, or compact "digests" that accumulate meanings through the history of their numerous social and material incarnations' (1948, cited in Corrigan, in Leitch, 2017: 30). Here, Bazin understands adaptive texts as forming assemblages with each other, with other variations of themselves, and with the social, cultural, political and industrial contexts that surround and condition them.[5] This is a particularly important principle within the contemporary field of adaptation studies and especially within those studies (for instance Hodgkins' (2013)) which explicitly utilize Deleuzian perspectives.

As alluded to, a particularly important development within the field, which has led into and crossed over with Deleuzian inspired studies of adaptation, is the shift towards considerations of intertextuality.[6] Reorienting adaptation studies along the lines of intertextuality involved perceiving adaptation as 'no longer an isolated, exceptional phenomenon' but as 'merely one particular instance of the intertextual impulse at the heart of every text that sprang from and in turn generated other texts' (Leitch, 2017: 4).

Under this perspective, scholars have been able to understand adaptation as a more dynamic process. If all texts are considered as intertexts, if 'every successive state of a written text functions like a hypertext in relation to the state that precedes it and like a hypotext in relation to the one that follows' (Genette, 1997, cited in Leitch, 2017: 4), then a more relational view of media and adaptation is formulated, free from the hierarchical languages of fidelity and the restrictive notions of medium specificity. More specifically, this development has allowed scholars, such as Elliot (2003, cited in Leitch, 2017: 4), to consider how deeply implicated novels and films are in the signifying systems of each other. Furthermore, scholars, through intertextuality, are able to consider more widely the interconnections formed between other mediums, beyond the traditional, novel and film relationship.

However, increasingly within the field, intertextuality has begun to be viewed as a limited concept, notably because there is no clear differentiation here between adaptation and intertext, nor a clear reasoning as to why certain texts should be considered adapted and others intertextual. This concept often 'threatens to dissolve adaptation studies into intertextual studies' (Leitch, 2017: 5). Thus, a more nuanced approach must be taken, one which allows for consideration of the differences between texts which more wholeheartedly draw upon a source and those which may make subtler, passing references to other works.

Assimilating and developing upon the ideas and principles formulated through intertextual studies, Stam and Raengo (2005) and Hodgkins (2013) have asserted that we must adopt a new ontology of thought within the adaptation studies field. Like other intertextual and adaptation studies, they assert we must think more relationally when discussing instances of adaptation or transmedia interconnection, we must think about how texts communicate, interconnect and transform one another in this adaptation process without resorting to the binaristic, hierarchical languages of incompatibility, loss and perversion. To help formulate this new ontology of thought, however, Hodgkins (2013) and Stam and Raengo (2005) uniquely highlight how 'Deleuze points to a new possible language for speaking of adaptations in terms not of copy but of transformational energies and movements and intensities' (2005: 10). As Deleuzian ideas, when applied to *Ju-On: The Grudge*, have already been proven to have the ability to incrementally transform elements of hermeneutic thought, it appears that their application here may also prove useful in the task of allowing adaptation and intertextual studies to diverge down different lines of flight.

Stam and Raengo specifically (in the aforementioned quote) appear to refer to Deleuze's ideas of becoming, a very interesting concept in relation to adaptive works, which can be reconceptualized as becomings of their source text, displaying transformations of their source's narrative, thematic and representational elements. These becomings form a dynamic, communicative assemblage with the source text and any further transmedia materials or adaptations of the franchise's core themes which may be produced (including websites, comic books, further filmic adaptations and even fan-made videos and films which may 'spin-off' from what are considered to be main narrative threads). By considering the novel, its adaptations and transmedia iterations as forming assemblages with each other, a conceptualization of a non-hierarchical relationship of communication between the forms can be achieved. This negates judgements being made about which form is superior and replaces the use of the language of 'lack' and 'loss' with the language of 're-direction' and 'becoming-other'.

In addition, as established within discussions concerning *Ju-On: The Grudge*, conceptualizing such a rhizomatic, non-hierarchical structure of assemblages can undermine judgemental notions about originals and remakes. For instance, derogatory perspectives on the American remakes of Japanese films can be challenged as they too (as within more conventional novel to film adaptations), under this conceptualization, become different potentials or becomings of a narrative core.

This rhizomatic, relational mode of thought is more informative for analysis today as it facilitates thinking about the heterogeneous, multifaceted, multimedial nature of present-day media ecologies. By utilizing hierarchical modes of thought in our adaptation analyses, where one pure text is considered to give birth to another, illegitimate copy on another medium, we limit our understanding of the many different influences (cultural, social, political as well as media-based) which impact all texts, including the source novel itself. The source novel may not be a source at all as it has, itself, been crossed and influenced by many other cultural, social and political, narrative and thematic constructs that have come before. As Stam and Raengo succinctly put it, 'any text that has "slept with" another text ... has also slept with all the other texts that that other text has slept with' (2005: 27). These considerations, namely what constitutes the source and what does not, are blurred within relational thought. Furthermore, these considerations are no longer relevant nor informative under this new ontology of thought.

This deterritorialization of concepts of source and copy under Deleuzian, relational thought is particularly pertinent, one could argue, to the horror genre and our understanding of it. This is because the horror genre, bearing the hallmarks of oral narrative, such as the free exchange of themes and motifs, is a particularly rhizomatic, impure genre, where there is, in some sense, no original at all, only variants (Clover, n.d, cited in Stam and Raengo, 2005: 166). Thus, original horror novels and films, in Japan as in countries across the world, are not original at all and instead are different becomings of numerous folkloric, cultural or religious tales, concepts, ideas and motifs which they have formed a dynamic assemblage with.

By considering all texts as becomings, a concept which specifically contends that no becoming can ever be an exact repetition of another, the idea of fidelity can also be transformed and deterritorialized. We can form analyses which un-judgementally map the different creative work each individual becoming is conducting. Whilst different becomings within a franchise may appear to have an abundance of common, creative features with each other (some more closely resembling each other than others) and it may therefore appear difficult to form discussions about what is different about each becoming, it is worth stating here that each becoming is, as Deleuze would argue, relatively autonomous, with their own particularities effecting the mode of expression, representation and, significantly, the qualities and intensities of affect generated. Thus, the same scene within a novel and a film, for instance, can be discussed as expressively, tonally, qualitatively and affectively different from one another. In particular, this book proposes that film is a more affective medium than literature, as it more easily taps into an audiences' bodily registers. As Stam and Raengo argue, 'while novels are absorbed through the mind's eye during reading, films directly engage the various senses ... films have impact on our stomach, heart, and skin, working through "neural structures" and "visuo-motor schemata", they are felt upon the pulse' (2005: 6). Adaptive films create spaces where the novel becomes more physical and fleshy. The scenes and characters we visualize in our minds when reading the book physically manifest in front of our eyes on the cinema screen.

Creating this differentiation between the two mediums could open this book to criticisms that it is invoking a hierarchy in the same manner as traditional adaptation studies, a reverse hierarchy. Even Hodgkins' (2013) consideration of adaptive, affective flows avoids addressing this idea for fear of this.[7] However, avoiding this trap, an affective, creative mapping of different relational texts and the work they are conducting, under Deleuzian perspectives, leads to a more celebratory viewpoint of difference. Difference in affective quality and intensity is important within today's mediums and media products as it is because of these differences that audiences engage transmedially with texts, which have the same narrative core, more frequently. Therefore, rather than reject those texts and mediums that do not seem as affective as others, it is important to map their qualities and levels of affective force and consider them as relational with other texts. Furthermore, under these perspectives of relationality, we can consider how different mediums communicate affectively and creatively with one another and how they can transform when confronted by their differences in expression and affect. Thus, it may be that the novel has the potential to become more affect-laden through its assemblage with its film counterpart.

This highlights another divergence from traditional adaptation studies. Rather than considering the communications and drifts between source and adaptation texts as just involving the one-sided (novel to film) exchange, within this reconceptualization of notions of source and copy, adapted texts too, can be perceived to transmit communications to and transform the source. In particular, a drifting of affective forces from the film to the novel, at the site of the audience member, who must have engaged with both of these texts for this to occur, opens it to mutations. An audience member will receive the novel differently upon reading it, realizing different affective qualities and levels of intensity if they have also experienced the affective qualities and intensities of the film. They may, for instance, recall their affective experience of certain scenes from the film and use these bodily memories to inform their experience of the same scenes of the novel. Not only this, as is discussed in the ensuing detailed mapping, creative, structural, thematic, representational and aesthetic elements of the film and our experience and perception of them, can also be layered over engagements with the novel and any other texts in the assemblage. This process, as would be expected, also occurs in reverse, with affective and creative elements of the novel transforming and mutating our experiences of the film.

Before such relational thought can be applied to the novel and film of *Audition*, however, a mapping of the creative and affective work that the novel conducts, separate from its assemblage with the film, must be conducted. This will feed into considerations of how and what the novel communicates to the film and vice versa, a discussion which predominantly takes place in the next section. In consideration of the novel, this chapter hypothesizes that it is more adherent to molar regimes of thought, predominantly issuing territorializing forces in its assemblages with audiences and other mediums and texts.

One particularly illustrative example of the more prolific adherence of the book to molar regimes arises at the very beginning of the narrative. In the film, Shigeharu is asked by his son why he has not met another woman and remarried. Shigehiko is prompted into this questioning through a fishing trip he takes with his father, leading him to ponder the similarities between catching a fish and a girl. This comment seems particularly questionable and alludes to some tendencies towards a degradation and disrespect of women; however, the same scene in the book is much more firmly planted within misogynistic discourse. Here, watching a women's marathon on TV prompts Shigehiko's question and, along with it, a number of added, disparaging comments between the two of them. These include comments on how plain the marathon runners are, how similarly ugly the female students at Shigehiko's school are and how beautiful women are rare and cost a fortune. This is quite a significant departure from the representations of Shigehiko and his father in the film who, in comparison, appear more liberal minded and more progressive. It could be argued that such views and their association with the main protagonist of the film and his son have been erased by Miike for his film in order to create a more profound, emotional impact on the audience when Shigeharu is tortured by Asami (a perceived avenging-female who rebels against the patriarchal system for a number of reasons). Rather than feeling that Shigeharu and his son are deserving of the violence they face, in the film, we feel more sympathetic towards these characters.[8]

Conversely, the film, in this respect, may demonize the character of Asami more profoundly, placing her more firmly within the monstrous-female paradigm than in the book, as she appears to prey upon the innocent. This therefore discredits, somewhat, the hypothesis that the film is less wedded to symbolic representations and the hermeneutic. However, by choosing not to re-interpret representations of such misogynistic ideas in relation to Shigeharu and Shigehiko, the film perhaps deterritorializes patriarchal regimes in a different way, allowing further, more nuanced and hybridized becomings of understanding for these two characters and the violence that is inflicted upon them. Through this, Asami is perhaps released from her role and subjectivity as the monstrous-female, violently reacting against patriarchal oppression, which now only constitutes one potentiality out of a multitude of possible subjectivities and motivations behind her actions. This notion is explored more prolifically within the next section of this chapter.

Linking in with Shigeharu and Shigehiko's discussion of women, in the book, Shigeharu begins to contemplate the state of Japanese society since watching a marathon during the 1964 Tokyo Olympics. He concludes that the years following the Second World War were hope-filled, linear, objective and mission-led. Today, he laments, things have changed, people are individualistic and lonely and as a result engage in extreme violence and sex. These assertions reflect upon actual Japanese national discourses and issues (discussed previously) as since the economic bubble burst in Japan in 1990, after years of prosperity, people have been stricken by unemployment and a sense of hopelessness, exacerbated by the transition of the economic model towards the production of information, communication and affect rather than material goods. For many (especially men), there appears to be no longer any purpose to life as there was when the economy was stronger. A prolific consumer culture, contributing towards the development of individualistic traits amongst people and thus, to their removal and isolation from traditional communal and familial bonds, was (and still is) also considered to be a significant problem within Japan. This consumer culture, particularly through the proliferation of more extreme forms of pornographic media, has also been criticized for warping people's views of sex, leading some men to harbour dangerous sexual proclivities. Shigeharu also appears to reference the growth in violent crime in Japan since the economic bubble burst, of which incidents like the Kōbe child murders are emblematic.[9]

Women, within these contexts, have often been blamed for the societal and economic malaise experienced. In particular, their struggle for equal rights, better education and employment opportunities has been considered as contributing to this economic downturn and to the emasculation of men from the workplace. Women, within Japan's consumerist society, have also become particularly central and powerful figures. This has led to further resentment amongst the male population of Japan, who, through consuming such media as more extreme, violent forms of pornography, seek to disarm, infantilize and subordinate women (Iida, 2002: 227).

As such lamentations are not as explicitly invoked within the film, once again we can perceive that the novel is more invested in creating molar understandings. Within both the film and the novel, however, attempting to combat feelings of loneliness which characterized Japanese society following the break with linear time, Shigeharu expresses a desire to meet a younger woman with a job, with some classical training in piano, dancing or singing and who can cook and clean for him and his son. These qualities expressed by Shigeharu, in both the film and the novel are emblematic of the *ryōsaikenbo* (the good wife, wise mother) figure, first popularized within Japanese social policy and popular cultural forms in the 1800s.[10] Thus, we can perceive, under a hermeneutic analysis, a specific positioning of Shigeharu's character within traditional, Japanese societal constructs which challenges notions that the film is not invested in producing molar thought.

Further compounding this positioning of Shigeharu within the novel, however, are the feelings of guilt he expresses at having not fulfilled his obligations as a father and a husband when his wife was alive. The novel reveals specific detail about how Shigeharu rarely saw his wife and son due to work and often visited strip clubs and engaged in affairs with other women. Invoking nationally specific forms of molar thought, Shigeharu's expression of guilt can be said to make reference to the traditional Japanese system of obligation or *giri*. This is a system, stemming from feudal times, where all citizens of Japan had a duty of care to those around them in their community, a duty to realize their happiness even if this meant self-sacrifice and a duty to repay debts of gratitude where they had received kindness (Davies and Ikeno, 2002: 95). Even in death this obligation system remains in force and those still alive have a duty to remember, honour and pay tribute to their deceased loved ones. If such obligations are not fulfilled, the offender will face punishment, bouts of bad fortune, hauntings, and chastisement from social groups and communities. Through such a culturally specific reference, Shigeharu, undergoing torture at the hands of Asami, can be considered to be being punished for his indiscretions against his wife, for not fulfilling his obligations to her.

The obligation system was a linchpin of the nation and its maintenance, from which Japanese people derived their sense of identity, role and function within the community (Iles, 2008: 36). Thus, by not fulfilling obligations to family, friends and colleagues and by not following traditional procedures to honour the deceased, the Japanese national community and its traditions are further deterritorialized and people become even more disconnected and isolated. This is the kind of society Shigeharu can be inferred, under such a hermeneutic analysis, to belong to and participate in.

As the film does not include these revelations about Shigeharu's marriage, it is much easier to establish such a hermeneutic interpretation in relation to the book. The film, in comparison, is more fluid and vague about whether Shigeharu has transgressed some specific, normative, national system or code. There are, however, allusions to potential guilt-feelings on the part of Shigeharu in the film. For instance, whilst looking at the audition applications at his desk, he places a photo of his wife face down. It is possible then that the film could be read as a tale about Asami's revenge against abusive males like Shigeharu, particularly if it is read in conjunction with the novel.[11]

Through revealing more explicit details about how Ryoko (Shigeharu's deceased wife) fulfilled her duty as a wife and mother, this narrative, in relation to Asami and her motivations, is further grounded within the novel. In particular, the novel includes information on her personality and nature, as a cultured, intelligent, supportive, self-effacing and modest wife, whose priority was first and foremost the well-being and education of her son, Shigehiko. Even, as the book states, when Shigeharu was found to have been extravagantly unfaithful to her, she had maintained a calm and collected air, she did not argue with or leave him, all for the sake of their son. Thus, Ryoko is depicted in the book as a stereotypical self-sacrificing *ryōsaikenbo* whose time and energy are focused entirely upon raising her son and keeping her husband happy. A sharp contrast between Ryoko and Shigeharu, who severely infringes the rules governing the obligation system, is created, and it follows that he must be punished. Rather than remaining as the sole property of the novel, however, Shigeharu's misogynistic views of women and the knowledge of him cheating on his late wife, could potentially drift from the book to the film so that audiences' responses (both emotionally and affectively) towards Shigeharu, of the film, are territorialized and affected by these elements.

A challenge, however, to the view of the novel as linear and primarily expressing rigid, nationalistic, molar regimes, can be established. Within the novel, a criticism of contemporary consumer culture and a pervading materialism is maintained throughout as this is seen, within the Japanese national imagination, to have contributed significantly to the disintegration of the system of obligation and to other traditional, national discourses. Often this criticism takes on a self-deprecating tone through the personal narrations of Shigeharu who laments that, within two or three years of the Second World War's end, starvation had been eliminated and yet the Japanese people continued to slave away in workplaces in order to obtain more things. He himself can be included within this discourse as he too worked long hours, never truly bonding with his son until his wife's death.[12] However, through Shigeharu's language, it appears that he sets himself apart from the Japanese people who indulge in this material culture and thus contribute to this disintegration of tradition and community. Contrary to the perceived interconnection that the novel has with Japanese national ideologies and contexts then, we may interpret the main protagonist as a becoming-other of the national narrative as he appears to not regard himself as part of such a subjectivity. He is diverging or pursuing different lines of flight from the rest of the people that inhabit Japan, avoiding a repetition of the same. Thus, perhaps the novel is more multifaceted than first suggested, presenting different, divergent ways of living and being within the Japanese nation.

Nevertheless, the invocation of well-established criticisms of contemporary Japanese society, whether Shigeharu distances himself from Japanese nationality or not, is a strong reterritorializing mechanism which must be considered in more detail. Perhaps the most significant instance in the novel, where criticism is levelled at the materialistic culture, occurs when, detailing a short time after his wife has died, Shigeharu, both in mourning and in search of redemption for issues he had within his marriage, travels to the small German town of Wittenberg. Here an idealistic simple life prevails, where food is rationed, and the townsfolk are at one with the nature around them. Far from the dazzle and buzz of hyper-modern cities, the novel details how the beauty of the scenery by the River Elbe, and the long walks Shigeharu would take had, rather than boring him, gave him a real sense of fulfilment that he had been missing in his consumerist, city lifestyle. This allowed him to heal and come to terms with his wife's death and the problems he had caused within that marriage. Thus, the book positions these naturalistic, pre-modern settings as aiding those from cities to rid themselves of the corruption that such environments breed, harking back (in a nationalistic manner) to a pre-modern past within Japan where people lived simply and were in touch with nature.

This is a very common trope within Japanese literature and film, for example, many of Miyazaki Hayao's animations, including *Tonari no Totoro* (*My Neighbour Totoro*) (1988), hark back to a pre-modern past and situate the countryside as having spiritual and healing properties. Thus, Shigeharu, whilst not partaking in one particular common, contemporary way of being within Japanese societal and cultural environs, partakes in another that has recently seen a resurgence within society as a counter measure against this dominant consumer culture. It is interesting to note that the alternative that Shigeharu partakes in can be conceptualized as a layer of the past (a previously dominant way of being and living) which has purposefully been recollected and made to clash with the consumeristic present. By being opened to such alternatives, Japanese people can imagine other potentialities for their existence, perhaps even allowing them to hybridize consumerist and traditional ways of being. Perhaps Shigeharu is even emblematic of an existence composed of both modern and traditional ways of being, as, despite him setting himself apart from his consumeristic countrymen, he himself, even after being spiritually awakened in Wittenberg, ignorantly participates in such a lifestyle. Notably, he treats women, especially Asami, as objects to be bought and consumed.

The most prolific display of Shigeharu's shallow, objectifying and consumeristic characteristics occurs during the latter stages of the book. Here,

Shigeharu takes Asami to a hotel in Izu, a peninsula to the west of Tokyo, where she initiates sex, requesting that Shigeharu love only her. In the ensuing passage, explicitly detailing the pairs' sexual encounter from the point of view of Shigeharu, a focus upon the expressions of anticipation and pleasure on Asami's face, the shape of her breasts and nipples, her pubic hair and her vagina predominate. Here, a generalization of the female form occurs and Shigeharu fragments Asami's body into a few objects of desire, so much so that she loses her wholeness, her individual identity. This does not go unnoticed by Asami who, drugging Shigeharu with sleeping pills, leaves the hotel and writes a note, which reads 'No forgiveness for lies – The woman who lost her name', the implication perhaps being that Shigeharu does not desire or love what is unique about her personally (characteristics like her dancer's feet and her scars from years of childhood abuse), but her general anatomy as a female. Thus, Shigeharu does not have the propensity to love and desire only her, as she demands of him; instead, women are interchangeable and replaceable to him, just like objects. This view of women, it is implied, is commonly held by men in patriarchal societies as details of Asami's violence against other men who sought to objectify her are also revealed.

However, Shigeharu's gendered subjectivity cannot be said to wholly belong within this misogynistic, patriarchal positioning. Instead he has the potential to fluctuate between different de- and re-territorializations, even within the more linear, truth-seeking novel. In particular, in relation to his detachment from this positioning, during the passage detailing Shigeharu and Asami's sexual encounter, Asami pointedly asks Shigeharu if he has paid attention to all of her body, particularly her feet, testing him to ensure that it is not only, as is perceived to be the case with most men, sex that he is interested in. Shigeharu passes this test, successfully describing her feet, and the reader is led to perceive Shigeharu as deterritorialized from Japanese national manhood and its tendencies. This clashes with his objectifying, derogatory actions and usages of language in relation to women throughout the rest of the novel. Thus, a hybridity to Shigeharu's character can be perceived, one that reacts against a territorialization of his subjectivity into one, single conceptualization. Therefore, the novel may not be as restrictive of becoming-others as the initial hypothesis suggested. However, the question of how radical such deterritorializations of character are does remain. Perhaps, as is discussed in the next section, more divergent and multifaceted becomings of Shigeharu's character within the novel are formed when the film establishes an assemblage with it.

Contrary to the hypothesis in its suggestion of the inherent grounding of the novel upon lines of segmentarity, whilst it may more predominantly lean towards this line and the molar regimes that characterize it, the novel is still crossed by lines of molecularity, giving rise to becoming-others of thought and understanding. Furthermore, it is possible that forms and their adherence to certain lines can change, especially when dynamic assemblages are established between different texts. Where one form was once primarily experienced linearly, conceptually and through molar regimes, upon a new encounter, after assemblages with other texts have been formed, the text may be experienced as molecular, at the level of the body, inducing new becomings of thought. This is the type of transformation that the novel potentially undergoes when it forms an assemblage with the film of *Audition*.

Exploring in more detail the ways in which the novel can be considered to be more complex and hybrid, it can be said to adhere more to lines of molecularity in one passage in particular, namely, the scene detailing Asami and Shigeharu's sexual encounter. The passage creates, through its descriptions of sexual intercourse, a sensual, immanent and even a-temporal rendering, resembling a filmic montage. Whilst the passage begins linearly, starting with the act of undressing and detailing Shigeharu's inability to take control from Asami, its descriptions suddenly end, as Shigeharu is drugged and falls into a troubled sleep. The next morning, Shigeharu struggles to remember the events of the night, and it is at this point that the reader is presented with eclectic passages of affective, sensual memory. These non-sequential snippets of information can be said to remediate the properties of filmic montage through their short, sharp and fleeting sentences, which quickly flit from describing one experience to detailing another entirely different one the next.[13] As these short descriptions do not create a linear timeline of the sexual encounter, they are confusing, eclectic, affective and contributory to deterritorialization. That is not to say, however, that an objective, sequential account would present us with a greater truth and understanding of the events. In fact, experiencing them within a fragmented montage allows us, the audience, to gain a more intimate, embodied insight into the events and how, specifically, Shigeharu experienced them (in terms of a memory loss and in short bursts of affect-inducing recollection).

These affective recollections of the sexual encounter are repeated in much shorter bursts at different points in the lead up to the novel's conclusion. These constitute further attempts by Shigeharu to piece together, in a sequential manner, the events of the evening (when had she first orgasmed? Before or after he told her he has a son?), something which, it appears, is quite impossible. Thus, Shigeharu has no option but to remain in a state of suspension over these events, understanding them only at the level of the body.

Such a-temporality and immanence within the novel, contrary to the initial hypothesis, serves to unground molar regimes, specifically, ungroundings related to gender take place here. Whilst the passages detailing the sexual encounter are written from the perspective of Shigeharu, we, as readers, through Shigeharu, are still aware of and attuned to the pleasures of Asami. Thus, we flit between an affective resonance with Shigeharu and Asami, male and female, confusing the distinctions and boundaries between the two. Shigeharu himself also highlights the deterritorialization of distinct gender boundaries occurring here through his assertion that, during the encounter, he could not differentiate where his own bodily boundaries ended and where Asami's began. Thus, he transcends his male subjectivity within the encounter, is ungrounded from his molar position and becomes more fluid and molecular, even, perhaps, becoming-woman.

This, as the most deterritorializing passage within the novel, highlights its hybridity, its adherence to lines of molecularity as well as to lines of segmentarity and molar regimes. However, its molecular elements and deterritorializations are significantly outnumbered by reterritorializing, molar aspects. Nevertheless, as is discussed in the ensuing section, this is something which can be changed through the formation of an assemblage with the film, a text which more prolifically aligns itself with molecularity. Nevertheless, we must not forget that the novel can similarly have the potential to territorialize the film within such an assemblage, causing it to become more grounded and linear like itself.

Audition the film: Mapping molecularity and drifts

The *Audition* film is composed along lines of segmentarity as well as molecularity, instigating both reterritorializations and deterritorializations of thought. It does, however, particularly in its latter half, lie more profoundly upon lines of molecularity, producing a-temporal, any-space-whatevers. This section seeks to map these a-temporal, ungrounded elements of *Audition* and the types of deterritorialization they instigate, including considering whether, in its assemblage with the novel, it produces ungroundings of this source text, transmitting molecularities to it (or, more accurately, the experience of it). In doing so, this section does not, however, neglect to consider the grounded molar regimes that inform the film and aims to read these in assemblage with the novel's molarities, exploring whether the film's lines of segmentarity become more firmly entrenched through its interconnections with the novel.

Producing this multifaceted mapping then, we first turn to a key scene present within both the novel and the film: the audition scene. This scene, within the novel, is hermeneutically coded, invoking stereotypes and well-established ideologies about gender especially. However, the film has the potential to deterritorialize these ideologies through the more fluid vision of gender it presents. Reading both the film and the novel in assemblage with each other, one would perhaps no longer be able to read the scene within the book without feeling the affective charge (a bodily memory) of the dynamic, multicoloured, multitextural montage from the film. Alternatively, the scene in the film may be reterritorialized by the novel's stereotype-laden interpretations of the auditioning women.

Outlining, first of all, the audition scene from the novel, Shigeharu describes nine women in detail, in terms of their appearance, backgrounds, personalities and occupations. He also briefly notes a number of other persons auditioning, including a nurse, baton twirler and a woman with a seventy-year-old 'sugar daddy'. Considering these very brief accounts of the auditionees first, whilst it appears that various facets or becomings of woman are captured within these descriptive passages, in fact they are quite simplistic, generalizing and limited, exploring only a few, select elements of these women's perceived existentialities and subjectivities. One cannot gain an adequate picture of these women's personalities, subjectivities, natures and behaviours through merely mentioning their occupation or age, thus audiences are likely to revert to dominant, pre-established hermeneutic modes of thought to infer information and gain a greater understanding of these characters. For example, audiences could infer (without much prompting) that the young woman with a seventy-year-old 'sugar daddy' is a decadent materialistic *kogyaru*, whilst the young nurse is a more traditional, virtuous female carrying out a more nurturing and caring role which is suited to her gender.

It could be argued that by limiting the information we are given about these women and by presenting these details in short, sharp bursts, Murakami attempts to create a sort of montage sequence. However, rather than having the effect of (as it may in film) ungrounding linear, cognitive responses, such as the invoking of stereotypes, these linear passages are more likely to instigate hermeneutic readings.

This invocation of stereotypes also occurs in relation to the nine women auditioning, who are described in more detail within the novel. For instance, one passage describes a woman who 'had appeared in over thirty adult films, had twice tried to commit suicide, had been institutionalized three times and was now, at thirty-three, a yoga instructor. She showed them the scars on her left wrist as if displaying her most valued treasure'. Such a nuanced description, ingrained with subtle judgements, explicitly draws upon wider, patriarchal ideologies of woman to fill the gaps in our (the reader's) understanding of this person, including notions of the harlot, the *kogyaru* figure who explicitly flaunts her sexuality, and notions of the unstable, erratic female, aligned with chaos, who cannot keep her emotions in check. Thus, we perceive this woman as decadent, immoral as well as potentially violent.

The film's montage sequence of the audition, on the other hand, is more affective, presenting an eclectic mix of sights, sounds, rhythms, tones and textures which could potentially transform the way in which we perceive and imagine the women described in the novel. From the moment that Yoshikawa declares 'let's begin', a joyful collage of female voices, clothes, accessories, hairstyles and bodies ensues, broken up by quick return shots to Yoshikawa and Shigeharu. Yoshikawa in particular acts as a node, linking all of these disparate women together, by asking various questions of them, including whether they have ever had sex with a man they do not like, whether they ever wanted to work in the sex industry, and even requesting them to stand and walk around the audition chair to show off their bodies. Shigeharu, whilst present, is not shown to ask any questions of the women; however, during some return shots to the audition table, he is depicted as giving a mocking look to Yoshikawa or else laughing with him at the expense of the women and their comments. Thus, Yoshikawa, through his questioning and requests of the women, performs a particularly significant and central rhythmic function. He can direct and influence the affective flows and the qualities of affect that are produced through his assemblage with the audition room environment and the bodies sharing that space (including the audience's). In particular, his tone of voice, body language and the choice of question he deploys within the montage dictate the response from the women, in terms of both action and affect, or their bodily responses (a change in their tone of voice, an unconscious touching of the hair or face, a tensing of muscles which betrays a reaction to an affective force).

As the sequence itself is so fragmented, it would not be far-fetched to suggest that, in a reflection of this, the audience's imaginings of such women become fragmented, hybridized and malleable with other shots of bodies and even literary descriptions from the novel. Such malleability and hybridization also extend to the way in which we perceive these women's identities, meaning that we no longer imagine the women in the novel as static and possessing one true subjectivity which informs their behaviours, attitudes and life choices. Rather than a wholeness of subjectivity and being, the film perpetuates that many different modes of appearance, being and subjectivity are possible, and that women can transform and become-other perpetually. For instance, within the novel, the self-proclaimed 'Queen of the Discos', who has always had men flocking around her since she was a little girl and is perceived to be exemplary of a decadent *kogyaru* figure, can be transformed through the assemblage made with the film. Through the audition montage, we may imagine that, as well as a keen disco goer, she is also very fond of playing sports (as one woman asserts within the scene), she has a friend working in the sex industry, her mother at two years old decided she would be an actress, she has dyed blonde hair, or a frumpy bobbed cut, brilliant white teeth, a dowdy knitted jumper or a fashionable skirt and blouse.

The film depicts, within this scene, a larger number of women and their multiple, hybrid, personalities and ways of being in the world, which serves to falsify and even ridicule the static singularities of woman that the novel presents. However, as the novel is written from the point of view of Shigeharu, these false views of women are perhaps territorialized to an extent as being personal to him. Furthermore, as Shigeharu metonymically represents the patriarchal structure, it may be that these falsities are territorialized as a-typical of the ignorant male within such a society, itself an over-generalization and falsity. Thus, within such an assemblage of novel and film, if this should be a potential becoming and reterritorialization of thought, perhaps the radical, transformative nature of the drifting between these two forms is somewhat lost, highlighting the multifacetedness of one (the women) whilst reterritorializing the other into a restrictive dominant order (the men whose assumed views have been falsified).

However, within the film, the camerawork often indicates that the eclectic montage of female forms, aesthetics and sounds is being witnessed, even constructed from, the point of view of Shigeharu.

Therefore, within the film, it perhaps appears that Shigeharu has, rather than a limiting, binaristic view of women, a much more complex viewpoint, which allows for a comprehension of the multifacetedness and hybridity of the women. It even appears that Shigeharu engages with the women through the body, relationally. He revels in the differing affective qualities and intensities each body brings to his audition experience, as do we, the audience, similarly engaging with the scene in an embodied way. Thus, this idea, formed through an assemblage between novel and film, that Shigeharu may be territorialized as ignorant and holding false, limiting views of women, can be challenged.

FIGURE 16 *Shot of an auditionee from the perspective of Shigeharu and Yoshikawa,* Audition *(Miike, 1999).*

Because of this male perspective within the audition scene taking precedence, scholars, adhering to hermeneutic methodologies, may be inclined to interpret the filmic montage sequence of the audition as voyeuristic in nature. These ideas could then even be transposed into the reading of the novel. Crucially the gaze of the camera or gaze of the audition holders, combines the intense, scrutinizing gaze that the audition process itself entails with the sexually charged, voyeuristic gaze that Shigeharu, through his intent of searching for a new wife, possesses. Accordingly, all shots from this subjective perspective can be interpreted as objectifying in a unique, dualistic sense, objectifying in that Yoshikawa is searching for a potential new commodity to sell on screen, and in that Shigeharu is searching for a new wife to objectify and use to serve himself and his family.

Nevertheless, the frequent entanglement of this potentially voyeuristic gaze with close-up shots of both Shigeharu and Yoshikawa may disrupt and challenge such an interpretation.

These shots challenge the notion that the camera is situated solely from the point of view of the two men and the camera here appears to have a mind and perspective of its own, one which can be interpreted as a-sexual, focusing on both men and women alike.

Perhaps strengthening the hermeneutic claim that these scenes are laden with voyeurism is the existence of a second, alternative camera's perspective. This camera, as we are shown on-screen, is operated by a male. Thus, the

FIGURE 17 *Shots of Shigeharu (right) and Yoshikawa (left) during the audition montage,* Audition *(Miike, 1999).*

gendered nature of the shots that this camera produces is perhaps difficult to deterritorialize and unground.

Perhaps if the shots produced by this camera were made to be indecipherable from the shots of the more naturalized, invisible camera then such a deterritorialization of its male coding could occur. However, shots from this camera significantly depart from the sleek, realist shots that pervade the rest of the film, ensuring that the audience understands them in the context of the camera operated by the male. The shots from this camera are of a much lower quality, they are quite grainy, and the figures and backgrounds appear quite blurry and saturated.

Further grounding this camera and its shots within the concept of the voyeuristic gaze, the images it produces are more sexually charged than the invisible camera's shots. On a number of occasions, the camera pans from a woman's face to her legs, consuming, in close-up, her whole body. Furthermore, in a much more erotic scene, where one candidate removes her clothes, the camera is quickly transitioned to and displays a close-up shot of the woman's breasts, producing her as an object of desire.

However, it is possible that this is not the only becoming, the only understanding, we can form from these shots. If the aesthetic, tonal, textural, audible and affective elements of this sequence are considered, such ideas of voyeurism can potentially be deterritorialized. We can consider these particularly voyeuristic shots as, due to their often incomprehensibility as part of the fast-paced, eclectic montage, becoming ungrounded from such

FIGURE 18 *Shot of the male operator of the camera (left),* Audition *(Miike, 1999).*

FIGURE 19 *Low-quality footage from the operated camera,* Audition *(Miike, 1999).*

FIGURE 20 *Voyeuristic shot from the operated camera of an auditionee's breasts,* Audition *(Miike, 1999).*

molar ideas. These shots, therefore, become part of the patchwork of this montage sequence, contributing differing qualities and levels of affect to the experience rather than languages and concepts of pleasure in the female body.

Within this montage sequence, the use of fast cuts to display an often ungraspable, exhilarating number of bodies, confuses and hybridizes what we, as the audience, are specifically, affectively resonating with. Furthermore, if we understand Shigeharu, especially, as receiving the audition in this way, his experience too is ungrounded and confused, no longer necessarily being informed by voyeurism. Ourselves and Shigeharu may well take pleasure in viewing the different bodies, registering their differing affective qualities and intensities. These pleasures may also combine with others, formed through a resonance with the editing rhythm, the cuts and transitions of image, the different colours, tones (opsigns) and textures (tactisigns) on display.

This feeling of suspension, of being unable to attribute pleasure, or tension (as it might more appropriately be termed in relation to affect) to a

FIGURE 21 *A collage of the range of bodies, colours, tones, textures, expressions and movements on show in the fast paced sequence at the end of the first part of the audition montage,* Audition *(Miike, 1999).*

particular object or subject, is at its greatest at the culmination of the first half of the montage sequence (just before the audition sequence stops and both men take a break from interviewing). At this point an even more fast-paced, indecipherable collage of images of various women flashes before our eyes.

This end sequence, bringing to the fore an eclectic sequence of colours, textures, bodies, shapes and movements, provokes our (the audience's) own bodies and senses into action, making us resonate with the affects generated. It also conditions us to receive other, subsequent scenes within the film in this way, particularly the second half of the audition process and the many a-temporal sequences that pervade the latter half of the film. We are even, perhaps, also primed to receive the novel, especially its audition scene, in this embodied manner when we next encounter it. Our affective experiences of the filmic audition may intermingle with our reception of the same scene from the novel.

This is not the only potentiality, however, that could be realized within the assemblage. Molar concepts could also drift from the novel to the film during the reception of its audition scene. Perhaps aiding this transmission of molarities, one can infer that the film translates, faithfully, a number of elements, characteristics and facets of woman expressed within the novel. Most noticeably, two characters have been transposed into the film, one a French studies graduate who, after a successful career in France and then in Malibu as a designer, returned to Japan to be a children's illustrator; and the other, a yoga instructor who had been institutionalized and had attempted to commit suicide twice. We can infer that these characters have been translated into the film because of the information that they give in the audition process. These two women, therefore, arguably retain the ideologies that formed an integral part of their reading within the more linear, hermeneutic-led passages of the novel. Thus, within the assemblage with the film, audiences may perceive the successful career woman as high-maintenance and materialistic, as she is presented as such within the book.

Furthermore, audiences may continue to perceive the yoga instructor as mentally unstable, chaotic and damaged (particularly when she appears to re-enter the audition room a second time as she had not finished what she wanted to say).

However, whilst these characters may be conceptually the same within both the film and the novel, as is true of all becomings, no two iterations can ever be identical, no two imaginings of character can ever be exactly the same. This, therefore, somewhat disrupts the potential of stereotypical ideologies of these characters, developed through the novel, becoming unproblematically transposed onto the film.

Whilst audiences may associate the auditionees in the book with those seen on screen, through such an association, some differences in imagining

FIGURE 22 *The successful designer auditionee transposed from the novel to the film,* Audition *(Miike, 1999).*

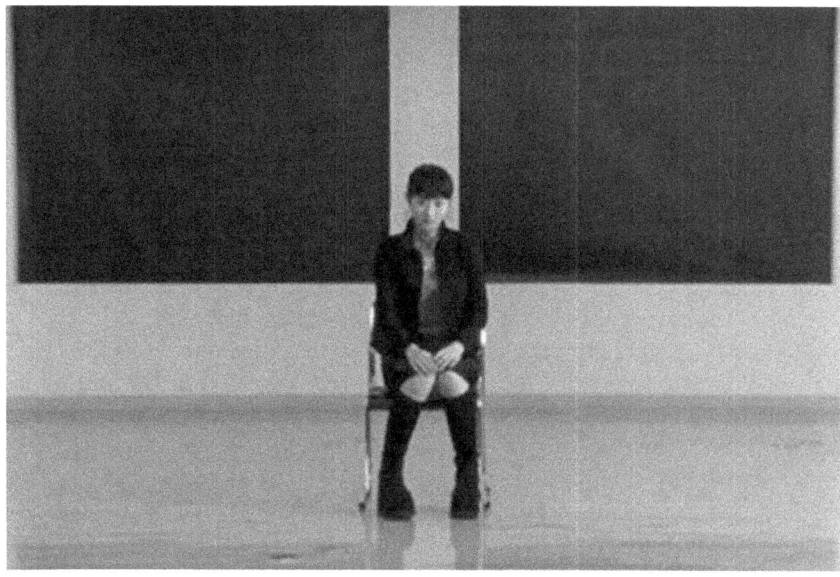

FIGURE 23 *Another character transposed from the book to the film, the suicidal, mentally unstable yoga instructor,* Audition *(Miike, 1999).*

can be perceived here. For instance, the designer, within the film, does not provide us with as much detail about her occupation and her personality, she does not state (as she does in the novel) that she was once a designer and had now become a children's illustrator, nor does she state the specific countries where she has worked and she does not wear an outfit of woven hemp, dyed in primary colours. Further to this, the mentally unstable woman, within the film, whilst similarly identifying her troubled past and institutionalization, does not discuss her role as yoga instructor, and crucially, nor does she discuss her role as an adult film star. These differences lead the audience to understand the characters as separate or as a variation or becoming. However, these differences also have the potential to falsify the ideas and stereotypes audiences use to understand these characters in the novel, opening them to wider becomings-other.

In particular, the designer, who, in the film, has little to say about her lifestyle and wears long dark clothing and little or no make-up, can no longer be strictly defined within the materialistic, high-maintenance, career-focused, modern woman paradigm, as she is so in the novel. Thus, rather than merely a deviant of the traditional role of woman, a humble, devoted wife and mother, here the character is open to become a much wider variety of subjectivities. Furthermore, in the film, through a lack of insight into the sexual history of the woman with a mental illness, a similar deterritorialization of discourses and ideologies associated with the monstrousness of female sexuality occurs. Here the character is again opened to potentialities for becoming-other.

The audition scene within the film, through assemblages formed with the novel, can be experienced as both reterritorializing and deterritorializing, molar and molecular. But what of the latter half of the film with its greater, a-temporal, ungrounding scenes? Can we understand these, at points, through molar regimes? Can the novel, despite diverging significantly from the film in its closing moments, still have some form of reterritorializing effect on the film here? What effect does the film, in turn, have upon the latter stages of the novel? To explore these questions, it is imperative that various scenes from the closing stages of the film are mapped.

The distinctly a-temporal, ungrounded scenes, characterizing the latter half of the film, begin shortly after Asami flees the hotel in Izu, becoming increasingly immiscible as the film reaches its climax. The first of these scenes occurs when, Shigeharu, attempting to find Asami, locates The Stone Fish, a small bar in Ginza, which Asami had previously said she worked at, helping out her friend. Upon entering the passageway of the small, seedy establishment, Shigeharu stares apprehensively down the stairs leading to the main door.

Taking a few steps down to the next landing, a scene, shot in point of view, ensues, building up affective intensity and tension, schizophrenizing the audience into the action (itself, as established in the previous chapter,

FIGURE 24 *Shigeharu stares warily down the staircase leading to The Stone Fish, a bar in Ginza,* Audition *(Miike, 1999)*.

a mechanism creating a confusion in temporality). Through this scene the audience can intimately experience the claustrophobia of walking down the narrow passageway and feel the tension at the prospect of walking into the unknown and unseen horrors of the bar.

Upon nearing the bottom of the staircase, Shigeharu is startled by a man, a resident of the apartments in the same building, who relays to him that no one occupies the bar. What is most interesting within this scene, however, is the reason given as to why the bar closed over a year ago, an account which marks the formal beginning of the a-temporal sequences of the second half of the film. The man tells Shigeharu that the bar owner was murdered, likely because of her association and problems with an unsavoury man in the music industry and her use of drugs, that her body was completely chopped up and that when the police tried to recompose it, three extra fingers, an ear and a tongue were found and could not be placed.

At this point, the scene quickly cuts to the inside of the bar where three fingers, an ear and a tongue lie in a pool of blood, the tongue, taking on a life of its own, writhes on the floor.

This scene deterritorializes the previously established linearity of the film, plunging audiences into an alternate temporality which is clearly not dictated by the normative laws of nature (it is quite surreal and unnatural to see a dismembered tongue writhing on the floor). Perhaps more surreally, this scene, as emblematic of the film's adherence to the body-horror genre,

FIGURE 25 *First person sequence leading down the narrow passageway towards the bar*, Audition *(Miike, 1999)*.

FIGURE 26 *Three dismembered fingers, an ear and a writhing tongue lie beneath barstools within the bar*, Audition *(Miike, 1999)*.

also serves to unground us, the audience, from notions of the wholeness of the biological body, falsifying the perception that we cannot be physically decomposed and fragmented.

Further compounding this deterritorialization, the assertion that extra body parts from another, perhaps even several humans were found, fragments us further and reconceptualizes us as transformational beings with interchangeable parts, rather than complete, static bodies. The bar owner, upon her re-composition, could be made up of any number of body parts that were not originally her own, her fingers may have become mixed up with those of another whom unwillingly provided the extras. Thus, through her fragmentation, the bar owner has become-other physically and even biologically. Not only this, but as our own bodily integrity becomes falsified, we too, as audience members, can imagine how we could become-other through such a break with perceived bodily wholeness, opening ourselves to new fluid imaginings of form, composition and being, where bodies and identities can be dismantled and reassembled in multiple different ways.

However, such an ungrounding of bodily wholeness, for both characters and audiences, is perhaps more profoundly achieved through the demonstration of the falsity of Shigeharu's bodily integrity. This is because, within subsequent scenes, we witness the process of Shigeharu's body being graphically decomposed by Asami.

After failing to locate Asami at the bar or at her former dance school, where, following a recollection-image, it is apparent that her dance tutor used to abuse her, Shigeharu returns home. Drinking from his decanter of whiskey, it soon becomes apparent that Shigeharu has been spiked by Asami who has snuck into his home. Shigeharu eventually regains consciousness to witness her, dressed in her virginal white dress with a black leather apron and gloves, removing various tools from her bag. Asami, after injecting Shigeharu's tongue with another drug, proceeds in her torture, first cutting the shirt away from Shigeharu's torso and then taking a number of long needles and inserting them deep into his chest, stomach and face.

This scene is punctuated by intensive sonsigns, namely, when we see the needles entering Shigeharu's body, we hear a squelching, visceral sound as it passes through his flesh. This is juxtaposed with Asami's joyful sing-song voice which cries '*kiri-kiri-kiri*' ('deeper'). The sounds and images of penetration, in our (the audiences') assemblage with the film, prick our own skin as if we too are experiencing this torture, once again challenging our own notions of bodily integrity.

The intense, affective experience does not cease following this, however, as Asami, retrieving more equipment from her bag, tightens a metal clasp around Shigeharu's ankle. She then stretches out a length of wire, and, wrapping it tightly around his ankle, gleefully begins to rotate it, cutting through Shigeharu's flesh and bone. The gut-wrenching sonsigns here are

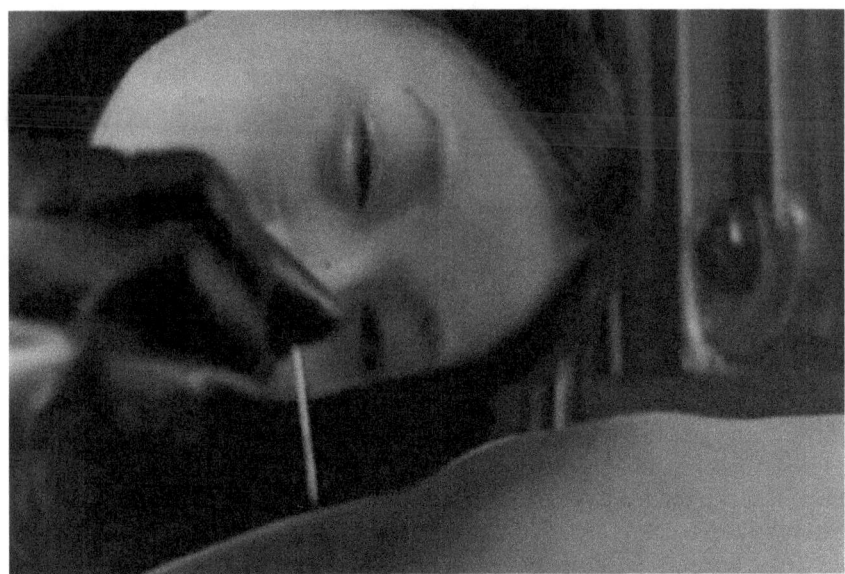

FIGURE 27 *Asami inserts needles into Shigeharu's chest, intoning the words* 'Kiri, Kiri, Kiri', Audition *(Miike, 1999).*

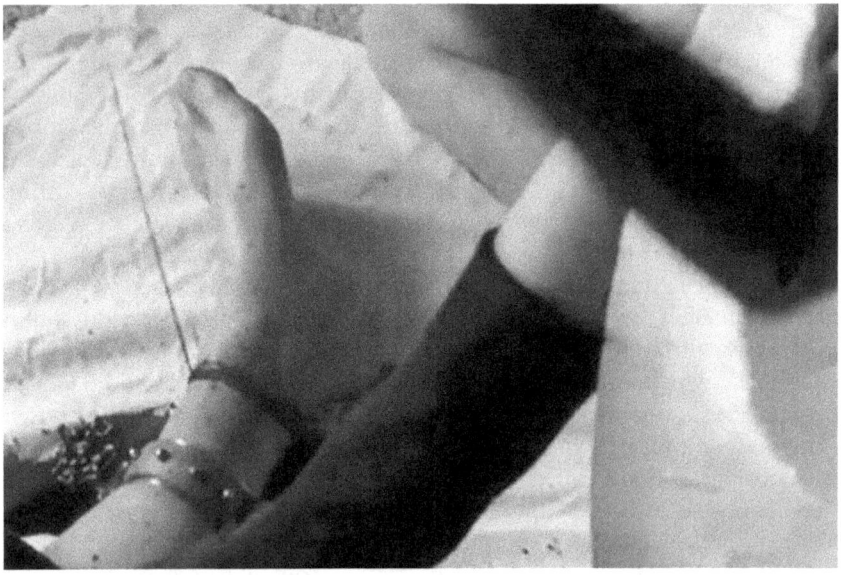

FIGURE 28 *Shigeharu's dismembered foot,* Audition *(Miike, 1999).*

accompanied by shocking images of the foot coming away from the leg and blood seeping and spattering out onto the white sheet underneath him.

Such scenes create an affective force within the audience who physically reel at the graphic nature of the torture, cringing, grimacing and clenching fists, mimicking the reactions and expressions of pain that Shigeharu displays.[14] Further to this, just like Shigeharu, paralysed by the drug Asami gave him, the audience are immovable within their seat, unable (in many cases) to detach themselves physically from the immanent moment of the torture, suspended in the position of, as is traditional of the horror spectator, both wanting to look and to turn away and cut off the visual and audible sense of what is happening.

Further heightening this immanence, this scene has the effect of schizophrenizing the audience into the action, allowing audiences to experience the torture and mutilation on a more intimate level. In particular, the close-ups of needles entering the skin, the wire cutting through the flesh and bone of the ankle and the point of view shots (from Shigeharu's perspective) of Asami's face as she commits these acts, facilitate this schizophrenization as it appears we are directly looking at our own bodily mutilation. Such an affective experience, as within the bar scene, leads to a falsification of the perceived impermeability and wholeness of the body.

However, as well as deterritorializing effects, these scenes of bodily disintegration also have the potentiality to be grounded and understood under molar regimes of thought. As McRoy has usefully pointed out, such 'cinematic representations of radical biological malleability or ... disintegration disrupt notions of identity (national, cultural, gendered) as "fixed" or "natural"' (2005: 89). Such scenes can represent fragmentations and dislocations of subjectivity which have occurred within society, such as those created within Japanese society upon the economic bubble bursting.

Reiterating and providing further credence to McRoy's (2005) suggestion is Ko (2004), who, in her paper, discusses how, characteristic of Miike's films, is 'the repeated use of the metaphor of the body, or, more precisely a concern with the metaphor of "a lack of bodily integrity"' (2004: 32). These metaphors, she argues, illustrate and render 'the break-up of the nation or, more appropriately, the break-up of the national body or *Kokutai* of Japan' (2004: 35). As discussed previously, upon the economic crash (the break with linear time), which was followed by a number of other disruptive, ungrounding events, many cultural commentators felt that people had become far too removed from the traditions, morals and values of the Japanese culture and nation and there was subsequent recourse to these ideas. Ko (2004), within her work, reads Miike's films as expressive of these concerns, prevalent during the 1990s and 2000s.

In relation to *Audition*, Ko's (2004) idea could be particularly informative. This is especially so if one considers the novel as forming an assemblage with the film. As already explored, the novel, through Shigeharu especially, often reflects upon and laments the way in which Japanese society has progressed and transformed, becoming an individualistic, secular, consumerist society where traditional forms of community have been dismantled.

This specific, grounded interpretation of Miike's works by Ko (2004), appears to, however, contradict further statements she makes about his films. In particular, she suggests, at other points, that Miike ascribes no hermeneutic meaning himself to the destruction and fragmentation of the coherent whole of the human body. She argues that there is no lamentation of this loss nor representation of hope for a rebuilding, he merely, she states, registers the fragmentation and notes its destructive impact, all whilst 'savouring the energies released by the destruction' (2004: 39). As Miike himself does not ascribe any clear meaning to his depictions of bodily disintegration, rather than territorialize them into one, singular national narrative, we can, instead, consider them as polynomial, as allowing for multiple interpretations based around other notions of subjective displacement and fragmentation (beyond the national and cultural).

The audience may infer these meanings, overlaying their own, personal experiences of deterritorialization and fragmentation onto these scenes of dismemberment. Interestingly, the characters of Miike's films themselves, through their molar groundings, may also contribute various meanings to these polynomial depictions. Especially, in the case of *Audition*, Asami and Shigeharu, who experience fragmentation, mutilation and dismemberment first-hand. These characters, as well as being representative of Japanese national identities and ideologies, can also be understood to embody other hermeneutic concepts (such as those pertaining to gender), which are sometimes closely interwoven with theorizations of Japanese nationality. Thus, these characters contribute to the multipotential ways in which *Audition*'s scenes of dismemberment can be interpreted or experienced.

It is not only through physical fragmentations and disintegrations, however, that these characters come to express various ideas about deterritorialization. It is also through psychological displacements and fragmentations, occurring when they are (in the latter half of the film) transported to different temporal layers and existentialities, that ungroundings come to be expressed. Arguably, these psychological displacements are more significant for Asami, as she does not undergo as profound a bodily dismemberment as Shigeharu (apart from when she breaks her neck at the end of the film having been kicked down the stairs by Shigehiko).

The deterritorializations of subjectivity that Shigeharu and Asami demonstrate in the film perhaps drift to the novel, challenging the more firmly grounded, hermeneutic perspectives of the characters perpetuated within it. Interestingly, the novel does contain scenes of bodily dismemberment, which may lead to some interpretations of symbolic ungrounding being formed. However, unlike the film, the novel does not contain such a large, concentrated section of a-temporality during the latter part of its narrative, significantly impacting its ability to induce, within characters, deterritorializations from linear conceptions of subjectivity. Nevertheless, as with the audition scene, those audiences encountering both the novel and film may never again be able to read the linear passages of the novel, detailing Shigeharu's torture at the hands Asami, without layering their ungrounded, a-temporal, filmic experience of this scene over the top of it. Alternatively, the more linear, static ideologies pertaining to characters in the novel, perhaps, have the potentiality to reterritorialize our experiences of the characters within the film.

One could easily perceive that, during the first half of the film, Asami represents a virtuous female, timid, honourable and polite, and that in the latter half of the film she undergoes a transformation into a monstrous, sadistic female. This is also true of the novel, however, within its narrative, there are more allusions to and more indications of Asami's violent nature within the first half, implying that her placid, gentle demeanour is a façade and that she only has one, true nature. The idea of Asami having one, true nature is expressed in one passage where Shigeharu meets with an old friend, an owner of a restaurant he attended with her. He questions the owner on what she thought of Asami and she relays to him that she believes Asami to be either a saint or a monster but not somewhere in between.

The film, however, captures the hybrid nature of Asami, as, rather than presenting her submissiveness as not being a true becoming of her character, it presents it, along with her violent nature, as equal transformations of her being, where one is not any truer than the other. As will be further explored, within the film, it is not just between these two polarities that Asami is positioned, therefore, such a multifacetedness of character further falsifies the idea that there are singular truths in subjectivity and nature.

The multifacetedness of Asami's being, in particular, is expressed within the a-temporal passages of the latter half of the film. These scenes depict Asami slipping into different layers of the past, including her childhood, where she becomes the young girl she once was. This is becoming diverging away from the polarities discussed previously, the virtuous, dignified female and the monster. This transformation into a child, for Asami, occurs when Shigeharu is suddenly transported from a restaurant, where he is eating dinner with the adult Asami, to a new layer of space and time, Asami's home. This space, it seems, is a void, much like the house in *Ju-On: The Grudge*, which does not follow the normative laws of time and nature. Here, the adult Asami hands a bestial man (a previous victim of Asami's who has had his tongue cut out, his ear and three fingers removed) a bowl of her vomit to consume. Following this, the child Asami appears in her place, kneeling in front of the man, ruffling his hair like a dog.

Within this shot, the child Asami, the bestial man and Shigeharu all occupy the same space and layer of time, an anomaly and temporal impossibility. This a-temporality is reinforced when the child Asami looks towards

FIGURE 29 *The child Asami pets the bestial man in this anomalous, recollection-image,* Audition *(Miike, 1999).*

Shigeharu and speaks in her adult voice. These anomalies have the effect of ungrounding the audiences' and characters' temporal and spatial moorings. Through this, subjective positionings and molar regimes of understanding are also deterritorialized. In particular, the transformation of Asami into a child deterritorializes and ungrounds understandings of her as a virtuous, ideal *ryōsaikenbo*, or as a desirable, yet threatening, femme fatale. These ideas are no longer informative of our understanding of Asami's being within the anomalous scenes. Asami exists here as a virtual, transformative being, a figure emblematic of becoming-woman, who is open to multiple potentialities of being.

Further illustrating the fluidity of Asami's character, she undergoes some other transformations at the site of her home, due to the convergence of other temporal layers, beyond the temporality of her childhood. Asami transforms into other beings during these a-temporal scenes, specifically, other women we encounter earlier on in the film. These transformations encapsulate the concept of becoming-woman, demonstrating women's malleability and fluidity as opposed to men, not featured within this series of transformations, who can therefore be conceptualized as more static. Asami undergoes these transformations when she begins to perform a sexual act on Shigeharu. First of all, she becomes Shigeharu's tearful secretary who bemoans the fact that he only slept with her once and did not start a more serious relationship with her.

FIGURE 30 *Asami becomes Shigeharu's secretary,* Audition *(Miike, 1999).*

A quick cut back to Shigeharu's reaction, and Asami is once again kneeling in front of him. She is then replaced, in the next instance, by Shigehiko's young girlfriend, Misuzu (Nakamura Misato). Shigeharu falls to the floor and backs away from this particular transformation, however, the schoolgirl pursues him, forcing Shigeharu to push her away and causing Asami's transformations to end.

These transformations, attributes and forms of subjectivity that the two women embody, drift to Asami, opening her character to further becomings or potentialities of being. Asami, like Misuzu (who offers to cook for Shigeharu when she visits his home), has the potential to become a respectful and virtuous female, willing to take on a more traditional role of woman. Conversely, she could become, like the secretary, an obsessive, downtrodden woman who is incapable of mustering the agency necessary for seeking vengeance against those men who have wronged her. Within this sequence, it is not only a fluidity of Asami's being that can be perceived, however. Understandings of the two women depicted alongside Asami can also be transformed. In particular, some of the most striking becomings occur for Misuzu, as previously she was depicted as a respectful, virtuous young woman who appeared almost pre-pubescent and sexually unenlightened. Here, however, we see her attempting to perform a sexual act upon Shigeharu and launching herself at him when he tells her to stop. Forming an assemblage with Asami and the secretary in this moment, Misuzu ungrounds previous subjective positionings and becomes-other.

FIGURE 31 *Asami also becomes Shigehiko's young girlfriend, Misuzu,* Audition (Miike, 1999).

Alternatively, these scenes can be read in more linear, molar terms. Rather than a fluidity and multipotentiality of character, these sequences of transformation, connecting to the ideas purported in the novel during the sex scene, can be interpreted as being emblematic of Shigeharu's misogynistic views of women, where women and their bodies are interchangeable with each other, their subjectivity irrelevant, as long as they can sexually perform and pleasure men.

Further to this, in another hermeneutic interpretation, these scenes, as theorized by scholars such as Balmain (2008) and Hantke (in McRoy, 2005), can be considered as a return of the repressed, dream sequence, expressing Shigeharu's guilty, tormented psyche. In particular, the secretary's presence expresses Shigeharu's guilt at his previous acts of misleading women and using them for sex. It could also be interpreted as expressing guilty feelings about being unfaithful to his deceased wife, that is, of course, if we consider the film in assemblage with the novel, which (unlike the film) outlines Shigeharu's marital indiscretions. The manifestation of Shigehiko's girlfriend in his guilt-laden dream alludes to his repressed desire and attraction for this girl. Here, then, a Freudian interpretation can be effectively applied, highlighting how Shigeharu's repressed, sub-conscious desire for Misuzu evidences a sense of competition he has with his son for mates.

Whilst these hermeneutic interpretations do offer some form of understanding of the sequence, they are, nevertheless, singular interpretations out of many other potentialities. Thus, these molar, reterritorializations can still be ungrounded, allowing for the realization of other meanings and experiences related to these scenes.

There is, however, perhaps one territorialized interpretation of the film that is particularly difficult to unground. At the end of the film Asami is kicked down the stairs to her death by Shigehiko, ensuring Shigeharu's survival and, as may be interpreted by scholars adhering to hermeneutic methodologies, ensuring a patriarchal restoration of order. Many would interpret this end as a final, damning territorialization of Asami into the role of the monstrous-female, who is finally vanquished by the male, re-establishing patriarchy's power over woman and the linearity of the patriarchal regime as the dominant, encompassing milieu. Perhaps, one could surmise, upon Asami's death, the a-temporal scenes cease, becoming replaced by linear action-images, once again detailing Shigeharu's mundane daily life (as at the start of the film). This interpretation is one which holds particularly well with the novel, as the linearity of its final chapters, never deviating into other layers of time as the film does, presents the idea that this is the only viable truth of the narrative, that the patriarchal order, through Asami's death and Shigeharu's survival, is and must be restored. If considered in assemblage with the novel therefore, these final scenes of the film may be even more likely to become territorialized as such.

Whilst the film may end upon Asami's death, this does not mean that a grounding of her character and the meaning of the narrative, bringing a conclusive end to the film, necessarily has to occur. The conclusion (if one can be conceived at all) can in fact be left open to multiple interpretations or becomings, once again, because of the anomalous, non-linear time-images that pervade the latter half of the film. In particular, the transitions to different layers of time and space which occur during Shigeharu's investigation into Asami and just before he is tortured, confuse the audience's sense of what is real and what is not, disrupting the formulation of any linearity and a definitive, grounded end. We cannot discern whether the layers of time we, along with Shigeharu, are transported to, in the bar, the restaurant, Asami's home and her former dance school, have more truth in them than the layers of time where Shigeharu returns home, is drugged and tortured, and where he and his son manage to reassert patriarchal dominance.

Adding further complexity to understandings of the film's conclusion is another scene, depicting another temporal slippage, which occurs just after Shigeharu has been mutilated and his son unexpectedly returns home. As Shigehiko looks upon his father in astonishment, Asami appears behind him and we are suddenly transported back to the hotel room where they had their first sexual encounter. Shigeharu awakens in shock as if he had been experiencing a bad dream. However, the torture scenes themselves, and the other transitions to different layers of temporality and existentiality that occur, are perhaps far too real and embodied to constitute a mere, dream. Shigeharu himself falsifies such an interpretation as, looking to the side and finding Asami naked and asleep next to him, he cries out in shock and backs away from her.

Asami's presence in the hotel room runs contrary to other layers of time where she flees. Furthermore, Shigeharu finds, much to his surprise and relief, that his foot has not been dismembered from his body, falsifying the other layer of time where he was tortured. Further, washing his face in the bathroom, Asami walks in, enquiring if Shigeharu is feeling ok, becoming the caring, softly spoken and slightly timid woman we encountered at the start of the film. This is a stark contrast to the violent, sadistic, overpowering woman she becomes in other layers of temporality and existentiality.

Once again, there is no more truth in one layer of time than another, the scene in the hotel room with Asami is no less embodied by Shigeharu and ourselves (as audiences) than other scenes, and it is thus impossible to ascertain which narrative discourse, which conclusion to the film is the one true interpretation. Does Shigeharu simply dream the horrific events and return to bed to lie next to his ideal wife to be? Is his nightmare, in fact, very real and Asami is a monstrous-female, brutalizing men and women, even transforming them into bestial forms? Or is Asami, in fact, a righteous figure, representing the concerns of all women (two of whom she transforms into during earlier, anomalous scenes), punishing those who would seek to violate and abuse her? Rather than being presented with an irrefutable idea of the truth of the narrative within these scenes, we are presented with multiple potentialities. The differing, potential timelines presented here, perhaps even open up the novel's narrative progression to duration, allowing it to be reconceived as multifaceted and falsifying rather than linear. On the other hand, as already discussed, it is possible that the film's multiple narrative threads could become falsified through the novel's assemblage with it, territorializing one truth of narrative where Asami is the monstrous-female. The scenes of the latter half of the film, despite them being much more non-linear than the opening scenes, rendering ungrounded any-space-whatevers, can be perceived to be experienced as both deterritorializing and reterritorializing, provoking molar thought (particularly if assemblages with the novel are established) and embodied, molecular responses at different points.

Presenting a similarly rhizomatic, a-temporal narrative, which is crossed by both lines of segmentarity and molecularity, is Kurosawa Kiyoshi's *Kairo* (*Pulse*). Akin to Asami and Shigeharu, the characters within *Kairo* (*Pulse*), especially the ghostly forms, are often ungrounded, fluid and mutable. They are perhaps more radically so, however, as through assemblages that are formed in the film between characters and digital technologies (reflecting the discourses of technologized societies like Japan), we see becomings which even challenge and diverge from what is understood to be human. Developing further upon the incremental transformations to thought that have occurred within this chapter and its predecessor, the following case study seeks to map out the affective, deterritorializing and molar, reterritorializing functions of *Kairo* (*Pulse*).

5

Kairo (*Pulse*) (2001): Cosmicism and 'becoming-machine'

Perhaps no other film discussed within this book sets out to as rigorously render and capture a crisis-laden, immaterial, technologized Japanese landscape as Kurosawa Kiyoshi's *Kairo* (*Pulse*). This text, whilst expressive of the break with linear time which occurred with the economic crisis of 1990, primarily renders (through its any-space-whatevers) the deterritorializations, transformations and intensities that digital media (especially the Internet) have instigated within Japanese society. The film represents an apocalyptic event whereby the realms of the living and the dead merge through a connection that has been forged via the Internet. Through the Internet, spirits begin to flood into the world of the living, causing those who encounter them to eventually die and become ghosts themselves. These renderings, an assemblage the film creates with the wider world, allow the audience to, as well as form a cognitive understanding, obtain a bodily apprehension of the ways in which digital media has mutated and accelerated the landscapes it is implicated within. This embodied understanding is perhaps informative for audiences living within Japan and even people living within similarly ungrounded, technologized and immaterial societies, providing them with a means to navigate these worlds.

As Eric White discusses, such Japanese horror films as *Kairo* (*Pulse*) and *Ringu* (which similarly represents media and technology):

> Depict a social milieu in which the family matrix no longer provides the exclusive basis for psychological structure. Instead, omnipresent information technology functions as a vast psychic apparatus, or better, psychotronic apparatus, randomly propagating affective dispositions, libidinal intensities, decontextualized personae and partial selves across the social sphere.
>
> (in McRoy, 2005: 45).

As digital media has become more pervasive within Japan, traditional forms of community and sociality, such as the family and local community groups, have transformed. Some scholars, such as White (in McRoy, 2005), argue that they have become more removed and distant from an individual's social networks, meaning that they no longer derive a sense of self from these groups. Instead they are perhaps being replaced by virtual sociality, affective communications with machines or with other humans that do not take place face to face. The potentially isolating effects that these forms of sociality have are discussed in more depth later within this chapter. In particular, the living characters of *Kairo (Pulse)* can be understood to be representative of such effects as these suspended beings, long before they meet their demise at the hands of the invading spirits and become like them, are ghosts in a social sense, finding it difficult to form close, interpersonal connections with others. *Kairo (Pulse)* features a number of living characters who each, at some point, encounters a supernatural being or event. Akin to *Ju-On: The Grudge,* rather than privileging a single grand narrative, *Kairo (Pulse)* 'accommodates numerous "petits récits" [little narratives], as Jean-François Lyotard calls them' (Brown, 2010: 5), which allows the film to explore a wider variety of more nuanced themes and issues centred around digital media and its collisions with our social, political and economic landscapes.

Japan, especially its capital city, Tokyo, under techno-Orientalist thought is understood to be particularly exemplary of a site conditioned and transformed excessively by new, digital, technological developments. As Tsukamoto discusses, 'Tokyo is becoming every day more like a sort of virtual reality world. People no longer communicate through contact but use technology for everything and this is progressively substituting communication itself' (cited in Brown, 2010: 111). The pervasiveness of digital media within Japan has led to the formation of (what is thought to be) a nationally specific pathology called *Hikikomori*,[1] where young males especially take the isolation that digital media offers them to new extremes, spending every waking hour locked in their rooms with only their PCs and digital devices for company. Through its living characters, *Kairo (Pulse)* makes reference to this pathology. However, this attribution of issues with digital media to one singular nation is problematic, particularly when such technologies are so adept at spreading globally. They are constitutive of, as will be explained, a transnational, posthuman condition. Thus, *Kairo (Pulse)* perhaps achieves a more global outlook on these issues than suggested.

Discussing the living characters in the film as simply barren, disengaged individuals, representative of the *Hikikomori*, is also a limited perspective to take and has implications for the way in which we view the spirits of *Kairo (Pulse)*. The living characters do not just simply become shells devoid of any emotion, feeling or humanity, but, through their assemblages with the spirits and their becoming-other, transform into inspirational, affective beings, able to, at certain points, reground themselves and form bodily interconnections with others. Nevertheless, there is a marked absence, within *Kairo (Pulse)*, of a goal-oriented hero who has the agency to vanquish the spirits invading the realm of the living and restore order. Two characters, Kudo Michi (Asō Kumiko), who works at a plant sales company and Kawashima Ryosuke (Katō Haruhiko), an economics student, do emerge as dominant within the narrative discourse, their stories eventually converging; however, they too are unable to reconstitute an encompassing situation. Any acts that the living characters carry out do not lead to the re-establishment of an all-encompassing, informative milieu which would break them free of the suspension that the apocalyptic event has caused. Their marginal actions, which have little significance or impact, are actually symptomatic of the deterritorialization of encompassing milieus. Long before the disruption of the spirits, invading the realm of the living, is introduced, these characters were perhaps already in a state of suspension and indetermination, not knowing how to act meaningfully in increasingly confusing, transformative spaces. They are beings, close to the body without organs, who are not constitutive of any singular molar regime.

The spirits within *Kairo (Pulse)* are arguably the more affective, transformative beings, however. Significantly, many of the spirits within *Kairo (Pulse)* are ontologically similar to digital media, being composed of code and behaving in very similar ways to these products. A number of spirits are pixelated, blurred beings who download themselves from the web and into the realm of the living. However, these spirits appear to be full of errors once they manifest in the realm of the living, glitching as they try to navigate their space.

Being composed of digital code, these spirits can usefully be discussed under the ideas and concepts of the posthuman and the transhuman. Congruent with Deleuze's concepts of becoming, posthumanism does not view the body as static and already fully formed, it can become-other, become-machine, through its assemblages with technology and realize different, heterogeneous existences and relational subjectivities. The spirits, through their assemblages with the Internet and their coded nature, are, like digital media, variable, where slight alterations in their code can transform them. Faced with such ambiguity, traditional, singular molar ideologies pertaining to gender, sexuality, culture, ethnicity and national origin become difficult to ground in relation to these spirits. Transhumanism, as is discussed, realizes a much more radical fusion between the human and technology than posthumanism, perceiving that the human and its organic body can be transcended (rather than just mutated). The merits of each perspective, in relation to an analysis of the spirits, are assessed in this chapter. Furthermore, how the living characters, through their assemblages with the spirits (usually via the medium of the Internet), can be understood as rendering the posthuman/transhuman condition and different becoming-machines is an important consideration. The living characters may be inspirational figures for audiences as through their assemblages with technology and the spirits they may become more flexible, relational and transformative. It must be noted, however, that *Kairo (Pulse)* perhaps does not prioritize a rendering of positive, affirmative becoming-machines. Instead, *Kairo (Pulse)* arguably envisions much darker, destructive outcomes from the assemblages people form with technology, informed by such key issues and events as the development of the *Hikikomori* pathology, the reorientation of the Japanese economy and various, violent, terrorist attacks occurring throughout the 1990s and early 2000s.

As is also explored in this chapter, these spirits are not restricted to interpretations based around their assemblages with digital media, they can also be understood in other ways, including as cosmic beings. They can be thought of as unknowable entities who cannot be conceptualized under a hermeneutic regime, such as psychoanalysis. Cosmic beings are emblematic of a paradigm shift that occurred within twenty-first-century horror, diverging away from the gothic. The resurgence of cosmic horror is widely understood to be symptomatic of breaks with linearity occurring within societies, like the one created by the bursting of the economic bubble in the 1990s and its interrelated, subsequent breaks. This is because cosmic, weird beings defy fixity, they cannot be understood through molar regimes, laws and milieus that belong to our world. Thus, they aptly express these breaks with linear time, the ungroundings of molar, hermeneutic regimes that they cause and the any-space-whatevers they create. Cosmic beings are unearthly forces that are not, as in the gothic and in traditional Japanese ghost stories for that matter, the spirits of deceased humans returning to the world of the living to exact revenge. They invade the realm of the living despite humans, not because of them, and they are not conducive to any moral or religious body, as in the gothic. Cosmic beings are post-familial, distorting the things we recognize, like media, genre tropes and motifs. Many of the spirits of *Kairo (Pulse)* too, through their strange inhuman forms, negate any straightforward application of a molar, linear or hermeneutic regime. They inhabit and are formed by the interstitial space between the realm of the living and the world of the dead, making them an indeterminate, affective presence.

These spirits then are polynomial, they can be interpreted in many ways, understood to represent and express a range of diverse, interrelated ideas, issues, crises and contexts, including economic hardship, technologization and terrorism, which pervaded Japan between the 1990s and 2000s. Many of the situations and issues that the spirits of *Kairo (Pulse)* express are transnational in scope. Although they are experienced differently in each national, cultural context, one must consider how facets of *Kairo's (Pulse's)* renderings may reach out and speak to audiences globally. Before such considerations of the polynomial spirits take place, however, this chapter begins with an exploration of the living characters of *Kairo (Pulse)* and maps out some of their most significant affective assemblages and becomings.

The living characters

The living characters of *Kairo* (*Pulse*), particularly Michi and Ryosuke, are not explicitly grounded within molar regimes when we first encounter them, instead, they are already largely deterritorialized. Unlike in engagements with the other films studied here, audiences perhaps do not come to apprehend the living characters' experiences of becoming ungrounded from molar positionalities. Such films, which more profoundly territorialize some of their characters into molar regimes, assume that we too are, or at least once were, grounded in similar types of static subjectivity, such as national, gendered and cultural identities, and can thus resonate or empathize with the traumatic transformations and deterritorializations that occur to them. However, the characters within *Kairo* (*Pulse*) appear to largely skip over such an ungrounding process and, without delay, the film renders them as already having undergone some kind of deterritorialization.

Michi is a good example of this. When we encounter her in the first scene, which, in terms of the film's timeline, depicts the conclusion, where herself and Ryosuke are escaping their doomed city on a ship, she stares over a railing out to sea, her back to the camera, as other passengers busy themselves plotting the course to South America (a supposed safe haven) and carrying out tasks on the deck around her. One man looks at Michi with concern and suspicion, informing us of her indetermination, as he cannot yet seem to understand her, to work out what the purpose of her inaction is. Furthermore, being denied sight of her face gives her a distant, ethereal feel. Much like the spirits of the film, we cannot know her or understand her through hermeneutic regimes, as we cannot form an emphatic connection with her. However, we can know her on some level, through a bodily, affective engagement, an assemblage which is very similar to one we form with the unknowable spirits of the film.

Even once her internal, reflective monologue begins, signalling the start of the telling of events leading up to her passage on the ship, we are still denied sight of her face. This is quite strange when one considers the determining nature of such a feature, setting up Michi as the purveyor of perspective on the forthcoming events of the film. However, as mentioned previously, Michi is not the sole source of knowledge on the events of the film and thus nor is she the sole protagonist. The use of this internal monologue, however brief, and the lack of sight of her face, therefore, takes on a new meaning. Rather than identifying and territorializing Michi into a specific, conventional narrative role of furthering the action of the story, it actually highlights her indetermination, her non-identity. She is an any-person-whoever here, an interchangeable, transformative being, able to become Ryosuke, become Harue (Katō Koyuki) (a young, computer science student who has a romantic connection with Ryosuke), become Taguchi (Mizuhashi Kenji) (a colleague of Michi's) amongst others and relay to us the recollection-images of their experiences of the crisis. At this moment, Michi is emblematic of posthuman subjectivity (an idea discussed in detail later within this chapter). She is fluid and relational and can tap into others' experiences of the events of the crisis and live them out.

This scene in which Michi's face is concealed, draws interesting links with Deleuze and Guattari's concepts of faciality and the deconstruction of the face within *A Thousand Plateaus* (1987). In this book Deleuze and Guattari (1987) assert that the face overcodes the subject and functions 'as the "black hole" into which individuality (and imperceptibility) is swallowed' (Rodrigues, 2012). Thus, by not revealing her face, by becoming 'defacialized' within these scenes, Michi cannot be coded under specific gender, or racial ideologies, which are limiting perspectives of the being. The figure of Michi here, fails to yield any sense of her wholeness and subjectivity to us, betraying our normative methods of reading and identifying a subject. We are thus suspended in our linear interpretations of her, making this scene particularly affective. Furthermore, this scene demonstrates that 'no entity is ever absolute. Rather, all are elements of more encompassing frames of reference; all are products of abstract, qualificatory work' (Rodrigues, 2012). Michi is a heterogeneous being within these scenes, through whom we can imagine a flux of identity and many different potentialities of existence, identity and being.

Whilst it could be argued that, at this point (the end of the film), Michi must have undergone transformation and deterritorialization at some earlier stage in the timeline and therefore there is nothing strange or novel about this depiction, in fact, Michi's suspension and indetermination appears not to be overturned within subsequent scenes. Some of these subsequent scenes occur prior to the collision of the worlds of the living and the dead and therefore prior to the formation of any suspending, any-space-whatevers informed by this event. There is no striking juxtaposition between how Michi behaved in the past, prior to the crisis and after. In the first few scenes, following the opening, we see Michi carrying out mundane tasks at work, filling in charts and moving plants, displaying little more life than when we first encounter her on the ship. Immediately after this, following her colleague Toshio's (Matsu Masatoshi) complaints that they need a disk that Taguchi has been working on at home, Michi picks up her bag without a word and then appears on an empty bus, staring unblinkingly into space, revealing no expression of concern at her colleague's strange, extended absence from work. These seemingly unnatural, robotic actions, displaying emotionless states, where no profound, personal interconnections are made between the characters, highlight their indetermination, their inhumanity.

This does not mean, however, that these characters are not affective and relational and cannot break out of their indeterminate state. In fact, their resonances with audiences as perhaps similarly suspended, indeterminate beings, potentially make for a much more profound, more closely interconnected assemblage between the two. Audiences perhaps even partially fill out these characters with elements of their own being, their own experiences of molarity, deterritorialization and molecularity, so that they can negotiate them in the space of the film, constituting it as an anti-environment (a term discussed later within this chapter).

Kusina, within her work on *Kairo (Pulse)*, has also highlighted the indeterminate nature of these living characters, discussing how 'each individual life is not shown to be especially distinct' (2008) and how these characters are perhaps even interchangeable. This is a very problematic idea however, as, whilst one could conceptualize that an entirely ungrounded, de-stratified being (a body without organs) would be interchangeable with other, similarly deterritorialized beings, as they possess the same qualities of malleability and the same abilities to perpetually 'become-other', these living characters are not completely de-stratified and elements of their being are subject to distinct molar regimes. Furthermore, bodies-without-organs cannot be interchangeable as, through their ability to become-other, they are fundamentally different from each other. Each body transforms, or 'becomes-other', differently, pursues individual lines of flight and transmits and receives unique qualities of affect.

Considering how the living characters are grounded upon lines of segmentarity, in parts of the film, it appears that Ryosuke and Michi may adhere to molarities pertaining to gender. For instance, Michi is sometimes positioned within a stereotypical caring, mothering role, taking care of the traumatized Junko (Arisaka Kurume) (another of her colleagues) in her home after she encounters a spirit.

FIGURE 32 *Michi taking care of Junko,* Kairo (Pulse) *(Kurosawa, 2001)*.

Ryosuke is also sometimes positioned within stereotypically masculine roles, for instance, rushing to save Harue, the damsel in distress, after she flees the train they were both travelling on, trying to escape the increasingly dire situation within the city. Ryosuke also utilizes the investigative gaze, coming the closest to finding some conclusion as to how and why the spirits have begun to enter the realm of the living.

Whilst these actions are illustrative of the characters' belonging to a milieu, positionalities which disturb and contradict such stratifications are much more common within *Kairo (Pulse)*. For instance, Michi is often positioned (much like Rika in *Ju-On: The Grudge*) within the traditionally masculine role of furthering the story, investigating what has happened to her colleagues as they gradually disappear and even saving her friend, Junko, from the clutches of a malevolent spirit. The female is not conceptualized as completely passive within *Kairo (Pulse)*, even minor female characters, such as Harue and Junko, display varying degrees of action and passivity. Furthermore, Ryosuke, and the other male characters in the film, can similarly be seen as fluctuating between varying degrees of passive and active becoming. Ryosuke, for instance, as well as being an active character, resisting becoming a spirit like those around him and denying the existence of ghosts right until the end, has moments of passivity. For example, he eventually succumbs to the transformative power of the spirit he encounters, sitting down on the floor as it moves closer towards him.

Whilst these characters do display some forms of agency, none of them fully fit into 'the hallmark role of hero as defender-of-humanity' (Kusina, 2008), able to reconstitute former milieus. In fact, these living characters, when they become ghosts themselves, transcend humanity altogether and become, therefore, unable to re-establish humanity's orders and regimes. *Kairo (Pulse)*, instead, presents audiences with multiple experiences of the crisis, none of which lead to a resolution. The encounters, or duels, of Toshio, Michi, Ryosuke and Junko with spirits are merely placed as a handful of experiences amongst thousands, perhaps even billions, when one considers, as the film tells us, that other places around the globe have similarly been affected by the intermingling of worlds. There is not one singular person whose agency can reverse the catastrophe of the realms of the living and the dead intermingling.

None of the characters appear particularly concerned with what is happening either, nor especially motivated to try and put a stop to the mysterious disappearances of those around them. They are placed within a situation in which they do not know how to act decisively and effectively, within increasingly a-temporal spaces where different existentialities intermingle. There is, therefore, no hope for progression it seems, only inevitable death. Perhaps many of the characters (especially Harue, as is discussed in the following section) come to accept this fate, explaining their inaction. This may be interpreted as a representation of Japanese subjects living under the conditions of the break with linear time, where people live within the moment, are not driven by encompassing milieus and are encouraged (or forced) to become, in different ways, fluid, adaptable and relational, ungrounding or erasing their identities constantly. These subjects, experiencing many micro-deaths when they partake in such discourses, may accept the prospect of a more absolute death more readily, perceiving it simply as another becoming-other.

As touched upon previously, the living characters of *Kairo* (*Pulse*) are also suspended and inactive in a social sense as 'even when ... [they] are presented with opportunities for genuine interpersonal connections, they seem inert and incapable of acting on them' (Kusina, 2008). For instance, Ryosuke and Harue have ample opportunity to create a profound connection with one another, but instead they are often aloof. Harue even suggests to Ryosuke that she could live very happily in the realm of the dead, away from her irrelevant parents.

Just like the glowing white orbs which feature in an experimental computer programme within Harue's lab at the university, each person/orb is an individual.

They never touch, interconnect or collide as they would die, but, as they drift and try to pull away from others around them, they are contradictorily drawn closer together. This programme is interpreted, within the film, as allegorizing the individualism and isolation that exist amongst

FIGURE 33 *The experimental computer programme within Harue's lab,* Kairo (Pulse) *(Kurosawa, 2001).*

subjects in the world of *Kairo* (*Pulse*) and, as such, it directly comments upon landscapes beyond it, in Japan and in other technologized societies. Through digital media especially, the characters of *Kairo* (*Pulse*), like people external to the film, have created their own virtual bubbles, where they can isolate themselves and cut themselves off from the real world. However, contradictorily, these technologies also have the ability to contract the world, bringing people from all over the globe closer together. Thus, the characters, long before they meet their demise through encountering a spirit, and subjects (beyond the film) alike, have, it is purported, become ghosts in a social sense (Kusina, 2008). They are empty, passive people who are losing the ability to form connections with other, bodily, non-virtual beings.

However, the idea that subjects (within and external to the film) and ghosts are empty and ethereal is highly debatable, especially when we consider that the spirits of *Kairo* (*Pulse*), as is discussed in the next section, are perhaps the most intense, affective, transformative beings in the whole film. Nevertheless, Kurosawa himself, not considering the affective force of these spirits, discussed in an interview how he thinks 'that ghosts are beings that lack human emotion and personality. They're human-like, but all the emotional elements of a normal person are missing. They're empty shells' (Brown, 2010: 117). Brown (2010), furthering this discussion, but again not considering the potential affectiveness of these spirits, highlights how, as empty shells, they are therefore, like the humans who encounter them and become suicidal, emblematic of the *Hikikomori* condition. Whilst the ghosts and the passive beings are perhaps useful allegories for this pathology, this is still, in some ways, a limiting reading of these characters.

One of the most basic criticisms of this interpretation could be made when one considers that the living characters do not always adhere closely to the symptoms of this pathology. For instance, Toshio, despite his depressed nature (after encountering a spirit close to Taguchi's apartment), still attends work every day and does eventually open up to Michi about how he has been feeling. This illustrates a further notion that while the characters on screen may not form especially intense connections with other bodily beings, contrary to what the computer programme renders, they nevertheless achieve some kind of assemblage with the bodies that they encounter. Connections that they create between each other do, in fact, lead to some changes, actions and reactions. Thus, these bodies are far from empty or passive. For example, when Ryosuke and Michi finally encounter one another, they become more vitalized, breaking out of their lifeless, static states. Here the two, through their assemblage, charged by the affective forces they have exchanged, regain a linear purpose. Using this force to become reterritorialized upon lines of segmentarity, they set out to find and rescue Harue together after she left Ryosuke on a train. These affective charges are also experienced by audiences and they feel invigorated by the creation of a new assemblage such as this.

Some of the most interesting assemblages that the living characters form, however, are with the spirits that they encounter. Through such encounters, the living characters are opened to more potentialities for becoming-other, most notably, different becoming-machines. By forming assemblages with the living characters and the ghosts on screen, audiences can also experience these multipotentialities of becoming. It is to an exploration of these interconnections that this chapter now turns.

The spirits and becoming-machine

The spirits of *Kairo* (*Pulse*) can be considered the closest beings to the body without organs that we have yet encountered within this book. These beings are transformative, fluid, polynomial and often indescribable or incomprehensible. Furthermore, when living characters, and audiences through them, form interconnections with the ghosts, the forces and intensities that drift to them are profoundly deterritorializing, causing them to eventually die (the characters that is), become ghosts themselves and take on their relational, fluid properties and ways of being.

Interestingly, as touched upon previously, many of the dispositions, movements and behaviours of these ghosts resemble the nature and languages of the Internet and its virtual landscapes and features. Thus, becoming-machine is a term which perhaps more adequately (than the term becoming-other) captures the digitally mediated nature of these spirits. However, as these spirits are polynomial they are exceptionally difficult to categorize into one, stable understanding. This section therefore explores a number of potential ways we can understand or know these spirits, for instance, under notions of cosmic horror, or as traditional ghosts or *yūrei*.[2]

The idea of the spirits within *Kairo* (*Pulse*) being particularly malleable, affective and mutable beings is similar to the one purported previously in the study of *Ju-On: The Grudge*, where the spirits, Kayako and Toshio, were conceptualized as close to the ungrounded body without organs. However, these two characters, through more profound anchoring elements of their subjectivities, such as their genders, are closer to reterritorialization or more grounded than the spirits of *Kairo* (*Pulse*). As these characters are, for the most part, grounded within deceivingly static human-like forms, Kayako appearing as a young woman and Toshio as a small boy, even though they transform their appearances throughout the film, they are far more territorialized and identifiable than some of the spirits that inhabit the world of *Kairo* (*Pulse*).

The spirits of *Kairo* (*Pulse*) are sometimes depicted as pulsating masses of shadow which are ungendered, unidentifiable and often unattributable to any hermeneutic regime or sense of identity. At points, it is even unclear

FIGURE 34 *A black, shadowy spirit Ryosuke encounters,* Kairo (Pulse) *(Kurosawa, 2001).*

if these masses are of human form. For example, in one particular scene, Ryosuke, returning to an arcade he frequents as the world crumbles around him, finds the place suddenly infested with dark shadowy figures, which slink between and behind arcade machines. One mass, in particular, that Ryosuke watches, appearing at first in a silhouette of a human form, begins to blur and distort as it turns around to face him, collapsing and morphing into inhuman shapes.

Nevertheless, precisely because of their heterogeneity these spirits can be understood under traditional Japanese narratives of *yūrei* or ghosts, a more comfortable, recognizable interpretation for audiences and scholars, which places these spirits into a culturally based, hermeneutic reading. These ghosts then can also be understood as forming assemblages with the *yūrei* of other Japanese horror films (such as Kayako and Toshio) or as becoming-others and re-imaginings of these other inflections of *yūrei*. However, we should hold this as only one potential interpretation or becoming of the film and the audience experience of it, which can be fused or hybridized with other understandings. The spirits within *Kairo (Pulse)* can be understood as *yūrei* as they mediate the gap between the afterlife and the land of the living, fulfilling the creation of the eponymous circuit (*kairo* translates as circuit in Japanese). The spirit that Junko encounters in her boss' apartment complex (after she visits him due to his absence from work) especially creates an explicit intertextual link with the *yūrei* of other Japanese horror

FIGURE 35 *The* yūrei *Junko encounters,* Kairo (Pulse) *(Kurosawa, 2001).*

films through its aesthetics. This particular ghost is female, has pallid skin and long dark tresses of hair which cover her face. These are all tropes associated with the *yūrei/onryō* characters of the likes of *Ringu* and *Ju-On: The Grudge*.

However, unlike the *yūrei* of traditional Japanese folklore and some contemporary Japanese horror films, the spirits within *Kairo (Pulse)* do not emerge in the realm of the living to fulfil a specific purpose such as seek revenge or care for the children they leave behind. In fact, it is very difficult to glean any motivation for their return. For this reason, as will be discussed further within this section, these spirits can be understood as post-familial rather than traditional *yūrei*. Furthermore, they are not always apparitions of a human spirit, their appearance resembling that of which they had in life. Thus, these spirits cannot be unproblematically understood under notions of the gothic and psychoanalytical regimes either.

One notable spirit, however, could be interpreted as adhering to the monstrous-feminine, vengeful spirit *(onryō)* and return of the repressed tropes. When Toshio leaves his colleague Taguchi's apartment after receiving strange phone calls from him (even though he has passed away), he comes across a red-taped-up door (which we later learn house spirits as they begin to manifest in the world). Upon entering it, a female spirit manifests. Within this sequence the horrific, abject female pursues Toshio, attacking him with her supernatural powers as he cowers before her, causing him to become nihilistic and suicidal. Here the female is uncanny, threatening and violent, challenging, much in the same ways both Kayako (*Ju-On: The Grudge*) and Asami (*Audition*) do, traditional notions of passive femininity. The focus that is placed upon her gazing eyes by the camera also poses a challenge to the male who, never an object of the gaze, is always positioned as the wielder. This is one psychoanalytic potentiality that could be realized by the audience once the spirit manifests into a recognizable icon of femininity, but it is nevertheless not the only potentiality.

It may be that, as Yoshizaki (Takeda Shinji), the graduate student sharing Harue's lab, surmises, the spirits have no specific purpose in entering the living realm, only that the afterworld is full, and they must seek more space. However, this hypothesis is neither proven nor disproven and thus (once again) it lies as one potentiality amongst many that could spark experiences of why it is that these spirits have manifested within this previously separate temporality.

These spirits, unlike Kayako and Toshio of *Ju-On: The Grudge*, are more profoundly embedded in a state of indetermination and suspension. In their shadowy, ill-defined state especially, these bodies exist as pure potentiality, masses made up of intense affective force which could be directed down any number of different lines of flight or manifest into any becoming of form. They are always on the verge of territorialization, always straddling the boundaries between worlds and thus becomings. These spirits, in this form, are never fully perceptible, are felt rather than seen and are therefore never fully explicable. They differ significantly from the traditional gothic ghost in this sense and are weird and unknowable, adhering to more post-familial, cosmic notions of horror.

The concepts of the weird and the cosmic, within culture, originate from the late Victorian period where writers of gothic fiction began to experiment with figures of monstrosity, departing from depictions of human, familiar, yet uncanny forms. The weird and the cosmic reached maturity in the 1920s and 1930s under the author H.P. Lovecraft who, influenced by the inexplicable horrors of the First World War, created obscure, alien-like creatures like Cthulhu (within *The Call of Cthulhu* (1926)). Since then, the cosmic and the weird 'has led an appropriately discontinuous and mutant existence', crossing many generic boundaries, including horror and sci-fi, and 'tracing its path across cultural forms from pulp magazines to film and from film to the graphic novel and more recently becoming the object of critical attention and even canonization' (Murphy and Noys, 2016: 117). Despite its fluidity as a form, central to its definition is the estrangement from reality that it induces within audiences. The weird and cosmic entities of certain horror texts, for instance, unlike uncanny monsters, are alien, unknowable and do not belong to our world. As such, they are imperceptible and cannot be classified under our systems of language, creating this estrangement. Fisher describes the weird as 'so strange that it makes us feel that it should not exist, or at least it should not exist here. Yet if the entity or object is here, then the categories which we have up until now used to make sense of the world cannot be valid' (2016: 15).

Particularly in their shadowy, pulsating forms, there is something cosmic and weird about the spirits of *Kairo (Pulse)*. Just like the alien beings within the tales of authors like Algernon Blackwood, especially his novella *The Willows* (1907), the spirits of *Kairo (Pulse)* are imperceptible in and as themselves, they cannot fully manifest within the world of the living, hence the dark, pulsating and the ill-defined, pixelated forms they take.[3] This unknowability of the spirits is what makes them fascinating yet terrifying, we cannot know what they truly are and what motivates their behaviours. Nevertheless, to come into contact with one, to know a spirit on some level, is to be destroyed by that knowledge. Within Lovecraft's works, characters who encounter weird, cosmic entities often experience breakdowns and psychosis. Similarly, in *Kairo (Pulse)*, those who enter a forbidden, red-taped room and find a spirit are driven to commit suicide. This discourse of the cosmic or weird is most explicitly expressed when Harue comes into contact with an invisible spirit, as, prior to this, she questions her understanding of the afterlife and the spirit beings that exist there. Finally understanding something of the nature of the spirits when she finds an invisible force in her apartment, she embraces it and exclaims joyfully that she is not alone. Soon after, however, Harue kills herself, destroyed by her connection with the spirits.

FIGURE 36 *Harue embracing the invisible force in her apartment,* Kairo (Pulse) *(Kurosawa, 2001).*

Through her joyful exclamations and embracing of the invisible form, this knowledge of, or encounter with, a spirit is interestingly not solely presented as horrific, nor completely destructive. This conforms to the discourses of other texts, particularly Lovecraft's, which present the capability of the weird or cosmic to induce a wide range of feelings and affects, including astonishment, ecstasy, as well as dread. The intense outpouring of energy from the invisible being, identified, in particular, by a sharp, electronic, ringing sonsign, feels invigorating for Harue who has been previously starved of the affective sensation of a close, intimate connection with some body or being. Thus, she embraces it rather than fleeing in horror, yearning for further affective bonds and sensations, something which it seems can only be achieved by becoming a ghost herself. This clashes with other encounters that occur within the film which are terrifying and horrific, not least Ryosuke's encounter with a spirit which, as later discussed in detail, is particularly destructive.

Akin to the weird, cosmic beings of *The Willows* who present themselves and exert their force through nature, the spirits of *Kairo* (*Pulse*) make their presence felt in an urban environment, twisting themselves into existence, by situating themselves within, appropriating and taking control of the interstitial, virtual spaces of the Internet. Here, like nature in *The Willows*, the Internet is made weird, it is a familiar space, yet it has a disturbing, unearthly force that works through it. The spirits open fissures in the living world, disrupting its linear flow and causing the spaces they infiltrate to, like them, defy fixity, categorization and cognitive understanding. As these shadowy or pixelated forms leak out from the space of the web and into the world of the living (a depiction of our own world, of Japan) we lose all sense of the natural laws that govern it, they throw it into chaos or suspension, creating an any-space-whatever.

Conversely, highlighting the differences between the cosmic and the gothic, the uncanny discourses of gothic texts work to reconstitute societal laws and values. The uncanny describes a category of things that are feared but which also lead back to what is known and familiar to the subject. In particular, impulses and desires that we have repressed in order to adhere to societal norms can be described as uncanny. Once they resurface in return of the repressed scenarios, they are familiar attractions to us that also invoke an anxiety that we will be punished for our deviance in taking pleasure in them. As Wood (in Nichols, 1985) argues, these uncanny things are conventionally returned to their repressed state at the end of a film, thus reaffirming certain milieus and their boundaries.

The weird or cosmic, rather than reconstituting milieus and upholding the human as the one true perspective on horror, defining what is to be feared based upon certain ideological and societal structures, actually presents us with our (the audience's) own inconsequentiality, in a discourse, established by Lovecraft, termed 'cosmic indifferentism'. What is disturbing in *Kairo* (*Pulse*) is often not coded as such through a hermeneutic signifier (such as some allusion to the unheimlich womb). Here, we, the audience, are insignificant, we cannot understand or define, through our societies and our languages, the cosmic beings that invade our once linear reality as they are not borne out of our societies. Thus, it gives audiences the impression that we have no special status within the universe, the spirits enter into our existentiality, our temporality, in spite of us, not because of our supposed repressions.

Furthermore, the threat that these cosmic forces pose is not conducive to any moral or religious bodies. Unlike the ghosts from the eighteenth century 'who tended to moralism and anti-Popish sniping, embodying as dread example lessons about virtue, justice, and so on' (Miéville, 2008: 116), there is no timeless good versus evil binary here. The ghosts, while horrifying, are not monstrous in the traditional sense, they are not sent here from any religious conception of heaven or hell. They appear, instead, to have sprung themselves from an indescribable void. Despite Yoshizaki's theory that the spirits have been spilling out of the afterlife as their realm is now full, there is no religious sentiment here and nor is this theory proven or disproven, it is simply a potentiality. Ultimately then this invasion of spirits is 'unprecedented, unexpected, unexplained, unexplainable – it simply is' (Miéville, 2008: 111).

Kairo's (*Pulse*'s) tendency towards weird, cosmic horror rather than classic, gothic horror can be considered as part of a wider resurgence of this form within literature, media, theory and philosophy in the twenty-first century. The term 'new weird' was coined in 2003 to describe this resurgence within popular culture. Specifically, the fiction and criticism of China Miéville from the early 2000s onwards can be considered to herald the emergence of the new weird; however, 'it can be traced back to the 1980s fiction of Clive Barker and especially Thomas Ligotti' (Murphy and Noys, 2016: 118–19). Ligotti's works, in particular, are interesting examples of weird, cosmic fiction with distinct allusions to Deleuzian thought. Unlike Lovecraft, who was preoccupied with detailing the alien, cosmic beings in his works, Ligotti is more concerned with exploring the subject's experience of the weird and how they are transformed, or become-other, through their encounters. The characters of Ligotti's works, encountering the weird, recognize within themselves a trace of something which is not human, leading to the realization that they are shaped and moved by non-human forces, ungrounding their sense of self and replacing it with the nihilistic idea that humans are not in charge of their own destiny, they are simply puppets.

It is not only within the new weird works of Ligotti, however, that we can perceive a distinct emergence of discourses of becoming-other. As Murphy and Noys argue, the new weird, in general, 'can be characterized as a new sensibility of welcoming the alien and the monstrous as sites of affirmation and becoming', the new weird, they say, 'treats the alien, the hybrid, and the chaotic as subversions of the various normalizations of power and subjectivity' (Murphy and Noys, 2016: 125), as a way to deterritorialize dominant, molar structures. Demonstrating these discourses of becoming-other, in Miéville's series of *Bas-Lag* (2000–) novels for instance, the 'Remade', a biological underclass, are subjects who, convicted by the criminal justice system within the fantasy world of Bas-Lag, are punished by having their bodies warped and transformed in various ways. Many have bizarre limbs and organs grafted to them or else are combined with machines, sometimes enslaving them to fulfil a certain purpose. Some Remade, however, manage to break free from their enslavement and use their mutations for their own gain, demonstrating a more positive, liberatory becoming-other. Through subverting normative biological construction and because of the sympathetic way in which Miéville treats these characters, the Remade within Miéville's novels, unground and 'interrogate the new racisms, misogynies, and class violence that characterize the time of the "war on terror," global financial crisis, and anthropogenic climate change' (Murphy and Noys, 2016: 126). Murphy and Noys (2016), through their reference to the 'war on terror', a global financial crisis and anthropogenic climate change, interestingly link Miéville's characters to elements of posthuman thought and the posthuman condition specifically.

The posthuman condition is a complex, multilayered conceptualization of today's global, societal climates and subjectivities, which identifies how certain social, economic, cultural, political, environmental and technological developments have introduced 'a qualitative shift in our thinking about what exactly is the basic unit of common reference for our species [(the human)], our polity and our relationship to the other inhabitants of this planet' (Braidotti, 2013: 1–2). Developments, such as accelerations in the processes of globalization, growing market economies, technological and scientific innovations, contemporary economic crises, global warming, natural disasters and modern terrorist threats (amongst other things), all inform and constitute a part of the contemporary posthuman condition. Crucially, the posthuman condition also prompts critical thought into what it is we, as humans, are becoming or will become in the future.

Murphy and Noys (2016), through their allusion to this body of thought, reference the widely held idea that weird, cosmic beings (beyond human biology and human comprehension) have recently proliferated within popular culture in light of various crises in the humanities and in conceptualizations of the human, caused by transformative events. As the posthumanist scholar, Rosi Braidotti, states 'the concept of human has exploded under the double pressure of contemporary scientific advances and global economic concerns' (2013: 1). As the concept of the human has fallen into crisis and the notion of the posthuman has emerged, weird, cosmic texts have proliferated as they render encounters where the human becomes ungrounded in the face of the weird or non-human, illustrating the posthuman condition of realizing that we have never actually been human in the traditional (humanist) sense that we thought. The mutable, weird characters of Miéville's fictions then, are perhaps positive, hopeful figures of the posthuman condition, allowing audiences to believe that deterritorializing issues and problems, characterizing our contemporary lives, can be overcome through new forms of subjectivity.

A particular issue, however, with this conceptualization of Miéville's characters specifically, and with Murphy and Noy's (2016) argument overall about the new weird and the becomings it engenders, is precisely its affirmative nature. Becomings within the new weird, as Ligotti's works demonstrate, are not always euphoric or liberatory. Encounters with other worldly forces can be toxic and induce nihilistic thought and suspension. Cosmic or weird beings unground subjects from their normative, molar ways of understanding the world around them and create any-space-whatevers. There is no guarantee, therefore, that a progressive, affirmative linearity for the subject will be reinstated immediately following the encounter. Once again this may directly reflect the way in which complex, often inconceivable events and issues are processed and received by subjects today (such as advances in globalization, terrorism, climate change and economic crises), ungrounding them, causing an inability to comprehend and act accordingly to a situation and engendering nihilistic feeling. As Braidotti highlights, one must not forget, in favour of pursuing more positive outlooks on these contemporary crises and transformations, that such posthuman conditions trigger significant destructive and inhumane discourses and thus 'extend[s] the death horizon to most species' (2013: 111), prompting morbid, nihilistic perspectives.

One central idea, related to posthumanism, which encapsulates this death horizon and highlights the nihilism inherent to many posthuman situations, is the Anthropocene, a label given to our current geological period, in which human activity has decisively changed the planet and affected all life on it. Humankind has finally become aware of the impact it has had on the planet and that we may have set in motion our own, eventual extinction, particularly through the profound changes in the climate we have instigated. Interlinking with this, advanced capitalism and the global market economy, which inform societies across the world, also 'threatens the sustainability of our planet as a whole' (2013: 64). It unifies all species, the planet and its natural resources under the imperative of the market, commodifying and exploiting them. Outbursts of violence and terrorism too, of the likes committed by the *Aum Shinrikyō* cult in Japan, are understood, in part, (by the likes of Iida (2002)) to have been a response to the dehumanizing processes of advanced capitalism and the market economy, contributing to and exacerbating the destructive, nihilistic facets of the posthuman condition.

The Anthropocene and the prospect of extinction, or a potential world without us, have transformed the way in which we understand ourselves, our societies, our relations with other humans and with other forms of life that inhabit our planet, deterritorializing humanist perspectives on such matters. For instance, Franklin, Lury and Stacey (2000, cited in Braidotti, 2013) discuss the idea of 'pan-humanity' which refers to 'a global sense of inter-connection among all humans, but also between the human and the non-human environment' (Braidotti, 2013: 40). The interconnections humans form between each other and their environments today are, as they discuss, based upon a shared sense of vulnerability, a fear of immanent catastrophes like the next natural disaster, environmental crises or terrorist attack. The Anthropocene constitutes a disruption or break with linear time, ungrounding the notion that the Earth is an infinite body of matter. It thus generates its own form of any-space-whatevers, causing suspensions in action and indecisiveness on exactly how to respond to the prospect of such a crisis.

Cinema and other cultural products from around the world have responded in different ways to the Anthropocene. Horror fictions (and other generic texts that are inflected with horror) especially have been adept at expressing these ideas and the fears related to them. Contemporary horror texts, such as *The Walking Dead* (2010–), *The Mist* (2007), *Cloverfield* (2008) and *Alien: Covenant* (2017), are rife with narratives about environmental breakdown, the collapse of civilization, survival and the near eradication of human life (or the prospect of it in some cases like *Alien: Covenant*). Cosmic, weird fictions, often crossed with the horror genre, can also be said to resonate with these ideas. *Kairo* (*Pulse*), for instance, through its depictions of the mass disappearance of people across Tokyo, Japan and (as the film alludes to at its climax) the world, the sudden crumbling of human civilization and society and the desperate attempts of individuals to survive, can be said to render fears about human extinction, the end of the world as we know it. *Kairo* (*Pulse*) then, is perhaps more in tune with destructive impulses, rendering a bleak picture of posthuman conditions within Japan specifically. However, as noted previously, Harue's encounter with the cosmic, weird entity in her apartment is quite interesting in this regard, as she is, at first, euphoric in her assemblage with the invisible being. This suggests that *Kairo* (*Pulse*) is much more nuanced in its perspectives on posthumanist conditions, breaks in linearity and the becoming-others that they instigate. It produces a dialogue on the tension between 'the celebration of chaos' on one hand, 'and the logic of nihilism' (Murphy and Noys, 2016: 127) on the other, between affirmative becoming and suspension, reterritorialization and deterritorialization.

It is important to note here that much of the posthuman thought that this chapter discusses is Western (especially European) in origin and thus comments specifically upon a Western context. However, this does not mean that it is uninformative as many of its assertions and ideas can be adapted to a Japanese, national context. We can, at the site of *Kairo* (*Pulse*) specifically, fuse posthumanist thought with specific, Japanese ideas, issues and contexts. For instance, our understanding of the break in linear time, occurring in Japan following the economic crash of 1990, can be expanded upon through posthumanist thought, linking Japanese conceptualizations of the break with transnational experiences and understandings of breaks.

The relation between resurgences in the cosmic, weird form and Deleuzian breaks in linear time is an element which, before going on to explore posthumanist thought in more critical detail, should be probed further. Today's breaks with linear time (whatever shape they may take, conditioned by both global and local contexts and events) are not the only occasions which have given rise to cosmic, weird fictions and creatures which defy comprehension, aptly capturing the contexts of the any-space-whatevers that surround them in the external world. As highlighted previously, the works of Lovecraft were significantly influenced by the First World War, which, in a European context, can be considered as a break in linear time. Miéville (cited in Fisher, 2016) has commented upon this connection between Lovecraft, the rupture of the First World War and, what he terms, the emergence of the new within his work. Miéville argues that the impact of the First World War, a traumatic break from the past, led to Lovecraft's creation of radical, alien creatures (sui generis, as he describes them) which are outside of any folkloric tradition (cited in Fisher, 2016: 21). Here, Miéville alludes to the capability of the any-space-whatever, created in such a break with linear time, to unground the repetition of the same (the depiction of previously established, familial monsters like the werewolf or the vampire) and give rise to becoming-others, the creation of the new (alien, cosmic creatures).

Similarly, we can perhaps consider certain events of the early twentieth century as breaks in linear time, influencing such weird, cosmic, deterritorialized works as Algernon Blackwood's. At the point of these early, cosmic, weird works emerging, the Victorian era had just come to an end, replacing peace, prosperity and a general feeling of national self-confidence with feelings of uncertainty and anxiety. This was due, largely, to changes in the political landscape, increasing Anglo-German estrangement, the politicization of the working classes, the growth in trade unions and the rise of women's suffrage.

Influencing *Kairo*'s (*Pulse*'s) renderings of the weird and the cosmic specifically is the break in linear time which occurred following the bursting of the economic bubble in 1990. This economic crisis within Japan coincided with other disruptive events and issues during the 1990s, including accelerations in the processes of globalization, technologization, shifts towards an immaterial, digital economy and various violent incidents perpetuated by individuals and cult groups. These complex, multifaceted events and issues amalgamated to constitute a break with linear time in Japan, spanning over a decade, creating any-space-whatevers or situations which people struggled to comprehend and act decisively within. The cosmic, weird spirits of *Kairo* (*Pulse*) then and the forbidden, red-taped rooms that they come to inhabit, can be understood as expressive of this break that began in 1990 and the states of suspension and incomprehensibility that it engendered. We can, however, expand upon and develop this viewpoint by looking towards posthumanist thought. Many of the facets of the break described in relation to Japan coincide with conceptualizations of the posthuman condition. Furthermore, it appears that *Kairo* (*Pulse*) explicitly draws upon such posthumanist ideas and renders them on-screen, thus, this is a particularly important body of scholarship to discuss.

Posthumanism critically questions the stance of humanism which came before it, a philosophy which emphasizes the value and agency of the human and entails 'a commitment to the search for truth and morality through human means in support of human interests' (Wolfe, 2009: XI). Such a stance, striving for and contributing to the progression of the human, has its interests firmly in line with hermeneutics. This methodology, in fact, has been profoundly influenced by the humanist stance, aiding it in its refutation of all other potential existentialities or interpretations of an event, culture, ideology or media text that do not align well with the image of the human that it constructs. Humanism presents a very specific vision of the human subject, 'they speak of the human in the accents and the interests of a class, a sex, a race, a genome' (Braidotti, 2013: 15). The human of humanism is a historical construct, contingent on certain locations and values, far from the natural law that it was once purported to be. What is recognized as human within humanism is the heterosexual, white, Western male, who stands in opposition to his 'sexualized, racialized, naturalized others and also in opposition to the technological artefact' (Braidotti, 2013: 26). Thus, humanist thought has been imperialistic, regulatory, exclusionary and discriminatory. The realization of its restrictiveness as a construct has been key to the formulation of posthumanist thought.

Posthumanism focuses upon the 'possibility of a serious decentering of "man", the former measure of all things' (Braidotti, 2013: 2) occurring, deterritorializing dominant humanist visions and perspectives on aspects of culture and society. This body of scholarship responds to widespread concern that the humanities is losing its relevance within contemporary fields of study. This concern, however, stems from the anti-humanist social movements of the 1960s and 1970s (feminism, anti-racism, decolonization and anti-nuclear movements for instance) and post-structuralist thought (also from the 1960s and 1970s), which aligned with such movements. These constitute important bases or sources for posthuman thought as a whole, but especially one particular strand which Braidotti (2013) advocates, 'critical posthumanism'.

Anti-humanist movements, like feminism and anti-racism, 'challenged the platitudes of Cold War rhetoric, with its emphasis on Western democracy, liberal individualism and the freedom they allegedly ensured for all' (Braidotti, 2013: 17), highlighting the inherent injustices within social systems for those who were not constituted as the ideal, white, heterosexual, Western male.

Similarly, post-structuralist philosophers, such as Deleuze and Derrida, interconnecting with these anti-humanist imperatives, 'argued that in the aftermath of colonialism, Auschwitz, Hiroshima and the Gulag – to mention but a few of the horrors of modern history – we Europeans need to develop a critique of Europe's delusion of grandeur in positing ourselves as the moral guardian of the world and the motor of human evolution' (Braidotti, 2013: 25). Stock of the subjugations, injustices and violence perpetrated in the name of humanism, in forwarding the moral, democratic values of the ideal human, needed to be taken and addressed. One way in which to deal with this was to give a voice to and take into account the multiple perspectives of those subjugated and othered within various strands of humanist thought. In post-structuralist philosophy therefore, the idea that the human (the white, heterosexual, Western male) is the sole authority, the only viable perspective on the world, was deterritorialized, allowing for diversity, multiple perspectives and multiple senses of belonging and subjectivity to emerge within critical thought. Within Deleuze and Guattari's *Anti-Oedipus* (2000) (emblematic of these shifts), for instance, the idea that there is a strict dichotomy and a hierarchy between the male and the female is challenged, positing that, rather than unitary, whole and static, the subject is more relational and transformative.

These ideas about multiple perspectives, belongings and relational, fluid subjectivity are aspects which Braidotti's critical posthumanism shares with anti-humanist and post-structuralist thought. As she states, the critical posthuman subject exists within 'an eco-philosophy of multiple belongings, as a relational subject constituted in and by multiplicity' (2013: 49). However, critical posthumanism extends, develops upon and transforms elements of these bodies of thought. Braidotti perceives the emergence of posthumanist thought as marking the 'end of the opposition between humanism and anti-humanism', tracing 'a different discursive framework, looking more affirmatively towards new alternatives' (2013: 37), new ways for thinking about the human species, our understanding of it and how it interacts with and relates to other forms of organic and non-organic life.

This formulation of new ways of thinking about and understanding the human subject, as multifaceted and transformative, is important within contemporary posthuman conditions as certain processes, forces and transformations within this context have caused subjects to become ungrounded, fragmented and fluid. The global market economy, for instance, and the processes of advanced capitalism, multiply 'deterritorialized differences which are packaged and marketed under the labels of new, dynamic and negotiable identities and an endless choice of consumer goods'

(2013: 58). Under such conditions, subjects are forced to become relational, more flexible, adaptable and transformative.

Market economies and the processes of advanced capitalism are global constructs, affecting societies worldwide, including Japan. Nevertheless, these processes and constructs are adapted to and mutated according to different national, cultural contexts, meaning that the conditions they engender are unique to certain contexts. These global processes intermingle with other, unique imperatives within Japanese societal and economic contexts, most notably perhaps, Japan's transition towards an immaterial economy of information, communication and affect. Thus, subjectivity and the transformations that its formulations undergo because of these conditions are also subtly different from context to context. In other words, it is important to not view the posthuman condition as a homogenous/homogenizing construct.

Within Japan, the processes of advanced capitalism and the growing market economy have been experienced (like many, globally, living under these conditions), since the 1980s, by youths especially, as a steady assault upon the empirical self, growing more violent and disruptive in the 1990s. Commercial penetration, at this time, reached the (once sacred) realms of subjectivity, (female) sexuality and the family, causing stable identity formation to become more difficult and leading many to lose a sense of purpose and meaning within Japanese society. The malaise, nihilism and lack of direction, caused by the processes of advanced capitalism and the market economy, led to reactionary discourses unique to Japan and Japanese youths in particular, including the formation and actions of the *Aum Shinrikyō* cult. There were, however, many discourses, including the practice of *enjo kōsai* amongst young girls, borne from capitalist processes and the detachments from meaning, context and the governance of self-consciousness and social morality that they engendered, which were experienced as liberatory.

Crucially, critical posthumanism does not ascribe to apocalyptic accounts of 'the end of man' (a perspective transhumanism purports) and it perceives humanist thought as still playing a role within formulations and understandings of subjectivity and the world. It can, adhering to Deleuzian and Guattarian notions, be reterritorialized or recapitulated. This coincides with this book's thoughts on how molar groundings can be reterritorialized within any-space-whatevers, such as the ones created by so-called posthuman conditions. Thus, this book, aligning with critical posthumanism, perceives, for instance, that it is possible for those fragmentary, fluid Japanese subjects, effected by the processes of advanced capitalism and the market economy, to become, at points, reterritorialized into more normative, stable forms of identity and understanding. Furthermore, following the notion of the art of dosages, by subsisting within posthumanist thought on subjectivity, humanist constructions can be more profoundly challenged and deterritorialized, hence it is important for them to remain within understandings. They can, in their inclusion, lead to the expression of 'the crisis of the majority and the patterns of becoming of the minorities' (Braidotti, 2013: 37–8).

Whilst critical posthumanism aligns with and mobilizes elements of post-structuralist thought, it tailors these perspectives specifically to address new issues, contexts and imperatives that have emerged in the twenty-first century, all of which constitute the posthuman condition. For instance, critical posthumanism attempts to address the distinct anti-intellectualism that emerged as part of the posthuman condition, it attempts to bridge the gap between the 'great explosion of theoretical creativity in the 1970s and 1980s' (overlapping the time when post-structuralist thought came to prominence) and today, overcoming the 'zombified landscape of repetition without difference and lingering melancholia' (ibid.: 5) that followed these great decades within scholarship. It therefore embodies and responds to a different scholarly context than post-structuralist thought from the 1960s and 1970s.

This critical posthumanism is an interesting strand of thought, however, it is not the only facet of posthumanism which can be utilized when exploring *Kairo (Pulse)*. In particular, what Braidotti (ibid.) terms as analytic posthumanism, stemming from science and technology studies, can also be discussed.[4] Analytic posthumanism focuses upon how contemporary science and biotechnologies 'affect the very fibre and structure of the living and have altered dramatically our understanding of what counts as the basic frame of reference for the human today' (ibid.: 40). This strand of posthuman thought is concerned with a specific aspect of the posthuman condition related to technology and science and how developments within these broad fields have deterritorialized our understandings of humanity, subjectivity and society.

Analytic posthumanism, of which the works of Rose (2007) and Verbeek (2011) are exemplary, perceives the subject as relational and transformative, much like the critical posthumanist strand. Within analytic posthumanism, however, it is the relationalities that are formed between human subjects and technological or scientific artefacts and the transformations and deterritorializatons that they engender specifically, which are the focus. Within Verbeek's (ibid.) work, for instance, an intimate and productive association between people, scientific and technological artefacts is conceptualized, which, he outlines, points towards the need for a post-anthropological turn (a potentially problematic viewpoint, as is explored in due course) and greater consideration of interconnections between humans and non-humans within scholarship.

The posthuman condition can be characterized by, in relation to developments within science and technology specifically, either widespread 'anxiety about the excesses of technological intervention ... or by [as Verbeek appears inclined] elation about the potential for human enhancement' (Braidotti, 2013: 57). These two contrasting perspectives on scientific and technological progression have become increasingly prolific within developed societies globally, as the relationships between humans and technologies have become more intense and intimate. As Braidotti states, 'the posthuman predicament is such as to force a displacement of the lines of demarcation between structural differences, or ontological categories, for instance between the organic and the inorganic, the born and the manufactured, flesh and metal, electronic circuits and organic nervous systems' (ibid.: 89). Increasingly, we have become closely entwined in assemblages with various scientific and technological artefacts and through this, deterritorializations and mutations in conceptualizations of the human and what it means to be so have occurred.

Discussions of assemblages formed with technological artefacts and the transformations they engender are relevant to Japanese contexts and the specific Japanese conceptualization of a break in linear time as the development and proliferation of new technologies are widely understood to be a contributory factor to a perceived disintegration of society and subjectivity. *Kairo* (*Pulse*), in fact, has been interpreted as a film which specifically comments upon the ills of technology on Japanese society. The convergence of the temporalities and the existentialities of the dead and the living within *Kairo* (*Pulse*) can be understood as allegorical of how the virtual worlds of the Internet have increasingly merged with our lived realities, disrupting their linearity, causing people to isolate themselves from others, forsake traditional familial and communal connections and even become ill and suicidal. Kusina highlights how 'Kurosawa makes no secret of this theme and he regularly suggests the failures of communicative technologies to halt the escalating trend toward loneliness and isolation' (2008) and the pathology of *Hikikomori* especially. One scene which is particularly indicative of this commentary is where Ryosuke visits Harue's research lab and comes across a strange computer programme which, as Harue suggests, represents a model of our world. In this programme, singular, glowing, white spheres move around a black screen, never connecting with one another, but, paradoxically, being drawn closer together as they push further apart. The program's behaviour represents how, as beings, we are all distinct, separate individuals who never really connect with one another in society despite the means for communication and interaction which we have at our disposal.

It is not only isolation and loneliness amongst Japanese citizens, however, that the proliferation of digital media has caused. Such technologies have also contributed to, and made possible, the often disruptive processes of globalization (also constitutive of the posthuman condition), bringing nations and cultures across the globe more closely together. *Kairo* (*Pulse*), again, can be considered to express these conditions and processes. The merging of the realms of the living and the dead, a polynomial discourse, can similarly be considered as allegorical of the convergence of different national, cultural, social spheres worldwide, occurring through digital media. Closer interconnections between different nations and cultures have been interpreted by many Japanese cultural commentators as damaging to constructions of a coherent, unique and unifying sense of Japanese national identity. *Kairo (Pulse)*, in its depictions of the eradication of the Japanese people and society, may be interpreted as a comment upon this. The living, Japanese people, through their interconnections with the spirits, become-other, become something horrific, foreign and incomprehensible (sui generis). Through their erasure, Japanese culture and its traditions, as we know them, cannot be maintained and thus, in *Kairo (Pulse)*, we witness the crumbling of Japanese society.

The fluidity and multiplicity of being that the spirits and, eventually, the living characters of *Kairo (Pulse)* demonstrate can also be interpreted as part of this commentary on globalization and its effects. Japanese people, because of globalization, have been opened to a multitude of different cultures and ways of being and thus can experiment and play with different forms of subjectivity.[5] This, however, it appears, according to *Kairo (Pulse)*, may be a destructive discourse to partake in. Those living characters who do become-other, become-ghosts, do not cease in their cries for help (as we often hear the whisper, '*tasukete*' whenever a character is close to the site where someone has perished), implying the horrific, traumatic nature of these transformations.

The transformative and fluid nature of these characters and the multiple meanings that can be potentially associated with them are further expressed in scenes involving the computer programme in Harue's lab. Interestingly, this programme mutates itself in response to the collision of the two worlds, the invasion of ghosts into the realm of the living and the increase in disappearances amongst the population. The programme transforms as it begins to display the orbs, which are more ethereal, blurred and distorted than in the previous encounter, blending, connecting and merging together to create ever more diverse shapes. Additionally, these orbs move in much more eclectic, random ways around the screen.

The orbs, representing people, express how subjects have become more fluid, relational and transformative following the merging of the two realms. This can have a multitude of interpretations attached to it, all of which relate to the posthuman condition and to the contexts of Japan (post-break) specifically. It could express, for instance, how, through advances and proliferations in different technologies, people have become more relational, mutating in their assemblages with different artefacts. Conversely, it could also express how nations and cultures now merge together, hybridize and transform because of the processes of globalization, creating new forms of subjectivity for people to flit between.

The idea of technology having ill-effects upon people and society, rather than an isolated, Japanese, nationally-specific claim, is a frequent

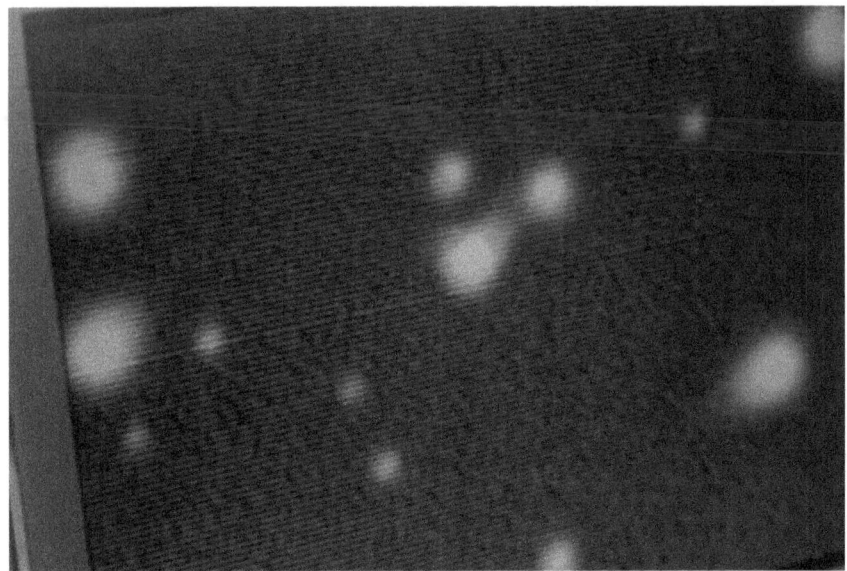

FIGURE 37 *The computer programme displaying the more fluid, malleable orbs,* Kairo (Pulse) *(Kurosawa, 2001).*

charge placed at technology's door by far-reaching sects of scholarship. For instance, Sherry Turkle, a scholar of digital media, has produced a large amount of commentary on the potentially damaging effects (particularly on the youth) of digital media (like social networking sites and email), impacting family life, education and romance. As she discusses in a lecture on the modern subject's constant need to be connected to their mobile phones, social media and the Internet, this need causes us to lose the ability to be separate, to cultivate the capacity for solitude and if we cannot be alone we become isolated as we lose the ability to connect meaningfully with people around us.

> How do you get from connection to isolation? You end up isolated if you don't cultivate the capacity for solitude, the ability to be separate, to gather yourself. Solitude is where you find yourself so that you can reach out to other people and form real attachments. When we don't have the capacity for solitude, we turn to other people in order to feel less anxious or in order to feel alive. When this happens, we're not able to appreciate who they are. It's as though we're using them as spare parts to support our fragile sense of self. We slip into thinking that always being connected is going to make us feel less alone. But we're at risk, because actually it's the opposite that's true.
>
> (Turkle, 2012)

Increasingly, it becomes difficult to avoid forming assemblages with social media and the web due to its proliferation in all aspects of life. Today, across the globe, people can become networked at the touch of a button on their phones and tablets. Such an expansion of digital media into people's everyday lives, reaching out beyond the static home or office computer units, has led to understandings of digital media, within scholarship, as viral or contagious. *Kairo* (*Pulse*) taps into this idea as the spirits spread through cyberspace unstoppably, like a virus.

Beyond social media and the Internet, there are many ways in which technology can augment and transform the human, sometimes unpredictably and uncontrollably. Eugene Thacker argues that we are well into a biotech century where computer technology is increasingly applied to life sciences research, producing such things as smart drugs, prostheses, artificial organs and bodily components, 'on-line genome databases, automated gene-sequencing computers, DNA diagnostic tools, and advanced data-mining and gene discovery software applications' (2003: 72). Such research has ensured the boundary between biology and technology, computer and genetic codes, is becoming increasingly blurred and that the human is increasingly networked through information technologies in attempts to augment and enhance the body, mind and human condition. It is hoped that, in its symbiosis with technology, the organic body can transform or update as quickly as new, digital technologies and their products, which are continually reforming and mutating their codes and algorithms to become more efficient or produce new events and experiences for the user/audience. A co-evolution of bodies and technologies may already be occurring as:

> A recent study which showed that young people's thumbs have overtaken fingers as the most muscled and dexterous digits among the under twenty-fives, simply as a result of their extensive use of handheld electronic game controllers and text messaging on cell phones. New generations of phones will be designed around this greater agility … The same kind of user-technology co-adaptation can occur at the deepest levels of neural processing. Such developmentally open brains are not just opportunistic but explosively opportunistic. They are ready to change themselves to make the most of the structures of media, and opportunities encountered during learning.
>
> (Clark, 2003, cited in Grusin, 2010: 93–4)

Thus, we are, as this strand of posthumanist thought suggests, through our assemblages with technology, transformative, heterogeneous and rapidly or explosively redefining the boundaries of the human, discovering different ways of being.

In relation to the complex neural processes that Clark mentions and how these can be adapted in assemblages with technology, Thacker discusses how 'one salient feature of such transformations includes the concept of "uploading" in which the parallels between neural pattern activity in the human mind and the capacity of advanced neural networking computing will enable humans to transfer their minds into a more durable (read: immortal) hardware system' (2003: 74). This idea holds some relevance to an analysis of *Kairo* (*Pulse*) which sees the spirits of the film uploading themselves to the web to infiltrate the world of the living. However, it is important to be critical of this notion which, rather than posthumanist, aligns more fully with transhumanist thought.

There is considerable confusion over the definitions of the two terms posthumanism and transhumanism and what each entails. As discussed by Braidotti (2013), critical posthumanism perceives that a decentering of 'man' takes place within the posthuman condition and it rejects anthropocentrism, the exceptionalism and instrumentalism of the human. On the other hand, transhumanist perspectives retain the centrality and importance of the human and view technologies as integral to human progression alone. Transhumanism also conceptualizes a transcendental view of the posthuman subject, whereas critical and analytic posthumanism, as discussed, perceive that the human subject and humanist perspectives can be reterritorialized within formulations and understandings of subjectivity and the worlds we live in. Transhumanist perspectives foresee that the human may one day be able to discard its contemptuously finite, fleshy body and become, essentially, a non-human being with greatly enhanced capabilities. This book aligns with the critical and analytic posthumanism that Braidotti (ibid.) conceptualizes as these strands are more closely interconnected with the post-structuralist perspectives of Deleuze in particular. This book has, throughout, advocated the Deleuzian and Guttarian (1987) notion of 'the art of dosages' and, thus, to now argue for an overturning of this perspective, to view the human as capable of transcendence, being able to reject all groundings, all reterritorializations, would not be in-keeping here. This does not mean, however, that such transhumanist perspectives cannot be accounted for or considered as part of the assemblage which makes up an understanding and experience of *Kairo* (*Pulse*). It is particularly important to acknowledge them here as they appear to have had some influence upon *Kairo* (*Pulse*) and, for that matter, upon a multitude of other, contemporary popular cultural products.

Thacker (2004) himself is critical of the idea of uploading because of its alignment with transhumanism. He argues that, within assemblages between technology and the human, 'the "goal" of biomedia is not simply the use of computer technology in the service of biology', challenging the anthropocentrism of such transhumanist thought, 'but rather an emphasis on the ways in which an intersection between genetic and computer "codes" can facilitate a qualitatively different notion of the biological body – one that is technically enhanced, and yet still fully "biological"' (ibid.: 7). Thus, the biological body does not use technology to supplant itself, as in this idea of uploading, it is still recognizable as a human body but is transformed by technology in different ways. Its 'material components and biological organization ... can in effect be reengineered, or redesigned' (ibid.: 11) and there are a multitude of different becomings or ways in which this can occur, producing alternative subjectivities and ways of being.

Thacker's (ibid.) views here align with posthumanism, rather than transhumanism, and there are therefore parallels which can be drawn between his comments on 'biomedia' and Braidotti's utilization of Deleuze and Guattari's concept of 'becoming-machine' (2013). Aligning with Thacker (2004), Braidotti argues that 'all technologies can be said to have a strong bio-political effect upon the embodied subject they intersect with' (2013: 90), they facilitate and induce transformations, becoming-others or, more accurately, becoming-machines. Like Thacker (2004), Braidotti perceives that, through these transformations, the human is not transcended and that this is an important distinction as the 'notion of the enfleshed, and extended, relational self [rather than the transcendental self] keeps the techno-hype in check by a sustainable ethics of transformations' (2013: 90). In the same sense as other becomings discussed previously, becoming-machine entails releasing the human from stratifying, molar regimes of subjectivity through technological assemblage, rather than some unsustainable transcendence of the body or human biology. As Braidotti discusses, 'the becoming-machine ... indicates and actualizes the relational powers of a subject that is no longer cast in a dualistic frame, but bears a privileged bond with multiple others and merges with one's technologically mediated environment'. She goes on to say that, 'the merger of the human with the technological results in a new transversal compound ... that generate new modes of subjectivity' (ibid.: 92).[6] It is possible, however, within this conceptualization (as is again the case with other forms of becoming), for traditional, molar, forms of subjectivity to be returned to or reterritorialized at points within an assemblage with technology. These molarities, however, may be restructured and transformed.

The becomings of the living characters especially, and some of the becomings of the spirits of *Kairo* (*Pulse*), may be better understood under the term 'becoming-machine'. However, within the conceptualization of becoming-machine, there exists an emphasis (as Braidotti (ibid.) is particularly useful at highlighting) on positivism, on the vitalistic, affirmative nature of assemblages with technology and the mutations they engender. This is problematic in relation to *Kairo* (*Pulse*) which expresses the potentially destructive nature of relationalities with technology and what is borne from them. It is therefore appropriate here, as Culp asserts in his discussions of Deleuze and becoming, to move away from an emphasis on the 'canon of joy', diverge from 'the joyous task of creation' and 'rehabilitate the destructive force of negativity' (2016: 1–2) within conceptualizations of becoming. This is discussed further, however, we first turn to how we might productively understand the characters of *Kairo* (*Pulse*) under the ideas of becoming-machine.

Some of the spirits of *Kairo* (*Pulse*) are, ontologically, very similar to digital media such as the Internet, webpages, apps and software programmes. This is a result of their method of traversal into the realm of the living where, forming assemblages with digital technology, specifically the Internet and the routers which forward data packets between networks and perform traffic functions on the web, the spirits have assimilated the properties of them, becoming transcoded. By becoming transcoded, the spirits can effectively navigate the rhizomatic, 'virtual, densely webbed, and infinitely complex' (Davis, cited in Brown, 2010: 122) circuits and connections of the Internet. They flow through them as if they were a computer virus, infecting people's PCs globally and inspiring suicides.

The assemblages that the spirits form with the Internet and its devices are most explicitly expressed in one scene where Yoshizaki is explaining to Ryosuke his theory of why and how the ghosts have entered this world. Here we are transported, in the film, to another temporality or to another potentiality, where a building surveyor, overseeing the demolition of a shipyard, enters a darkened room and proceeds to tape up its entrance. The audience is instantly aware, through their bodies, that there is a strange affective force within this room due to the deep, resounding bass and electronic, ringing sonsign used. These electronic sounds are the first indicator of the nature of these spirits and their composition. However, just as the spirit begins to enter this world and become more visible, the room is demolished by a crane, halting its transition. Instead of having its affective force dissipated and diffused, however, the spirit manages to transfer itself into a small electronic device amongst the rubble.

At this point we hear the distinct, unmistakable sound of a dial-up Internet modem connecting to the web, signaling to us that the spirit has entered the modem and has begun to upload itself, translating itself into computer code.

Through their assemblages with the Internet, their transcoding, these spirits also inheret the property of variability. Digital media, because of their coded composition, are inherently variable, never fixed and always changing, they are autopoietic. As Manovich explains: 'every time you visit a webpage something will have changed, the number of views, comments or posts' (2001). Changes even occur immanently while we are exploring a webpage as new code and algorithms will have formed to accommodate new additions of information. Similarly, we witness the rapid, immanent transformations that these spirits constantly undergo when we see the throbbing shadowy masses within the arcade taking different shapes, from human to non-human forms.

The constant, immanent changes that occur within a digital media's composition highlight how webpages, for instance, can exist in potentially

FIGURE 38 *The electronic device through which a spirit transfers and transcodes itself,* Kairo (Pulse) *(Kurosawa, 2001).*

infinite versions or as infinite potentialities. Slight changes in coding and algorithm can alter the way in which a digital media looks and works and these changes can be archived, creating a database of different versions of a particular webpage, app or software, which can be returned to at any point. So too, then, can the spirits of *Kairo (Pulse)*, assimilating this principle of variability, exist as infinite versions or have the potential to infinitely become-other, changing their form, sex, shape, colour and even their species. This is reflective of elements of the posthuman condition, borne out of interconnections with technological artefacts that humans form. As Braidotti highlights, 'the nature of the human-technological interaction has shifted towards a blurring of the boundaries between the genders, the races and the species' (2013: 109). Through technologies like the internet, subjectivity can become more fluid, people can experiment with many different ways of being and living. People can, for instance, create avatars, online persona, within chat rooms or gaming worlds, which can allow users to play with different subjectivities and forms. One must not forget, however, as discussed previously, the potentially negative, traumatic way in which people may experience such openings to multiplicities of subjectivity. In the face of such multipotentiality, people may become suspended, unable to act or actively experiment with different ways of being.

As coded beings, the spirits can perhaps all be regarded as variations of each other, as part of the same source code or, in this case, source energy, which has infinitely branched out or variegated itself, forming a rhizomatic web of many different potentialities of form, behaviour and being. Slight changes in the coding and algorithm that have generated a spirit in one instance, cause them to take on a different form in another, resulting in the many different aesthetics, behaviours and even speech patterns of ghosts within *Kairo* (*Pulse*). The spirits then have the potential, as bodies of code, to have their formula and specific numerical values stripped down, causing them to become the black, ill-defined, writhing masses of the ilk that inhabit the arcade, until new codes determining their form, behaviour and aesthetic are generated.

Epitomizing the coded nature of the spirits is a ghost that Ryosuke encounters in a disused factory, which he enters during his and Michi's search for Harue. Entering a forbidden room in the final throes of the film, Ryosuke finds a ghost that appears semi-transparent, pixelated and blurred from a distance and remains so, even when he surprisingly manages to grab it as though it were flesh.

Ryosuke, who falls to the floor in shock, then observes the ghost moving towards him, glitching like a computer programme or video game might, mutating and blending its composition and colour with the dark, shadowy environment as it does so. Upon close inspection, as the ghost's face leans in towards Ryosuke's and our own, rather than becoming sharper and clearer, it actually becomes more distorted, blurred and ill-defined.

FIGURE 39 *The blurred, pixelated spirit Ryosuke encounters,* Kairo (Pulse) *(Kurosawa, 2001).*

FIGURE 40 *A close-up of the pixelated spirit,* Kairo (Pulse) *(Kurosawa, 2001).*

This pixelated being is made up of small packets of data, each containing its own values pertaining to colour and tone. The spirit, however, is not a static image and it is imbued with an affective force, causing the values of its pixels to constantly change and its form to ebb and flow with an intensity.

The glitchy, jumpy movements of the spirit are also a particularly interesting envisioning of becoming-machine. Here the spirit mimics the malfunctioning of digital images, videos and game sequences, when the execution of their code pertaining to a particular behaviour, action or transition hits a snag, an error in translation or is miscoded or when connections to the web, powering the reception of this data, are disrupted. This glitching that the spirit experiences occurs when it executes some sort of movement, which, it seems, requires a lot of energy or processing power. However, it is not only its behaviour and movement that we can conceptualize as a glitch, in fact every spirit themselves, as beings, are fundamentally errors of the system that should never have been able to twist themselves into the interstitial spaces of the web. Therefore, the spirit itself, and its malfunctioning, fragmented movements represent a failure in communication, the horror of mediation. They are noise, 'abject information and aberrant signal within an otherwise orderly system of communication' (Nunes, 2011: 3). An orderly system of communication that now dictates many of our social interactions within the networked age. Any error or disruption occurring within such a system is abject and must be negated, neutralized or contained as part of a feedback process, so as not to compromise the ideal of 'an error-free world of 100 per cent efficiency, accuracy and predictability' (ibid.). These disruptions in the digital media systems we are using, where once seemingly functional, seamless extensions of ourselves falter and damage our sense of their infallibility, can be disturbing and affective experiences, just like our encounters with the spirits of *Kairo* (*Pulse*), where we are suspended, resonating with their affective power, unable to fully comprehend what they are.

Some scholars have argued that glitches or errors are potentially more affective than the semiotic, representational or narrative content that is contained within digital media products. As Picard (1997) demonstrated in a study of the video game *Doom* (1993), where a subject's neurological and bodily responses to playing the game were recorded, 'none of the violent events in the game aroused the player as much as the software problem' (Grusin, 2010: 112), as when the game unexpectedly froze or crashed. Similarly, the unprecedented error that has occurred within the Internet in *Kairo* (*Pulse*), allowing spirits to spill into the realm of the living, creates the most disturbing, affective encounters. The errors in the movement of the spirit Ryosuke encounters further the affective impact. Here, the ghost is trying to bridge the gap between the world of the living and the dead, but fails. It never fully resolves or manifests into a human form, it instead remains as affective noise.

This conceptualization of the spirits as disruptive, computational errors or horrors of mediation, can be productively linked to the work of Thacker (in Galloway, Thacker and Wark, 2014), who explicitly discusses *Kairo* (*Pulse*) and other iterations of Japanese horror cinema in relation to these ideas. These spirits, as incomprehensible, unresolvable errors, embody the idea of excommunication, 'the fantasy of an absolute end to all communication' (Galloway, Thacker and Wark, 2014: 16), the idea that there will be no more (normative) mediated messages, that the state of things has become inexpressible. They (as discussed previously in relation to cosmic horror) make the Internet, its spaces and peripherals (for instance, webcams) a weird media, or, as Thacker terms it, a 'dark media', as they highlight its powers to allow for connection and communication with the previously inaccessible, supernatural realms of the dead, things that 'we are normally "in the dark" about' (in Galloway, Thacker and Wark, 2014: 85). The Internet is portrayed, therefore, as a normative technology that is behaving in abnormal ways, revealing the 'ambivalent boundary separating the natural from the supernatural, the uncanny from the marvellous, the earthly from the divine' (ibid.: 91).[7]

The Internet, within *Kairo* (*Pulse*), can negatively span different ontological orders, producing, 'very little at all, not objects but things receding into an obtuse and obstinate thinglyness' (Galloway, Thacker and Wark, 2014: 18), things which cannot be communicated or understood, namely the mediated spirits. The mediated spirits lie between the two ontological orders in the interstice, thus, they can never fully enter the world of the living and become human (as is demonstrated by their coded, pixelated forms), and nor do they belong, anymore, to the realm of the dead. By not belonging to either order they are incomprehensible, no molar understanding can be unproblematically attributed to them as these regimes are dependent on and formulated from clear, grounded milieus. They can, however, perhaps be usefully understood under the notion of 'electronic presence', a term, coined by Jeffrey Sconce, describing the living quality of technologies like the web, their thrumming and pulsating, their invisible circuits, which give rise to 'to fantasies about invisible entities adrift in the ether, entire other electronic realms coursing through the wired networks of the world' (Brown, 2010: 123). The spirits cannot be perceived through sight and comprehended cognitively, instead their pulsating, electronic, affective presence can be apprehended on the body.

The interstitial, in-between nature of these spirits aptly reflects the current condition of subjectivity under various posthuman conditions or in suspended any-space-whatevers following the break in Japan. Ungrounded from static conceptualizations of subjectivity and opened to multiple potential ways of being through these multifaceted conditions, subjects become centres of indetermination, they perpetually become-other in response to different situations and assemblages they form. Thus, like the spirits, subjects today are always in-between or on the threshold of becoming something else, they are not fully grounded within a singular molar, conceptualization of subjectivity. *Kairo* (*Pulse*), as polynomial, can reveal multiple, different ways in which people, particularly Japanese subjects (although one must not neglect to consider the transnationality of some of these subjectivities and conditions), exist interstitially, between different positionalities, according to the assemblages they form with social, technological, cultural, global and economic landscapes and bodies.

In the face of such incomprehensible mediations as the spirits, the living characters become excommunicants, suspended beings, unable to respond to the presence of these spirits in any meaningful way. They too come to exist interstitially as, to possibly be reconciled or to be able to understand the spirits, these living characters must transform themselves, become ghosts by killing themselves and, further to this, partake in a becoming-machine as the spirits have. Thus, the spirits, as embodiments of error and excommunication, do not simply destroy communication but instead evoke the 'impossibility of communication, the insufficiency of communication as a model', they are 'prior to the very possibility of communication' (Galloway, Thacker and Wark, 2014: 16) or catalyze and engender potential new forms of communication (just as they can engender new forms of subjectivity through their becoming-machines). They are, once again, reflective of the posthuman condition, illustrating that to avoid being excommunicated from the contemporary, technologized landscapes that people now globally inhabit, they must become-other or become-machine.

A conflict between positive, affirmative and negative, destructive becomings can be discerned here. Are the spirits suspending, destructive beings that excommunicate the living? Or do they offer the possibility of being opened to new ways of being and communicating? Relatedly, is the Internet a weird media, producing negative becomings and connections with different ontological orders (the realm of the dead)? Or is it a haunted media, affirmatively spanning different orders and producing 'artefacts, relics and other divine objects' (ibid.: 18)? These are difficult questions to answer conclusively as there are many instances in *Kairo* (*Pulse*) where connections between the realms of the living and the dead and the new becomings (in terms of being and communication) that they foster are presented as destructive. On the other hand, there are indications, particularly in the case of Harue's assemblage with a spirit and the realm beyond, that the intermingling of the two ontological orders and the becomings that this engenders, can be productive and part of the Deleuzian canon of joy (to use Culp's (2016) term).

Returning to the terminology of glitches or errors used to describe the spirits and their coded, computational nature, whilst these terms may appear to incite a negative viewpoint, emphasizing the unproductive, disruptive nature of the spirits, there is a growing body of work which emphasizes the potentially productive, affirmative nature of errors and glitches within digital media. This therefore provides impetus for the argument that positive assemblages and becomings can be fostered between the living and the dead in *Kairo* (*Pulse*) and, thus, the human and the non-human. Scholars, such as Nunes (2011), propose that, rather than reject and ignore errors as irrelevant miscommunications, we should embrace them and investigate them further. Nunes, adopting a Deleuzian approach to explore the role of glitches and errors within our global networked societies, argues that the disruption, the suspension in linearity that glitches create 'provide creative openings and lines of flight that allow for a reconceptualization of what can (or cannot) be realized within existing social and cultural practices' (ibid.: 4). They, as discussed previously through Galloway, Thacker and Wark (2014), do not destroy communication but can open up new possibilities for different forms of communication. Glitches open us up to multipotentialities of what a networked system of social communication could be or become, how our interactions, communications, engagements and the products we produce from these can become-other from what has already been realized within existing, dominant systems. In other words, the codes, algorithms, logics and mechanisms in place within digital media lead to a restricted number of outcomes for engagement and communication which serve the imperatives of the different social systems that they are a part of. Errors or glitches then, unhinge and unground milieus, they are 'a vagabondage or wandering of the mind' (Nunes, 2011: 8), which is far from unproductive.

Reid (2012, cited in Hammer, 2014) proposes that glitches are, in fact, necessary conditions of the composition of objects and so should be respected as such. A rhetoric which embraces glitches, 'prepares us for "an ever-stranger compositional environment where the rhetorical roles we imagined for ourselves as *modern* humans will not function"' (ibid.). Here Reid (ibid.) directly refers to the posthuman condition and the changes that various processes like globalization and technologization have instigated, creating any-space-whatevers where our previous models for understanding and acting within the world become erroneous. What Reid proposes here is not just a cognitive acceptance of glitches, however, as this sort of response can only go so far in helping to produce such a preparatory outcome. Through a bodily acceptance or reception of the errors, through absorbing their disrupting, affective qualities, people can become primed to absorb the impact of further glitches or suspensions in linearity and ready to adapt to suit new situations and living conditions which are difficult to traverse via the models that people have previously understood the world through.

As errors or glitches therefore, the spirits may have a similar, productive function. By forming a bodily assemblage with the spirits, audiences can potentially acclimatize themselves to their affective impacts, learn to absorb them more quickly and use these intensities to transform themselves to suit different contexts and assemblages. Thus, when audiences encounter glitches and suspensions in their lived world they can perhaps, because of this, more effectively and swiftly engage with them, adapt or become-other. This is particularly important for those living under posthuman conditions, which are understood to be rife with disrupting, suspending forces (conditioned, of course, by specific contexts like the national). Similarly discussing the value of affective media works today, Shaviro asserts that they can 'help and train us to endure – and perhaps also to negotiate – the unthinkable complexity of cyberspace, or the unrepresentable immensity and intensity of the world space of multinational capital' (2010: 138).

Perhaps then, *Kairo (Pulse)* can be conceptualized as a premediating text, a concept coined by Richard Grusin (2010), which has interconnections with the idea of time-image cinema. Emerging, Grusin (ibid.) asserts, after a (Western) break in linear time, when the events of 9/11 occurred, premediating texts, like time-image cinema, suspended audiences and opened them to multiple ways of envisioning the future. However, unlike time-images, which simply immerse audiences in affective experiences, premediating texts posit that audiences should be fearful of such immediacy. Premediating texts, therefore, aim to pre-empt immediate, affective events and condition audiences to them so that they will not be as profoundly shocked and suspended if another break in linear time, like 9/11, were to occur. They create, for the audience, at the level of the body, 'a low level of anxiety ... in order to protect them', in a fashion 'similar to what Benjamin has described cinema as doing in training the human sensorium to deal with the shocks and traumas of modernity' (ibid.: 17). Therefore, *Kairo* (*Pulse*), perhaps achieves a similar feat, generating an affective force that conditions audiences and prepares them for the perpetually transforming, disruptive society beyond the film.

However, this idea of conditioning and the qualification of the reception of affects into a discourse of fear inducement can be contested. Affective experiences are different each time we encounter them, we always, even if we are watching the same film or TV programme for the second, third or even eleventh time, experience different qualities and intensities of affect. Scenes that were particularly intense previously may not be upon the second viewing, and scenes that were rather mundane could be particularly impactful. Furthermore, whilst some audiences may indeed react to the affective stimulants of certain media products in ways deemed negative, others may react in less definable ways. For instance, faster heart rates, galvanic skin responses and feelings of tension can be categorized as both negative and positive reactions, understood as part of feelings of both fear and excitement. Thus, this poses the question, how can we be prepared for profound affective shocks that might occur in the future, in the way that Grusin (2010) imagines? Rather than pre-empt the level of intensity and the specific qualities of affects that might befall us during such significant events, premediating films, as suggested (aligning with Shaviro (2010)), may prepare us by conditioning us into relational, fluid beings, more open to affective bodily resonance. We become, through these texts, more competent in receiving information in this bodily way, rather than cognitively, which can become an impossibility in such disruptive, suspending events.

The idea of *Kairo* (*Pulse*) being a productive, affirmative conditioning force could be disputed by highlighting that people do not need to train to become fluid, transformative beings here when they can do so in the real world, an environment which is equally as filled with disruption. However, as McLuhan and Fiore state 'one thing about which fish know exactly nothing is water, since they have no anti-environment which would enable them to perceive the element they live in' (1968, cited in Hammer, 2014). Thus, to apprehend our environments, what we are and what we might become, we must create anti-environments. Horror cinema, in general, has a profound connection to this idea of an anti-environment. As psychoanalysts like Kristeva (1982) and Creed (1993) highlight, horror fictions have a long-standing tradition of performing cathartic functions, allowing us to work through issues, confront fears and negotiate the abject things that pervade our societies.

Kairo (*Pulse*) then, can be convincingly conceived as one such anti-environment, helping Japanese audiences to reflect upon, in an embodied manner, their own lived worlds. However, one must question whether *Kairo*'s (*Pulse*'s) power to function as an anti-environment may have depleted in the present day as it was released in 2001. Arguably then, the filmic anti-environment is time-sensitive. *Kairo* (*Pulse*) perhaps productively functioned as such at a time when Japan was still to convincingly recover from the economic break of 1990, when it was transitioning towards a more immaterial, affective economic model and form of sociality, and when the violent acts of such groups like *Aum Shinrikyō* were still raw.

As a polynomial anti-environment, *Kairo* (*Pulse*), envisions many different transformations that can occur through assemblages with technology and technological environments (many ways, as previously discussed, people exist on the threshold between subjectivities, as interstitial or indeterminate). The character, Taguchi, for instance, demonstrates a quite distinct vision of becoming-machine and becoming-ghost from the encoded spirits. Taguchi, encountering a spirit via some strange webcam footage that is inadvertently accessed each time the user logs on to their PC, slowly begins to mutate and deteriorate following this experience. In a direct comment upon the ills of digital media (creating isolation and mental illnesses like depression), Taguchi becomes detached from those around him, stops attending work and then, eventually, he commits suicide, leaving only a black stain behind in the place he hung himself. This is not the last we see or hear of Taguchi, however. Toshio, Taguchi's work colleague, begins to receive strange phone calls from Taguchi following his death, where he repeatedly cries '*tasukete*' (help). Here, Taguchi becomes mediated in a different way to the encoded, computerized ghosts. He has tapped into and appropriated a different form of media to transmit his message (highlighting his relational, fluid nature), the cellular networks of mobile phones. He therefore re-constitutes this as a dark media, like the Internet, which can bridge the two realms, of the living and the dead, together.

This particular inflection of becoming-machine, demonstrated by Taguchi, reflects the different ways in which, beyond the film, users engage with and are transformed through electronic forms of communication. Like Taguchi, within our assemblages with mobile telephones, web chat rooms and email, we partake in a 'ghosting of human interaction along the virtual pathways of electronic presence' (Brown, 2010: 125), which compresses space-time, fragments us and opens us up to multiple potentialities of being. As Derrida (1981, cited in Brown, 2010: 125) discusses, 'the present moment is always being split, always shadowed by an "elsewhere" that takes up every moment of time not filled by some immediate activity' and this is so when we are communicating with absent others through such media. We are, increasingly, in our assemblages with electronic communications, splitting ourselves between two spaces and temporalities, or sometimes more in the case of larger, group communication forums on the web. The distances that we split ourselves in such assemblages vary widely, however, often great distances are compressed and different time zones are traversed. We exist as multiplicities within these situations, inhabiting different existentialities as fragments, as just a disembodied voice, just an image or just text. Through these scenes of ghostly communication, *Kairo* (*Pulse*) perhaps provides an anti-environment for people to understand and apprehend the types of splitting and fragmentation they undergo through these communications.

Within *Kairo* (*Pulse*), another becoming of Taguchi's is also quite interesting. While investigating the phone calls he is receiving, Toshio visits Taguchi's old apartment, where he finds the black stain on the wall. The stain, as Toshio turns away, turning off the light, disappears and Taguchi stands there, as he was when he was alive, but motionless and unresponsive.

Taguchi appears, in this scene, to be unmediated by any form of technology, he appears as a more familiar ghost, taking the form he did in life. It appears that, in this instance of becoming, rather than a media artefact, the space of the apartment itself (the black stain especially) is a point of mediation, a portal, between the realms of the living and the dead. We can also perceive within *Ju-On: The Grudge* that spaces become points of mediation between two ontological orders. In this film, as discussed in an earlier chapter, the house is an a-temporal void which does not follow the normative laws of the outside world, it is a weird space where 'impossible becomings suddenly present' (Thacker, in Galloway, Thacker and Wark, 2014: 93) themselves. In regards to *Ju-On: The Grudge* and space as mediator, Thacker notes that

FIGURE 41 *Taguchi appearing where the stain, left after his suicide, once was,* Kairo (Pulse) *(Kurosawa, 2001).*

'the tight spaces of a bedroom, a shower, even one's own bed, all become occasions for a sudden dilation of physical space' (in Galloway, Thacker and Wark, 2014: 93), for the mediation of a ghost. Similarly, within *Kairo (Pulse)*, Taguchi's apartment constricts to focus upon one particular corner of the bedroom, one particular wall with a dark stain upon it, and it is here, in this space, that a weird mediation occurs, where Taguchi crosses over into the realm of the living.

In *Kairo (Pulse)*, there are further examples where places become a mediator between the two realms. The forbidden rooms, taped up and sealed away from the rest of the world by those living persons who have already encountered a spirit and are about to die, are spaces which fulfil this function. They, much like the a-temporal voids in *Ju-On: The Grudge,* are interstitial, disjointed spaces, they are sites of rupture, belonging to neither of the two realms but bridging the space between them. There are multiple forbidden rooms within *Kairo (Pulse)* which compel the living characters to enter them. Even though they are warned not to go in, and they try to resist, something unnatural takes hold of them and gravitates them to these spaces. As audiences, we too enter and experience the forbidden rooms through our assemblages with the living characters on screen, our sense of linear time and existence is disrupted along with theirs and we become deterritorialized and suspended between different layers or worlds. In these spaces, molar regimes of understanding are uninformative and characters cannot act according to them.

Some of the forbidden rooms, it appears, are more a-temporal and disorientating than others. One of the most interesting instances lies within the abandoned factory Ryosuke visits in his search for Harue. This room's exterior, the vast factory floor, is filled with the imperishable remnants of the material industry it once served: lifting equipment, machinery, large steel constructions, shelving units and scaffolding.

In this factory, time, perhaps long before the worlds of the living and the dead collided, was suspended when production ceased. The factory, it could be presumed, may have closed as a result of the *Heisei* recession following the bursting of the economic bubble. It may also have ceased production due to the shifts in the Japanese economic model towards one focusing upon service industries and 'the immateriality of communication, information and affect' (Allison, 2009: 91). This factory floor then, like the forbidden room, is an a-temporal void, filled with the preserved yet suspended and sleeping bodies of machinery that await the resumption of linearity, action and progress. It is a portal or a gateway into another layer of temporality, the past.

The forbidden room that lies within this factory is a void within a void, a portal within a portal. It presents audiences with a mise-en-abyme, a term 'used to describe a story within a story, a film within a film ... or any figure, image, or concept that self reflexively disrupts the logic of identity or

FIGURE 42 *The abandoned factory floor,* Kairo (Pulse) *(Kurosawa, 2001).*

renders meaning unstable by repeating the whole in multiplied reflections in an apparent feedback loop of infinite regression' (Brown, 2010: 126). This motif of the mise-en-abyme is repeated at various points throughout *Kairo* (*Pulse*), for instance, within a photograph of Taguchi in his apartment, standing next to his PC, we can see that his computer monitor is displaying the same image we are beholding in the photo, and so on infinitely.

This repeated motif is an expression of the portals, the wormholes that have been created between the two realms, either through media artefacts or space. It expresses how different (usually incompatible) layers of time and existentiality can merge together infinitely, can become relational. It also expresses the 'dissociative relationships among body, mind, space, and time' (Brown, 2010: 127) that have been borne from the collision of these different ontological orders, these formations of any-space-whatevers. Once again this may be linked to the multifaceted posthuman condition and the break within Japan. Under the processes of globalization, advanced capitalism, the market economy and technologization, subjects have become more relational and fluid, crossing into many different situations and adapting themselves to them. Spaces then, constituted by the actions that take place within them and the relationships that people form with them, have similarly become more relational, fluid spaces in response. These expressions of different layers of time and existentiality blending together can be considered to render this relational, fluid condition of space. Furthermore, they express the disruption and deterritorialization that occur when subjects come into contact with

FIGURE 43 *The mise-en-abyme image featuring Taguchi,* Kairo (Pulse) *(Kurosawa, 2001).*

these spaces, not knowing how to act in them due to their disassociated, ungrounded nature.

As mentioned previously, whilst this chapter primarily utilizes posthumanist thought to discuss *Kairo (Pulse)*, transhumanist thought should also be acknowledged and briefly considered. This is because, whilst many becomings of the characters within *Kairo (Pulse)* entail a redesigning of human properties (into a vision of posthuman subjectivity) so that they are still largely recognizable as such, in other instances of becoming, *Kairo (Pulse)* questions to what extent the human can be transformed in its assemblages with technology, 'whether the human as human can survive its translation into digital information' (Herbrechter, 2013: 133). Through its depictions of the malformed, unidentifiable entities in the arcade and the black, in-human shaped stains left behind by those who have died, the implication is that many of the characteristics of humanity struggle to persist within these becomings, presenting to us how they can be a horrific, traumatic and debilitating experience rather than liberatory and enhancing of our current condition. Within such becomings, humans have become something fundamentally inhuman.

Audiences of *Kairo (Pulse)* come to apprehend these traumatic, horrific becomings when they come directly into contact with the pulsating, black figures. In the arcade, audiences experience first-hand the throbbing, pulsating actions of these masses and can feel their affective force upon their skin. Audiences can become truly disturbed, suspended and deterritorialized by this encounter, the black masses are akin to the malleable piece of wax that Descartes vividly describes. For Descartes (cited in Kusina, 2008), a piece of wax is disturbing to no end as he seeks a clear presence of mind that is troubled by the seeming non-identity of a candle and its shrinking, melted incarnation. Just like the wax, these masses are unidentifiable and have the unnerving potential to morph into any shape, size or composition.

The disintegration or transcendence of the human (transhumanism) that these dark masses and stains are emblematic of, links well to ideas of cosmic indifferentism. As Lyotard discusses, the human/brain system, from the beginning of time, was always an unlikely material realization of the energies and elements that were created at the moment of the big bang and is thus simply 'part of the continuing cosmic struggle between entropy and complexity over the allocation of energy' (2001, cited in Herbrechter, 2013: 9). The human is merely a means to an end within this struggle, the triumph of complexity over chaos and in this pursuit the cosmos 'asks not for the perfecting of the human, but its mutation or its defeat for the benefit of a better performing system' (ibid.: 6). The humans of *Kairo* (*Pulse*) are also subordinate to this struggle and insignificant, they cannot resist the contagion delivered through the spirits which forces them to commit suicide, as this is the catalyst through which the human will either transform itself into a more fluid, molecular being, able to survive in a new technological era, or be broken down and eradicated.

The pessimistic and nihilistic character of *Kairo*'s (*Pulse*'s) perspectives on transcendence has perhaps been borne out of specific Japanese contexts and events (contributing to a posthuman condition) occurring during the break in the 1990s. Iida, for instance, suggests that the climate of commercialization and technologization within Japanese society during the 1990s, as well as inspiring euphoric hopes for transcendence, spiritual renewal and an alternative future amongst some people, also created anxieties over 'the loss of an end, death or the absolute, the loss of a structuring frame for cognition and a system of meaning authorized by a sense of the finite' (2002: 234). Due to the advancement of the consumer culture and the rapid development and proliferation of new technologies during the 1990s, things that were once sacred, including the body, sexuality and subjectivity, came to be exploited and manipulated by these processes. This led, as detailed previously, to profound shifts in conceptualizations of the body, the human and existence. It appeared that, people were 'no longer bothered by injury or violations of the interior self' (ibid.: 233), as is evidenced by the various violent outbursts during this time and phenomena such as *enjo kōsai*. Increasingly, people began to seek to consume the self and erase it. Many have mourned the loss of structuring principles, like morality, self-consciousness and the value in life that these discourses represent. *Kairo* (*Pulse*) may also be part of these discourses, presenting transcendence or consumption of the self, via technology, as, not euphoric, but destructive, immoral, painful and horrific.

Additionally, *Kairo (Pulse)* may have been influenced in its pessimistic outlooks on technological assemblage and transcendence, more specifically, by the *Aum Shinrikyō* cult which, in its teachings, manifest and activities, explicitly appropriated science and technology and created visions of a euphoric, transcendental, new human. As discussed previously, a psychically gifted few were believed to be capable of inheriting the world once a global nuclear war had occurred. The cult believed that enlightenment and the achievement of a higher sense of self (to survive the nuclear war) could be reached through the aid of technologies and scientific experiments. This is perhaps not surprising when one considers that the inner-most circle of the cult was made up of some of the most gifted science and technology graduates from some of Japan's highest-ranking universities (Iida, 2002: 240). Those disciples who tried to run away or tried to speak to the press about the cult's activities were the ones most often subjected to horrific torture, mutilation and experimentation. The cult also developed in its labs, different chemical weapons, including the nerve agent, VX, mustard gas and the sarin gas it used in the Tokyo subway system attack (ibid.: 241). It is these instances of science and technology being used in malign ways which have created pessimistic, nihilistic and fearful feelings, such as those expressed within *Kairo (Pulse)*, towards these fields, their processes and developments. These challenge the idealistic visions presented by some enthusiasts, who laud the extraordinary transformations that sciences and technologies may be able to achieve in their assemblages with the human.

Challenging the grounding of these transhumanist perspectives in an interpretation of *Kairo (Pulse)*, however, it appears that, once humans, within the film, have become ghosts or transcended into a machine, this does not mean that they cannot be reterritorialized into once lost codes pertaining to human characteristics (such as speech, gender and human bodily form). There are instances within *Kairo (Pulse)* where the spirits appear to transcend their assemblages with technologies, ceasing to be so predominantly defined by their properties and, instead, becoming re-coded within normative conceptualizations of the human and the human body. One particular instance of this occurs when Toshio encounters a female spirit within Taguchi's apartment complex. This spirit is, at first, visibly encoded, much like the spirit Ryosuke encounters, as her face is pixelated and blurred.

However, walking towards Toshio, the spirit suddenly stumbles forward, ceasing the strange tempo and gait of her movements and allowing her to become a much clearer vision, no longer blurred and clearly identifiable as a seemingly living human.

This spirit transcends the logics and ontologies of digital media technologies to become human. She can even be considered to become

FIGURE 44 *The pixelated figure Toshio first sees,* Kairo (Pulse) *(Kurosawa, 2001).*

FIGURE 45 *The discernible face of the spirit Toshio encounters,* Kairo (Pulse) *(Kurosawa, 2001).*

grounded in molar conceptualizations of subjectivity, particularly those to do with gender and more traditional, classical notions of horror and the spirit (the return of the repressed), as was discussed earlier within this chapter.

However, transcending the ontologies of digital media and becoming more grounded do not mean that molecularity is left behind. This spirit, along with the others, still retains the potential to become-other once again, and not just through forming assemblages with digital media technologies, but all kinds of different conditions, bodies and spaces. This is, once again, reflective of the posthuman condition and the Japanese break in linear time, which are experienced by subjects as a flux between different deterritorializations and reterritorializations, engendered by the different assemblages with social, cultural, global, technological and economic landscapes that are formed. As highlighted in this book, the films *Ju-On: The Grudge* and *Audition* align with *Kairo* (*Pulse*) in such renderings of contemporary conditions. It is to a summary of each of these films, how they interconnect and the developments in thought on them which have been produced, that this book now turns.

Conclusion: Reconceptualizations of Japanese horror and beyond

This book has developed new avenues of thought for Japanese cinema, and Japanese horror cinema studies more specifically, incrementally transforming and going beyond hermeneutic film theory. This particular field (of Japanese horror cinema), developing significantly within Western scholarship after the transnational Japanese horror boom of the late 1990s and early 2000s, has been dominated by the hermeneutic methodology and its concepts, more specifically, notions pertaining to psychoanalysis, national, transnational and world cinema. Whilst this methodology and its various concepts have yielded many fruitful insights into Japanese horror cinema and Japanese cinema more generally, it was perceived here that for them to continue to provide insightful commentary, they must be extended and developed in new ways.

What was identified as being particularly problematic with hermeneutic concepts was the fact that they seek to formulate singular, generalizing truths about film texts. They search for the hidden, encoded meanings of texts, overlaying interpretations onto them, even if this means that elements of them, not aligning with a concept, are ignored. They therefore occlude alternative ways in which we may be able to understand film texts. This is an issue when one considers the hybridity and complexity that all film texts display, including Japanese horror films. Of course, hermeneutic concepts have been continually reformed and adapted in relation to mutations within cinema, ensuring their continued importance to scholarship. However, there are still registers of film, particularly the affective, which cannot be accounted for through this methodology. As affect is an important, expressive facet of film (particularly within time-image cinema), rendering, for instance, the indescribable any-space-whatevers created in the wake of breaks with linear time (such as the Japanese economic crash of 1990), it is imperative that scholarship become more attuned to these elements. An alternative ontology of thought was therefore perceived to be required to introduce incremental changes into the fields of Japanese cinema and Japanese horror cinema studies specifically, one that diverged from the hermeneutic.

This book mobilized the taxonomy of Gilles Deleuze to formulate alternative perspectives on this area of cinema, drawing also upon some of his collaborative works with Guattari. Furthermore, this book found the works of film scholars, including David Martin-Jones (2006, 2011) and Anna Powell (2005, 2007), who have utilized Deleuzian perspectives for their own studies, invaluable to the formulation of ideas regarding how this taxonomy may be productively applied to the areas of horror cinema and national, transnational and world cinema scholarship.

Deleuze's perspectives are fundamentally different to hermeneutic concepts as they allow for understandings and ideas about films to arise out of the texts themselves. Deleuze perceives bodies (organic and machinic) and the meanings attributed to them as unfixed and mutable, they transform in response to the different assemblages that they form with other bodies. Thus, film texts, perpetually forming assemblages with a range of different bodies, including industrial, authorial, social, cultural, political and audience bodies, are transformative and can be experienced and understood in many ways. However, some bodies and film texts are more adept at forming relationalities than others. In particular, time-image cinema, which presents the whole of duration and the multiple potentialities of meaning, being and becoming that characterizes it, is especially relational and rhizomatic, forming innumerable interconnections with different bodies and thoughts. Time-image cinema, unlike movement-image cinema, is much more ungrounded or deterritorialized from linear pathways of progression and molar, hermeneutic regimes of thought, it engenders indetermination and multiplicities of progression and perspective. Not dictated by lines of segmentarity, it is able to form multiple, fluid, affective and divergent assemblages with different perspectives, bodies and ways of being or becoming.

Nevertheless, this book has not advocated a dismantling or disregard of molar, hermeneutic regimes, and time-image cinema has been conceptualized as forming assemblages with such bodies of thought, despite its molecularity, thus allowing for potential reterritorializations into dominant ways of thinking. This perspective was founded upon Deleuze and Guattari's notion of 'the art of dosages' (1987), which emphasizes the need to retain small doses of molar thought in order to more effectively challenge and disrupt their assertions. By exposing doses of molarity to molecular, affective perspectives and expressions, these regimes can, potentially, be transformed. They can be made to diverge from dominant, entrenched lines of thought, producing alternative understandings.

This can be seen at work within the case studies. For instance, both the study of *Ju-On: The Grudge* and *Audition* highlighted how normative, hermeneutic understandings of the female characters on-screen can be ungrounded, allowing for other potentialities of subjectivity and being to be explored. More specifically, the monstrous-feminine motif, which is present within interpretations of both films, can be deterritorialized and transformed, becoming more nuanced and hybridized with other notions and perspectives about subjective positioning. Nevertheless, one must not rule out the potentiality for motifs to be more wholly reterritorialized at points during the films. Thus, the time-image films discussed are experienced as both deterritorializing and reterritorializing, molar and molecular. This, as explored, reflects the day-to-day experiences of people within Japanese society following the break with linear time.

Time-image cinema, specifically that which emerged as part of the Japanese horror genre in the late 1990s and early 2000s, is symptomatic of the break in linear time which occurred when the economic bubble burst in Japan in 1990. This break coincided with other disruptive, ungrounding events, issues and processes during the decade, including (but not limited to) developments in the consumer culture, advancements in the processes of globalization and increases in violent crime and terrorism. Many of these issues and events, as discussed in the case study on *Kairo (Pulse)*, have also been linked to and conceptualized as part of the posthuman condition that informs modern societies. Following this multifaceted break, there was a proliferation of any-space-whatevers, situations within which people no longer knew how to act, where normative, molar ways of understanding society were no longer informative. Many Japanese people, particularly the once vaunted 'salarymen', became unemployed and thus disconnected from the progressive, national mission of economic expansion. Furthermore, many youths, graduating high-school or university, found themselves ill-equipped to find their place within the now volatile job market, which sought to increase employment (due to shifts within the economic model) in the immaterial, service industries. Various outbursts of violence within society, committed by both individuals and groups, served to further disconnect the general public from the Japanese state, the sense of national progression, Japan's mission and understandings of their individual place within these contexts. Time-image films, specifically those within the Japanese horror genre from this period, therefore express these traumatic, disruptive contexts, the feelings of unease, suspension and indetermination that many experienced in subtly different ways.

Nevertheless, within Japanese society there were various attempts to reinstate linear regimes, not least from those commentators, scholars and politicians who sought a recourse to traditional, national cultural ideologies and ways of being. Such a recourse was perceived as being able to remedy economic hardship, the increasing violence within society and communal and familial disconnection created through the prevalent consumer culture. This consumer culture however, whilst ungrounding familial and communal subjective positionings, served to create alternative reterritorializations of identity and place within society. Many found new, fulfilling ways of being through the consumer culture which allowed them to experiment with many different subjective positions and escape the overwhelming pressures of daily life. Thus, the time-image cinema from this period also captures these moments of molarity and linear progression that people experienced, whether they be national, cultural groundings or more eclectic, consumer-based territorializations.

The time-image cinema discussed here, as well as rendering these conditions within its content, also partakes in these deterritorializing/reterritorializing discourses. Not just simply holding a mirror up to the world, these films have the potential to deterritorialize and reterritorialize audiences who form assemblages with them, allowing them to explore different ways of being, understanding and becoming-other. Audiences, in their assemblages, are not static or fully formed individuals, they are fluid and mutable.

Within this book, three time-image films from the Japanese horror genre, the relationalities they form with various bodies and perspectives, how they can be understood under certain molar concepts and how, conversely, they can be conceptualized as affective and molecular, were mapped out in detail.

Shimizu Takashi's *Ju-On: The Grudge*, a film frequently discussed in Japanese horror cinema studies, provided a useful platform for initial tests of the application of Deleuzian methodologies. In particular, Deleuzian ideas about the any-space-whatever, recollection-images and how slippages between different layers of time and space occur were explored in the first part of this case study. Most notably, the cursed home, inhabited by the ghostly Kayako and Toshio, was conceptualized as an ungrounded, a-temporal any-space-whatever. Detached from the temporal coordinates of the external world, the home facilitates the characters' traversal into different layers of the past and future when they come into contact with the space. This space was also perceived as being able to grow or expand. Kayako and Toshio, able to leave the confines of the cursed home, in entering other spaces, similarly unground these environs from normative, linear ways of understanding and navigating them. Pre-empting discussions of inter-medial assemblage in the study of *Audition,* considering other, transnational iterations of the *Ju-On: The Grudge* franchise as forming an assemblage with the original film also led to understandings of how the any-space-whatever of the cursed home could extend its reach, ungrounding spaces situated beyond the borders of Japan.

Another of the primary focuses in this study was upon previous psychoanalytical interpretations of the film within scholarship, centred especially on notions of the uncanny, the return of the repressed and the monstrous-female. Through *Ju-On: The Grudge*'s rhizomatic narrative structures and its rendering of any-space-whatevers, such psychoanalytical perspectives could be ungrounded. Focusing upon the character of Kayako for instance, who has commonly been understood under the concept of the monstrous-feminine, through her perpetual mutations, instigated through her assemblage with the a-temporal void of the cursed home, this perception of her subjectivity can be falsified. Kayako, within this study, was conceptualized under Deleuze's notion of becoming-woman, a fluid, transformative being who cannot be understood fully through one, singular molar regime of thought. Whilst the concept of the monstrous-female could be reterritorialized in relation to Kayako in the course of the film, this interpretation becomes hybridized with other notions about her identity and being, for instance, as a victim figure, as being able to take the form of living, human characters (such as when she transforms into Katsuya to torment Hitomi) and even as an invisible, cosmic entity whose malign force is transmitted through the cursed home. The fluidity and transformative ability of Kayako speaks to fears permeating Japanese society during the 1990s and early 2000s, pertaining to the agency of women in the societal and economic landscapes of the time. In particular, the prevalent consumer culture of the 1990s and into the 2000s has been perceived by scholars, including Iida (2002), as being liberatory for women, endowing them with the ability to experiment with different subjectivities. Women's ability to displace men from the workplace at a time of economic hardship and high unemployment rates was also perceived as threatening to the patriarchal regime, creating concerns about the power of women.

Other characters within this film, including the heroine, Rika, and Kayako's son, Toshio, were also conceptualized as fluid and mutable beings, ungrounding different, yet interlinked, hermeneutic, psychoanalytical notions of their subjectivities. Toshio, for instance, can be ungrounded from his positioning as the eternal foetus, tied to Kayako and her monstrous motherhood, and be understood as a bakeneko, a shapeshifting being who can transform, most notably, into a cat. Rika also can be understood under Clover's (1992) concept of the final girl; however, her divergence from characteristics of this motif highlights her hybridity, her fluidity of subjectivity. In her death (unconventional for the final girl motif) Rika potentially becomes part of the curse herself, she perhaps becomes a malevolent, vengeful spirit like Kayako, able to mutate her form perpetually.

The applications of the concept of becoming-woman demonstrated here and how it can deterritorialize normative understandings of female characters have potentially wider implications for studies into gender and horror cinema. Applying this Deleuzian and Guattarian notion to studies of the female figure in horror films beyond Japan, particularly within Western and Hollywood cinema (upon which many of these filmic, psychoanalytical concepts are based), can complexify our understanding of such characters, extending it beyond the parameters of concepts like the monstrous-feminine and the final girl.

Exploring the concept of becoming-woman through *Ju-On: The Grudge* laid much of the groundwork for similar considerations within the subsequent study on *Audition*, which, again, because of its prominent depictions of women, had also previously been understood under psychoanalytical notions, such as the monstrous-feminine.

Considerations of becoming-woman were not the main focus of the second case study, however. Alternative avenues of thought were opened up through an exploration of this text. As a film adapted from a novel of the same name, this study could explore the wider relationality that the film has with its source text. Highlighting how Deleuzian perspectives have the potential to incrementally transform wider spheres of thought beyond (trans)national and psychoanalytical models, this case study explored how adaptation studies and its concepts could be rethought. By considering the source and the adaptation as relational spaces, the normative conceptualization of a one-way flow of material and affect from the source to the adaptation could be ungrounded. Instead a two-way flow can be conceptualized, where the adaptive film has the capacity to transform and mutate the source novel or, more accurately, the experience of it at the site of the audience. It was hypothesized that, as the more ungrounded and nonlinear of the two texts, the film *Audition* has the potential to unground the molarities of the novel, particularly those, once again, pertaining to notions of gendered subjectivity. However, the novel was similarly conceptualized as having the capacity to reterritorialize such notions within the film through its relationality.

As highlighted, some adaptation studies scholars (particularly Hodgkins (2013) and Stam and Raengo (2005)) have already perceived the value in Deleuzian perspectives for instigating incremental change to concepts within their field. The *Audition* study therefore positioned itself in amongst these developments within adaptation studies scholarship. As a relatively underdeveloped strand of thought within this field, however, this case study contributed an expansion to these Deleuzian reconsiderations, offering developments upon the insights of previous scholars and bringing world cinema into purview of these discussions.

Thinking further about the external relationalities that filmic bodies form, within the *Audition* case study, the relationalities formed between the auteurs of the novel (Murakami) and of the film (Miike) were also considered. Through this, new transformations to the concept of the auteur were formulated. Instead of a distinct individual with their own static, generalized style, the auteur can be considered as a fluid, transformative being who re-creates their style each time they undertake a creative project and form different relationalities with other bodies (including other auteurs and industrial bodies such as studios).

The final study of the book explored the film *Kairo (Pulse)*, where fresh perspectives on bodies, subjectivity and molecularity of being were produced. The spirits especially were the source of such perspectives as they were conceptualized as the most deterritorialized beings, the closest to the body without organs, that had yet been encountered across the three case studies. To try and understand these spirits, a number of perspectives were appropriated, including notions of cosmic horror. Under this perspective, the spirits of *Kairo (Pulse)* were conceptualized as weird, indescribable beings who cannot be understood through molar regimes and can only be apprehended upon the body. Constituting these beings as such and, thus, the film *Kairo (Pulse)* as a cosmic text meant that it could be situated within the recent trend for new weird fictions. In light of breaks within linear time the world over (including those seen within Japan upon the economic crash in 1990), cosmic works have proliferated as a means to express the suspending, indescribable any-space-whatevers that have formed within societies.

Through another, interlinking perspective, it was conceptualized that these spirits and the living characters to an extent, may be expressive of the posthuman condition (or a specific facet of it) and its deterritorializing processes and contexts. The notion of the posthuman condition was understood in this study to link separate conceptualizations of disruptive events and processes, or breaks with linearity, together, including such things as the processes of globalization, technologization, advanced capitalism and the Anthropocene. The notion of the posthuman condition is transnational in its scope, creating generalized conceptualizations about the contexts and situations of societies globally, which are all subject to certain disruptive processes, events and issues. These posthuman conditions connect to other culturally and nationally specific disruptive breaks (in Japan specifically) discussed within this book, including the bursting of the economic bubble in 1990, developments in the consumer culture and various outbursts of violence within society. It has been conceptualized that these spirits are expressive of the posthuman condition primarily because, at points, they appear to be very ontologically similar to the digital technologies that they use to traverse the boundary between the realm of the living and the dead. They inherit the coded properties of these technologies and the property of variability, giving them the ability to perpetually mutate or recode themselves. As conceptualized, these spirits demonstrate a range of becoming-machines, transformations instigated through assemblages formed with technology. This aptly reflects the posthuman condition as people in their daily lives increasingly form complex assemblages with different digital technologies, become more flexible and mutable and transform themselves through them.

Rather than presenting a positive, affirmative view of the becomings that can be fostered through assemblages with technology, as per the posthumanist perspective, *Kairo (Pulse)* instead comments upon the destructive impact that digital medias especially can have upon Japanese society. Such a commentary perhaps has been created in light of nationally specific events and issues related to technology within Japan, such as the rise in cases of *Hikikomori*, a pathology associated with over-indulgence in digital media, and the *Aum Shinrikyō* group's use of technology to develop chemical weapons to use against Japanese society. These technologies within *Kairo (Pulse)*, invoking the idea of the Anthropocene, ultimately lead to human extinction, not to any euphoric, enhancing becoming where the human remains intact.

It was considered therefore that transhumanist perspectives may allow further, more nuanced insights into *Kairo (Pulse)* and the nature of the assemblages it renders between technologies and the human. However, these perspectives, whilst having some resonance with the film which appears to, in parts, depict the transcendence of the human, could not account for why it is that these spirits, in some cases, can reground themselves within seemingly, static human forms. It was concluded then that a negotiation, an assemblage between all of these different understandings (cosmic horror, posthumanism, transhumanism etc.), rather than grounding *Kairo (Pulse)* within one singular interpretation, is most appropriate, an approach which can be achieved through the utilization of Deleuzian, relational thought.

As detailed, Deleuzian perspectives already have prolific connections with many of the principles of posthumanist and transhumanist thought, particularly the notion of becoming-machine. However, the ways in which these bodies of thought utilize Deleuzian perspectives are still open to development and transformation. As highlighted through this case study and as Culp (2016) has argued, a more rigorous consideration is needed of the pessimistic, destructive implications of Deleuzian thought which, as emblematized by many posthuman theories and transhumanist perspectives, has become too closely associated with affirmation, euphoric assemblage and positive becoming. If consideration is given to how assemblages and becomings can be traumatic and cataclysmic through, as Culp (2016) terms it, a dark Deleuzian taxonomy, the understandings of the relationalities between humans and technology within these fields can perhaps be developed. Such fusions between dark, Deleuzian perspectives and posthumanist and transhumanist thought would have wider implications for understandings of cinema and other media beyond *Kairo (Pulse)*. As Thacker (in Galloway, Thacker and Wark, 2014) has highlighted, a number of other Japanese horror texts and, of course, their American remakes, from the late 1990s and early 2000s have thematically explored the ills of technology, situating media such as video, television and mobile phone networks as dark media, bridging the gap between the living and the dead.[1] Thus, these films too can potentially be reconsidered through posthumanist (specifically related to technology) and transhumanist thought and Deleuzian notions of destructive, traumatic becoming-machines.

Further Deleuzian studies into Japanese horror cinema are crucial if the dominance of hermeneutic thought in this area is to be more significantly challenged. It is particularly important if there is, as some commentators (e.g. William (2016)) have predicted, to be a resurgence in the form, that more scholars revisit Japanese horror films from the boom years and prior, rethinking the ways in which they have been understood through Deleuzian perspectives. This will enable the field to meet new trends in the genre with a range of innovative, developmental concepts which can produce new knowledges and perspectives from those commonly seen within scholarship to date. A revitalization of the genre must be accompanied by advancements in the thought and scholarship upon it, of which, as this book has demonstrated throughout, Deleuzian perspectives can certainly most be a part. In fact, a more thoroughgoing embrace of Deleuzian perspectives in wider fields of cinema scholarship (e.g. wider horror film studies and national, transnational and world cinema studies), as hopefully has been expressed here, can allow scholars studying a range of topics (beyond Japanese horror) to transform existing thought and more fully address the complex, affective, molecular and hybridized dimensions of contemporary societies.

NOTES

Introduction

1 Affects or intensities (as they are also sometimes referred to) are a bodily reaction to an external stimulus which prepare the body to complete an action in response to the stimulus. As the philosopher Gilles Deleuze would say, affects are 'a motor tendency on a sensitive nerve' or 'a series of micro-movements on an immobilised plate of nerve' (2005: 89). When receiving or generating affect in response to a stimulus, the body is in an immobile, suspended or receptive state, preparing itself for a subsequent action.
Films can act as a stimulus for instance and have an affective impact upon audiences' bodies, creating sensations such as goosebumps upon the skin and increases in heart rates. They allow the viewer to experience film through bodily contact rather than simply visually, creating a sense of immediacy, as though the audience member is a direct participant in what is occurring on-screen. Affects, Deleuze argues, can also enter into 'intensive series', where their intensity changes or passes 'from one quality to another, to emerge on to a new quality' (2005: 92). Thus, when engaging with a film, audiences find that they experience a wide range of different qualities of affect which fluctuate according to the oscillations or mutations of the moving stimulus of the film. Each time an audience member encounters a film, the affective qualities generated will be different, even if the audience member views a film that they have seen before, the intensities will vary from their last experience. Affects also differ significantly from emotional responses and cannot be qualified in language. As Massumi, an affect theorist, argues, emotions are the 'sociolinguistic fixing of the quality of an experience which is from that point onward defined as personal' (2002: 28). No language can fully express the experiences, qualities, ranges and fluctuations of affect, they are 'unqualified … not ownable or recognisable' (2002). If these sensations are fixed within a language their full essence is largely lost and repressed. They are, in other words, pre-cognitive as they are generated in situations detached from spatio-temporal coordinates which would give them a language and a purpose. As they cannot be fixed within language, the affective is a dimension of film which has largely escaped the attention of hermeneutic-based studies.

2 This idea that there is a cinema exploring the affective dimensions of particularly disruptive events or processes within society is an extension of Steven Shaviro's insights within *Post Cinematic Affect* (2010). Shaviro (2010), discussed in more depth later, highlights how certain media (from the West)

render, affectively, the disruptive processes and effects of globalization which he perceives as facilitating a movement away from 'experience conceived as a continuous cumulation, towards an experience of momentary shocks that bombarded and shattered subjective experience like hand grenades' (Charney and Schwartz, 1995, cited in Standish, 2012: 12). Departing from Shaviro (2010), however (as is discussed at length later), this book emphasizes the nuances of territorialization (e.g. national and cultural groundings) that remain within media texts, rendering, for instance, Japanese nationally and culturally inflected discourses of globalization and societal and economic transformation. In other words, this book does not unproblematically consider such disruptive events as globalization as just causing a deterritorialization of linear, hermeneutic regimes or ways of understanding and navigating society. Many facets of such disruptive events and processes can perhaps be successfully negotiated within hermeneutic language. In this book, unlike within Shaviro's (2010) work, there is a focus upon tensions between the national/cultural and the global, the molar and the molecular (for a definition see below), reterritorialization (where molar regimes are reinstated to dominance) and deterritorialization (where molecularity becomes dominant), and how these manifest in a variety of ways within the films considered.

3 The term 'assemblage' means arrangement or fitting together. It is where bodies, objects, territories and various conceptualizations of time can come together (perhaps for a limited period) and transmit various forces, affects, ideas and concepts between each other to transform ways of functioning. Elements which come together have 'the ability to rearrange, fragment continually and in new and different patterns or configurations' (Deleuze and Guattari, 2000: 7).

4 The term 'transnational' has been utilized by many recent studies (including this book) rather than other, very similar terms, such as 'international' or 'global'. This is because the term 'international' implies that processes, interactions, products, individuals or institutions, whilst extending beyond their nation of origin, are still to be understood as belonging to a specific national framework and set of ideologies. This becomes problematic when one considers how they may transform within different environments and under different cultural conditions. Furthermore, the term 'transnational' 'has merit over "global" … [as it] sounds too all-inclusive and decontextualized … Transnational draws attention in a more locally contextualized manner to the interconnections and asymmetries that are promoted by the multi-directional flow' (Iwabuchi, 2002: 17). In other words, the term 'transnational' embodies a balance between considerations of the ungrounding of national paradigms and the emergence of new formulations of subjectivity, conceptualization and understanding and the retention of the local and the national.

5 'Molar' is a term linked to the hermeneutic which can be used to describe a body or space which is coded as whole or is fixed within language. 'Molecular', on the other hand, is a term linked to Deleuzian thought which can be used to encapsulate the affective, fluid or transformative nature of bodies, spaces and territories and their identities or the ways in which they are understood.

6   Gilles Deleuze and Félix Guattari, a psychotherapist and philosopher, wrote a
    number of collaborative works together, including *Anti-Oedipus* (1972) and
    A Thousand Plateaus (1980). Whilst these works especially are utilized within
    this book for various purposes, not least for challenging psychoanalytical
    ideas, it is Deleuze's solo works which take precedence here.
7   'Deterritorializing' is an important term within the Deleuzian taxonomy
    which details how meanings ascribed to a particular body or space (a
    territory) can be unmade, disrupted or become disassociated. The term
    'becoming' is also important to the Deleuzian corpus which encapsulates the
    idea of thought becoming different or presenting the world anew rather than
    as a repetition or a representation of the same world once again. Becomings or
    becoming-others occur when there is extreme contiguity between two or more
    bodies without resemblance.

Chapter 1

1   There are, of course, other bodies of thought beyond psychoanalysis which
    have been utilized to examine horror cinema, for instance cognitivist
    perspectives from the likes of Cynthia Freeland (2000) and Noël Carroll
    (1990). However, psychoanalytical theory has arguably been one of the most
    prolific, contributing some of the most interesting and critically successful
    concepts to horror cinema scholarship. There has always been an evident
    kinship between horror film and psychoanalytical ideas, making it a valuable
    tool for analysis. This stems from an intimate relationship between gothic
    literature (which has and continues to be the source of many tropes, aesthetics,
    themes and narratives within horror films) and, in particular, the works of
    the founder of psychoanalytical theory, Sigmund Freud. Both gothic literature
    and Freud provided complimentary 'responses to the problems of selfhood
    and identity, sexuality and pleasure, fear and anxiety as these were manifested
    in the nineteenth and early twentieth centuries' (Schneider, 2004: 8). Whilst
    psychoanalytical works decoding the horror film have primarily focused
    upon horror cinema from Europe and America, recently, with the advent
    of increased transnational filmic flows, scholars have begun to apply
    psychoanalytical thought to films from a diverse range of countries,
    including Japan.
2   *Noh* theatre dates back to the fourteenth century and its plays are
    characterized by their use of masks and their fusions of song, dance and
    music. *Kabuki* on the other hand dates back to the seventeenth century and
    is renowned for its elaborate costumes and make-up and its special effects
    (Hand, in McRoy, 2005: 20, 21). *Bunraku* is a traditional puppet theatre from
    the late seventeenth century and many of its plays are thematically similar to
    Kabuki theatre's (Japan-Guide, 2016).
3   For instance, within Japan, many cultural discourses and communications,
    including film, can be argued to express the state-sanctioned ideologies
    of *Nihonjinron* and *Nihonbunkaron*, or the idea of the 'uniqueness and
    superiority of the Japanese people and culture' respectively (Iles, 2008: 42).

4   Within Ruth Benedict's *The Chrysanthemum and the Sword: Patterns of Japanese Culture* (1946) for instance, an image of an eternal, unchanging Japanese culture is presented.
5   Stuart Hall provides a useful definition of globalization, an elusive term which has many different facets. He states: 'Globalization is the process by which the relatively separate areas of the globe come to intersect in a single imaginary "space", when their respective histories are convened in a time-zone or time-frame dominated by the time of the West; when the sharp boundaries reinforced by space and distance are bridged by connections (travel, trade, conquest, colonization, markets, capital and the flows of labour, goods and profits) which gradually eroded the clear-cut distinction between "inside" and "outside"' (1995, cited in Iwabuchi, 2002: 15).
6   As Higson highlights, 'the concept of national cinema still has some meaning, as governments continue to develop defensive strategies designed to protect and promote both the local cultural formation and the local economy' (in Hjort and Mackenzie, 2000: 69). Thus, states and governments within nations maintain internal industries and keep national production contexts alive.
7   A good example of these processes at work can be found in the American remakes of Japanese horror films which proliferated at the same time as the 'J-horror' boom. American films, such as *The Grudge* and *The Ring*, reworked their Japanese originals, perceivably because retention of obvious Japanese elements from the originals would not appeal to the producers' intended, Western audience. In terms of both *The Grudge* and *The Ring*, main characters in the film were Westernized and, perhaps more profoundly, *The Ring* relocated the setting of the film away from Japan to Seattle. Elements of 'Japaneseness' are still present, however, in these remakes, for example, in the folklore that informs the vengeful spirits of these films.
8   This makes reference to a concept Iwabuchi explores in his earlier publications. Cultural 'odor' is something that is imbued within cultural products, an essence which identifies their specific origins. This 'odor', signalling the culture from which a product derives, as well as being suppressed, can become attractive, appealing and a selling point for a product. Iwabuchi describes the experience of an attractive cultural odour as 'the moment when the image of the contemporary lifestyle of the country of origin is strongly and affirmatively called to mind as the very appeal of the product' (2002: 27).
9   Orientalism, a term most famously coined by Edward Said, describes the process within cultural and communicative discourses of 'the ontological and epistemological distinction made between "the Orient" [the East] and "the Occident" [the West]' (2003: 2), where the West is positioned as dominant and superior to the East which comes to objectified and stereotypically represented and perceived as primitive, exotic, erotic, seductive, feminine, inscrutable, brutal, savage, irreducibly other and uncanny to Western perspectives. These binary distinctions between the West and the East are useful within social and cultural discourses for building notions of national, cultural identity in relation to the differences of others.
10 This does not mean, however, that hegemonies and imbalances of power need to be removed from scholarly purview, as is alluded to in the following paragraph.

11 This book, following Shaviro (2010), utilizes the terms 'map' and 'mapping' to describe the films under consideration and the analyses that are produced here. This is because these terms embody the affective, fluid and transformative nature of this alternative media regime, 'they are not static representations but tools for negotiating and intervening in social space ... [they] actively construct and perform the social relations, flows and feelings that they are ostensibly about' (2010: 6).

12 Although not explicitly stated, Shaviro (2010) discusses Western media products and thus how they affectively map a specifically Western experience of society and transformative forces. This book extends this line of thought by arguing that Japanese horror films from the late 1990s and early 2000s too can be considered part of this growing body of works which are particularly adept at rendering the hermeneutically unrepresentable through affect. Japanese media products may be especially important texts within this novel media regime that Shaviro (2010) proposes. As Zahlten suggests, 'Japan has for many decades been, both for self-reflection within Japan and views from the "outside", an arena where discourses of globalization are dramatized' (in Miyao, 2014: 439). According to Zahlten, Japan and its cultural products have become particularly important spaces it seems where 'the crisis of dealing with the phenomenon of "the worlds"' (Miyao, 2014) can be negotiated.

13 It is also important to note that contemporary media products do not just express these complex social processes, but also, as Shaviro (2010) notes, participate actively in them. They are, themselves, 'machines for generating affect' (2010: 2–3) which comes to constitute part of the functioning and flows of these processes.

14 An *Onryō* is usually a female spirit who returns from the dead to exact revenge on those who have wronged her. It is a term for a character motif that was established first within the traditional theatres of *Noh* and *Kabuki*.

15 However, within various *Noh* plays, it is also men who experience betrayal by the women they love, returning in some form to punish them. For instance, in *Koi no Omoni* (The Deadweight of Love) a gardener, taking care of the retired Emperor's chrysanthemums sees a consort of the Emperor's and falls in love with her. Noticing his affection for her, the consort sets a task for the gardener to carry a large package around the garden hundreds of times. If completed she would appear before him. However, the package is too heavy for the gardener to lift and he is filled with bitterness and rage at this cruel trick, vowing, as he passes away, that the consort will pay (The-Noh.com, n.d.).

16 The play *Kanawa* (Iron Trivet), for instance, tells the tale of a woman who travels to a shrine every night to curse her ex-husband for abandoning her and taking a new wife. A priest tells the woman that if she dons a red kimono, spreads red powder on her face, puts an iron trivet on her head that burns with three flames and holds rage in her mind, she will be able to turn into a daemon. The woman's former husband, suffering nightmares every night as a result of the woman's prayers, seeks help from a diviner who begins to exorcize the couple, placing the curse into two dolls resembling the pair. Appearing at the couple's house, the woman, now transformed into a daemon, attacks the two dolls; however, the diviner manages to exorcize the daemon

who disappears whilst promising to return to seek revenge once more (The-Noh.com, n.d.).
17 These commentaries, however, may do a disservice to Japanese horror films (particularly between the late 1990s and early 2000s) which equally have the capacity to influence the cycles, themes and aesthetics of global cinemas. The impact that Japanese horror cinema had upon Hollywood horror productions in the 1990s and early 2000s is most obvious with the various American remakes that surfaced, such as *The Ring*, *The Grudge* and *Dark Water* (2005).
18 Furthermore, just as the woman is both abjected and desired, other cultures and constructions of nation are subject to this contradiction. Within national cinema studies it has been theorized that images of Eastern cultures become objectified by a dominant Western perspective, coded with an exotic, mysterious, primitive 'to-be-looked-at-ness'. The East, within Western, Orientalist perspectives, is perceived as unalterably other and therefore abject, as well as fascinating and alluring. As an abject entity then, the East must be mastered by the West for it to maintain its distinctive, subjective boundaries. One way in which it achieves this mastery is through employing 'the gaze' within cinema which lessens the threat the East poses to Western subjectivity and morality.
19 The term *hibakusha* refers to survivors of the atomic bomb who have been affected by radiation or else burned by the fires that broke out in the immediate aftermath. Many *hibakusha* have experienced discrimination within society as many believed that radiation exposure was an infectious disease. This led *hibakusha* to being excluded from work and from social life (Youth Arts New York, 2013).
20 The term *Pika* refers to the blinding flash that occurred when the atom bombs exploded, scorching imprints of shadows onto the earth and melting bodies (Deamer, 2014: 21).

Chapter 2

1 Many other scholars have also picked up on this new, affective media environment. As Parikka and Tiainen (in Barrett and Bolt, 2012: 216) argue, advertising no longer needs to recognize "particular target groups" in that they can tap into the 'sensation of an excess of possible meanings with respect to a given image/product'. Stern concurs by stating 'rather than selling an actual product and what it does … commercials can simply sell an abstract idea of fulfilled desire through their product. Provide us a powerfully affective image in an advertisement …. and we will give the product our own meaning. Couple product power with the supposed infinite choice of interactivity, and credit card details will be very forthcoming' (2013: 47).
2 This challenges Bergson's negative perception of cinema which he felt was incapable of producing the movement-image. However, as Deleuze (2005) highlights, Bergson came to this conclusion by observing a primitive form of cinema where the camera was static. Once the camera became mobile

and dynamic, moving shots, altering perception, depth and dimension were possible. Deleuze (2005) perceives this as an emancipation allowing for the emergence of the movement-image within cinema.
3   Objective perception is one where 'all the images vary in relation to one another, on all their facets and in all their parts' (Deleuze, 2005: 79), as opposed to subjective perception where images vary according to a central, privileged element or body within the film.
4   Deleuze (2005) suggests, however, that perception is not as polarized as this and is perhaps more complex. A character, acting on-screen, is assumed to perceive the world in a certain, subjective way, however the camera sees the character and the world from another point of view which has the potential to transform the character's perception. Deleuze terms this a 'camera consciousness' which identifies 'a very special kind of cinema which has acquired a taste for making the camera felt' (2005: 76). This camera consciousness is a decentred, objective perspective, which is 'no longer tailored to solids' (2005: 82), the subjective or the molar. It is instead a molecular, fluid mode of perception. Such a mode of perception, placed within a montage of affection and action-images, 'perceives all the points on which it acts, or which act on it, however far these actions and reactions extend' (2005: 83). It is therefore a mode of perception that opens onto duration and its multiplicity. As such, this molecular, camera consciousness may be most prominent within time-image cinema, however, it is also present within the movement-image, but, as part of this image, it is more likely to be reterritorialized into a molar, subjective perception through subsequent perception-images. One must not, however, rule out the potentiality of it becoming deterritorialized from such a molar positionings again within the discourse of the film.
5   The face, Deleuze argues, is expressive of affect, it conveys 'all kinds of tiny local movements which the rest of the body usually keeps hidden' (2005: 90). Deleuze (2005) also asserts that a feature of the face, expressed in an extreme close-up, has just as much intensity as if we perceive the whole face. Any perceivable backgrounds beyond the close-up of the face similarly lose their spatio-temporal coordinates and become any-spaces-whatever or part of the affective force of the image. Furthermore, close-ups of objects are also affective.
6   The Second World War can be considered to constitute a break in concepts of linear time for Japan. This is evidenced by the attempts of the Japanese state, throughout history, to re-write and erase elements of the past and fabricate the continuation of the ideal nation. A practice Robertson calls *nenpyōlogy* (*nenpyō* literally meaning 'year-chart') or the art of creating new genealogies of timeline which 'disrupts, and discourages rigorous historical analysis. The magic of *nenpyō*logy ... is, the creation of a pervading, dreamlike synchrony, or what I call "relentless presentism"' (2010). This relentless presentism within Japan was, in 1942, as in the nineteenth century, achieved through the revitalization and redefinition of a sense of *Nihonbunkaron* and *Nihonjinron* (a sense of the superiority and uniqueness of Japanese culture and people). 'This cultural essence, or "Japanism", was perceived as something that existed outside of history and that, therefore, was impervious to sociohistorical

transformations; it was something that was always already continuously present' (2010). Revitalizations of these idealistic notions meant that anything within Japanese history which did not adhere to or disrupted this relentless presentism or 'Japanism' were erased from the Japanese historical timeline. For instance, since 1945 the majority of Japanese people have not been exposed to the full extent of Japan's own brutal colonizing history. 'Only in 1997 did the Ministry of Education approve school textbooks that began to acknowledge ... such acts of aggression as the Nanjing massacre, the existence of biological warfare laboratories, and the state-sanctioned coerced prostitution' (2010). An admission that was short-lived and soon replaced by a reversion back to a perpetuation of the victim status of Japan as a nation brutalized by the United States.

7 This is because the Japanese economy, seemingly only just recovering in 2010, has since experienced a number of other disruptive events. Most notably the global recession which occurred in 2008, dubbed the Lehman crisis, and the *Tōhoku* Earthquake and Tsunami in 2011, which became the costliest natural disaster in history after losing the economy 235 billion US dollars.

8 Groups of young people (usually males) who see themselves as social outcasts because of their obsessive interests in manga, anime, videogames and technology (amongst other media forms).

9 A female fashion subculture characterized by promiscuous, materialistic young girls wearing outfits based upon high school uniforms (such as short skirts, blazers and knee-high socks).

10 This perception of consumer cultures is shared transnationally, as Shaviro highlights in his consideration of the West in the twenty-first century, 'the market forces traversing our world are so intense and so disruptive that one's very identity [as in Japan] is continually under threat' (2010: 53).

11 Where Japan resented its involvement in funding the war and began to question its position, past and present, vis-à-vis the United States. In particular, it began to question the utility of Article 9 of the Japanese constitution (instated during the allied occupation) which barred Japan from having a military force and from engaging in war to resolve disputes.

12 The cult perpetrated other acts of terrorism and violence in the years and months leading up to and following the sarin gas attack, including kidnappings, murders, torture, sending a parcel bomb to the governor of Tokyo's office and even planting numerous hydrogen cyanide devices in the subway system of Tokyo which, fortunately, were found or failed to detonate.

13 Deleuze himself formulates his own categories of cinema to challenge the restrictiveness of traditional, genre categories. These include the encompassing (including American Western films and the films of Kurosawa Akira), the flat (including the films of Joseph Losey), the empty (including the films of Ozu) and the stratographic (including the films of Jean-Marie Straub and Daniéle Huillet) (Herzog, in Brown and Martin-Jones, 2012: 138). These are based, not on 'more traditional generic and national groupings', but on 'specific affinities or certain stylistic consistencies that might otherwise escape notice' (Brown and Martin-Jones, 2012) namely 'consistencies arising from the expressive materiality of the filmic event' (Brown and Martin-Jones, 2012: 139).

Chapter 3

1. A semblance given particular legitimacy when the two manga adaptations of *Ju-On: The Grudge*, released in 2003, are considered.
2. Citing Japanese hieroglyphs and *Kabuki* theatre as influences on his own pictorial development.
3. This discourse of the void or house, drawing people in and transforming them into these molecular beings, may not be a positive one, preparing the characters and ourselves for an increasingly complex, multilayered, affective world which requires perpetual adaptation and transformation to occur. In fact, the transformations occurring within this void may be debilitating, horrific, traumatic and destructive. This is an interpretation much more akin to the way in which Andrew Culp in his book, *Dark Deleuze and the Death of This World* (2016), re-conceptualizes Deleuze's concepts and ideas which have become too closely associated, he argues, with joyous affirmation, creation and ecstatic assemblage. He purports that we should reconsider the negative, pessimistic side of Deleuze's theories pertaining to how affects can be cruel rather than intense, becomings can be cataclysmic rather than restorative, and how subjects can be unravelled within assemblages. This is a point discussed further, in relation to *Kairo (Pulse)*, within the third case study.
4. These ideas about such extended, transmedia spatialities along with notions about originals and remakes are picked up again in the next case study on *Audition*.
5. This idea is discussed more fully in the case study on *Kairo (Pulse)*, a film which more explicitly explores extended, relational assemblages with digital media.
6. Using the term 'whole' is, however, quite problematic as engagement with these extended sites of communication and production means that the whole perpetually transforms and expands as more and more materials are produced around it, warping our understanding and comprehension. The whole of the film and its affiliated media perpetually mutate and take flight down different paths of becoming as is discussed more prolifically in the next case study on *Audition*.
7. As gendered ideologies are intertwined with other, wider Japanese national, social structures, concepts and dynamics, the film, appropriating a non-linear, affective, time-image structure, perhaps cannot help but also deterritorialize other forms of molarity. These include (but are not limited to) the ideas of *Nihonjinron* and *Nihonbunkaron*, *Shintōist* ideologies, Confucianism and Neo-Confucianism, 'a particularly conservative strand of Confucianism … [which] in the Japanese interpretation [stressed] absolute obedience to authority' (Buruma, 2003: 17).
8. They can perhaps also be understood through Guattari's perspectives. Although Guattari's elaborations upon the concept, beyond his collaborative works with Deleuze, are beyond the scope of this book.
9. An especially abject function of woman according to the Japanese religion *Shintōism* which proliferated ideas of *aka fujo*, or red uncleanliness, leading to the exclusion of ritually unclean menstruating or pregnant women from sacred sites such as temples (Kobayashi, 2013: 20).

10 Kayako can transform herself into a wide variety of perceivable, whole human forms. This further attests to her role as an inspirational figure for all becomings not just those of women. Gender distinction here is increasingly deterritorialized.
11 This is where singularities, 'described as incompatible elements which are welded together, intersect' (Powell, in Brown and Martin-Jones, 2012: 181).

Chapter 4

1 The Japanese New Wave Movement is a term used to describe a group of loosely connected filmmakers who emerged between the 1950s and the 1970s. These filmmakers rejected the traditions and conventions of Japanese cinema and opted to portray controversial, often taboo subject matter, such as sexual violence, delinquency, youth culture, radical left-wing ideas and discrimination against Koreans living within Japan.
2 Tarantino has even starred in one of Miike's films, *Sukiyaki Western Django* (2007), a film, arguably, directly influencing Tarantino's *Django Unchained*.
3 A book focusing upon the story of the character Ryū and his friends, who live in a Japanese town, where their lives revolve around sex, drugs and rock and roll. The narrative is an intensive journey through tales of group sex, overdoses and suicide.
4 Within *In the Miso Soup*, twenty-year-old Kenji, a Japanese night-life tour guide for foreigners, receives a phone call from Frank, an American, seeking his services for three nights. Kenji guides Frank around the Shinjuku district, all the while his suspicions grow that Frank might be responsible for the gruesome events reported on the news.
5 Diverging from early perspectives on adaptation in different ways, one other tendency within the field has been to try and (developing upon fidelity-based studies) distinguish between 'different possible approaches to adaptation and different ways to describe these approaches' (Leitch, 2017: 3), considering, for instance, how film texts try to, in different ways, remain faithful to their source or else try to rewrite them. Andrew's considerations of 'borrowing, intersecting, and transforming' (1984, cited in Leitch, 2017: 3), for instance, are emblematic of this trend in the field, deterritorializing the negative, hierarchical languages that pervaded medium-specific and fidelity-based commentaries previously.
6 This shift towards intertextuality has been in response to recent developments in digital technology and media which have transformed the processes of adaptation. Notably, digital technologies have transformed our culture from, as Lessig (TED Talks, 2007) would say, 'read-only' to 'read-write', where anyone, anywhere with access to these technologies can partake in producing, reproducing and adapting (or remixing) cultural products themselves. Developments in digital technologies and media have also contributed to the trend of 'transmedia storytelling', where franchises, their themes and narratives, are adapted or spread across multiple platforms.

7   Within the book, *The Drift: Affect, Adaptation and New Perspectives on Fidelity* (2013), Hodgkins, unfortunately, does not go beyond stating the existence of differences between intensities issuing from a source text and its adaptation and how they thus 'comment differently on our disarticulated age' (2013: 20).
8   In fact, as Balmain states, 'Aoyama is fundamentally a respectable and sympathetic character, providing a possible point of identification for the (male) spectator' (2008: 110).
9   In 1997, two children, Yamashita Ayaka and Hase Jun, aged ten and eleven respectively, were brutally murdered by a fourteen-year-old boy in Kōbe.
10 It is worth noting that since the Second World War, however, the figure of the *Shufu*, a term meaning housewife, has replaced the *ryōsaikenbo* within the popular imagination of roles for women.
11 The notion of Asami seeking revenge against males, motivated by past abuses she appears to have experienced at the hands of her stepfather, in the novel, and her dance instructor, in the film, means that, according to scholars like Balmain, she must be not only contextualized in relation to rape-revenge films such as *I Spit on Your Grave* from the West but also 'in relation to the violated bodies of female victims of Japanese sadomasochistic pornography and, from the 1960s onwards, pink cinema' (2008: X). Whilst these films can rightly be discussed as forming assemblages with *Audition,* we should not, as Balmain (2008) does, simply consider that they drift molar elements to our experience, grounding our understanding of Asami and the narrative into discourses of the wronged, vengeful female. These films also drift affective, molecular elements to our experience of *Audition*, potentially ungrounding territorializations. Furthermore, perhaps not all of the molar, linear regimes centred around the violated body that are expressed by these soft-porn and rape-revenge films, necessarily contribute to a territorialization of Asami and *Audition* into this rhetoric. These ideas about drifts, within assemblages, between different texts are discussed in detail at various points throughout this chapter.
12 Such comments and opinions on Japan's consumer culture and such allusions to the nature of Shigeharu and his son's relationship are never made within the film, however.
13 Perhaps adhering to Bolter and Grusin's (2000) conceptualization of remediation, Murakami's novel remediates the filmic montage in order to reassert itself in face of the perceived domination of cinema and even challenge the view that novels cannot, unlike film, induce the same intense, affective resonances and engage the audience at the level of the body in the same way that film can. However rather than considering this in such static terms, as a novel's assimilation of static, irrefutably filmic mechanisms into its once pure, literary body, Deleuze would refute this term remediation and consider the novel as becoming-other as transforming itself through its and its author's (Murakami) assemblage with the wider, affective fragmented world and wider mediums like film which drift affects and new potentials for being and becoming between each other. Thus, the novel is realizing a potential within itself (for expression through montage) that was always there but rarely ever realized.

14 The affective impact of these scenes is epitomized by the reports of numerous audience walkouts from theatres and film festivals, perhaps most notoriously the Rotterdam film festival in 2000. These scenes induced such an unbearably intense affective response from some that they could no longer stand to be in assemblage with it.

Chapter 5

1   A term literally meaning pulling inward or being confined which describes a contemporary cultural phenomenon where youths (particularly males) avoid all social contact, confine themselves to their rooms, stop going to school, college or work and stop maintaining their relationships with friends and family. As is discussed further within this chapter, *Hikikomori* is often considered as a specifically Japanese issue caused by the more profound development and integration of technology into society there, feeding into Western techno-Orientalist ideologies of Japan 'that sees it only as a technological dystopia or occasionally as a utopia' (Napier, 2005: 24).
2   *Yūrei* is an encompassing Japanese term for spirit or ghost, used to describe those who have departed and then returned to the realm of the living. *Yūrei* may return to the realm of the living for various reasons, including if they have not had the proper funeral rites performed for them or if they were murdered out of revenge, jealousy or hatred. This term is distinct from the other Japanese word used within this book to describe spirits, *Onryō*, which specifically means vengeful spirit and pertains to those deceased (usually murdered) persons who return to the world of living to right the wrongs they experienced when alive.
3   *The Willows* tells the tale of two friends who are travelling by boat down the river Danube. Landing their boat on a sandy island to camp for the evening, the two find that there is a sinister, unseen force lurking in the nature that surrounds them, particularly the dense willows that populate the edge of the river.
4   There is a third major strand of posthuman thought which Braidotti (2013) identifies, one that she describes as a reactive form. This reactive form, however, is largely incompatible with this book and the positions, in terms of alternative ways of understanding transformations within societies and subjectivities (deterritorializations and reterritorializations), it seeks to forward. The reactive approach to posthumanism 'develops a thorough contemporary defence of humanism as the guarantee of democracy, freedom and the respect for human dignity' (ibid.: 38). It rejects anti-humanist and post-structuralist perspectives and calls for a full reinstatement of humanist visions of the subject which can overcome the posthuman condition. Nussbaum (1999, 2010), for instance, considers that there is no room 'for experimenting with new models of the self' (Braidotti, 2013: 39) and that there is a need for universal humanistic values which can provide stable, moral foundations for subjectivity within contemporary societies across the globe.

5   This discourse of the film can also be understood as polynomial, however. For instance, the fluidity and multiplicity of being demonstrated by these characters can be interpreted as a commentary on technologization and technological assemblage. As analytic posthumanism suggests, by increasingly forming intimate connections with different technological artefacts, people become transformed through these assemblages in different ways.

6   Drawing upon Clark's envisioning of co-adaptation, Braidotti (2013) also highlights how machines can become-other within their assemblages with organic bodies. She discusses Guattari's notion of machinic autopoiesis, which conceptualizes how machines have the ability, like organic cells, to reproduce and maintain themselves, and highlights how this establishes a qualitative link between organic matter and technological artefacts. Machines, like organic bodies are thus 'intelligent and generative. They have their own temporality and develop through generations: they contain their own virtuality and futurity' (ibid.: 94). It is possible therefore to perceive of becomings-other for such machines which can adapt and mutate their ontologies and character.

7   Thacker (in Galloway, Thacker and Wark, 2014) notes that Japanese horror fictions, in particular, are rife with depictions of media negotiating the space between the natural and the supernatural, signal (coded meaning) and aberrant noise (affect). For instance, within *Ringu* it is the cursed video tape which mediates between a supernatural realm and the real world. Thacker also notes that other examples of Japanese horror cinema 'move beyond the use of technology devices and show us the ways that the human body can serve as a medium' (in Galloway, Thacker and Wark, 2014: 92), as a bridge between two different ontological orders. *Rasen* (*Spiral*) (1998), for instance, presents the corpse as a medium, 'with DNA and informational code eerily emerging from the organs of the body' (Thacker, in Galloway, Thacker and Wark, 2014: 93). Furthermore, in other iterations, like *Uzumaki* (*Spiral*) (2000), it is thought which becomes haunted or a point of mediation between the natural and the supernatural, creating madness. One can even discern a final stage beyond this, within films such as *Nagai Yume* (*Long Dream*) (2000), where 'it is, finally, being itself that mediates the supernatural' (Thacker, in Galloway, Thacker and Wark, 2014: 94). Within *Nagai Yume* (*Long Dream*), the character cannot stop dreaming, loses all sense of time and his body begins to twist and mutate in grotesque ways.

Conclusion

1   These include *Ringu, The Ring, Chakushin Ari* (*One Missed Call*), *One Missed Call* and even video games such as the *Project Zero* (2001–) series which, part of the Japanese horror boom, situates the camera as a dark media, which allows the various protagonists to see spirits through it and defeat them. The recent American film, *Rings*, a sequel to *The Ring* and *The Ring 2* (2005), could also be considered through these ideas as here, within this film, we see the return of the cursed videotape.

BIBLIOGRAPHY

Allison, A. (2009), 'The Cool Brand, Affective Activism and Japanese youth', *Theory, Culture & Society*, 26 (2–3): 89–111.
Andrew, D. (2006), 'An Atlas of World Cinema', in S. Dennison and S.H. Lim (eds), *Remapping World Cinema: Identity, Culture and Politics in Film*, 19–29, London: Wallflower Press.
Anderson, B.O.R. (2006), *Imagined Communities: Reflections on the Origin and Spread of Nationalism*, Revised edn, London: Verso Books.
Appadurai, A. (1996), *Modernity at Large: Cultural Dimensions of Globalization*, Minneapolis: University of Minnesota Press.
Athique, A.M. (2013), 'Leaping the Demographic Barrier: Theoretical Challenges for the Crossover Audience', in S. Khorana (ed.), *Crossover Cinema: Cross-Cultural Film from Production to Reception*, 107–22, Oxon: Routledge.
Bâ, S.M. and Higbee, W. (eds) (2012), *De-Westernizing Film Studies*, Oxon: Routledge.
Balmain, C. (2008), *Introduction to Japanese Horror Film*, Edinburgh: Edinburgh University Press.
Barker, J.M. (2009), *The Tactile Eye: Touch and the Cinematic Experience*, Berkeley: University of California Press.
BBC (2009), 'Religions – Shinto: Kami', *BBC*, 4 September. Available online: http://www.bbc.co.uk/religion/religions/shinto/beliefs/kami_1.shtml (accessed 26 May 2020).
Benedict, R. (1946), *The Chrysanthemum and the Sword: Patterns of Japanese Culture*, Boston: Houghton Mifflin Company.
Bergson, H. (1954), *Creative Evolution*, London: Macmillan & Co.
Billig, M. (1995), *Banal Nationalism*, London: Sage Publications.
Blake, L. (2012), *The Wounds of Nations: Horror Cinema, Historical Trauma and National Identity*, Manchester: Manchester University Press.
Blouin, M.J. (2011), 'A Communal Haunt: "Synchronicity" and "Betweeness" in the Atemporal films of Shimizu Takashi', *Asian Cinema*, 22 (2): 178–95.
Bolter, J.D. and Grusin, R. (2000), *Remediation: Understanding New Media*, Cambridge, MA: MIT Press.
Booth, P. (2010), *Digital Fandom: New Media Studies*, New York: Peter Lang Publishing.
Braudy, L. and Cohen, M. (eds) (2004), *Film Theory and Criticism*, 6th edn, Oxford: Oxford University Press.
Braidotti, R. (2013), *The Posthuman*, Cambridge: Polity Press.
Brinkema, E. (2014), *The Forms of the Affects*, London: Duke University Press.

Brown, S.T. (2010), *Tokyo Cyberpunk: Posthumanism in Japanese Visual Culture*, New York: Palgrave Macmillan.
Brown, W. (2012), 'There Are as Many Paths to the Time-image as There Are Films in the World: Deleuze and the Lizard', in W. Brown and D. Martin-Jones (eds), *Deleuze and Film*, 88–103, Edinburgh: Edinburgh University Press.
Burch, N. (1992), *To the Distant Observer: Form and Meaning in the Japanese Cinema*, Revised edn, Berkeley: University of California Press.
Buruma, I. (2003), *Inventing Japan: 1853–1964*, New York: Modern Library.
Carroll, N. (1990), *The Philosophy of Horror or Paradoxes of the Heart*, Oxon: Routledge.
Cazdyn, E. (2014), 'Japanese Film without Japan: Toward a Non-Disciplined Film Studies', in D. Miyao (ed.), *The Oxford Handbook of Japanese Cinema*, 13–32, Oxford: Oxford University Press.
Charney, L. (1995), 'In a Moment: Film and the Philosophy of Modernity', in L. Charney and V.R. Schwartz (eds), *Cinema and the Invention of Modern Life*, 279–96, London: University of California Press.
Charney, L. and Schwartz, V. R (eds) (1995), *Cinema and the Invention of Modern Life*, London: University of California Press.
Chaudhuri, S. (2005), *Contemporary World Cinema: Europe, the Middle East, East Asia and South Asia*, Edinburgh: Edinburgh University Press.
Choi, J. and Wada-Marciano, M. (eds) (2009), *Horror to the Extreme: Changing Boundaries in Asian Cinema*, Aberdeen, Hong Kong: Hong Kong University Press.
Choo, K. (2013), 'Playing the Global Game: Japan Brand and Globalization', in A.Y.H. Fung (ed.), *Asian Popular Culture: The Global (Dis)continuity*, 213–30, London: Routledge.
Clark, A. (2003), *Natural-Born Cyborgs: Minds, Technologies, and the Future of Human Intelligence*, London: Oxford University Press.
Clover, C.J. (1992), *Men, Women and Chainsaws: Gender in Modern Horror Film*, Princeton, New Jersey: Princeton University Press.
Clover, C.J. (2002), 'Her Body, Himself: Gender in the Slasher Film', in M. Jancovich (ed.), *Horror, the Film Reader*, 77–90, London: Routledge.
Coates, J. (2016), *Making Icons: Repetition and the Female Image in Japanese Cinema, 1945–1964*, Aberdeen, Hong Kong: Hong Kong University Press.
Corrigan, T. (2017), 'Defining Adaptation', in T. Leitch (ed.), *The Oxford Handbook of Adaptation Studies*, 23–35, Oxford: Oxford University Press.
Creed, B. (1993), *The Monstrous-Feminine: Film, Feminism, Psychoanalysis*, Oxon: Routledge.
Creed, B. (2005), *Phallic Panic: Film, Horror and the Primal Uncanny*, Australia, Carlton: Melbourne University Press.
Crofts, S. (1998), 'Concepts of National Cinema', in P. Church-Gibson and J. Hill (eds), *The Oxford Guide to Film Studies*, 385–94, Oxford: Oxford University Press.
Culp, A. (2016), *Dark Deleuze and the Death of This World*, Minneapolis: University of Minnesota Press.
Davies, R.J. and Ikeno, O. (2002), *The Japanese Mind: Understanding Contemporary Japanese Culture*, Vermont: Tuttle Publishing.
Deamer, D. (2014), *Deleuze, Japanese Cinema, and the Atom Bomb: The Spectre of Impossibility*, London: Continuum Publishing Co.

Deleuze, G. (1968), *Difference and Repetition*, France: Presse Universitaires de France.
Deleuze, G. (2005), *Cinema 1: The Movement-Image*, London: Continuum.
Deleuze, G. (2013), *Cinema 2: The Time-Image*, London: Bloomsbury Academic.
Deleuze, G. and Guattari, F. (1987), *A Thousand Plateaus: Capitalism and Schizophrenia*, Minneapolis: University of Minnesota Press.
Deleuze, G. and Guattari, F. (2000), *Anti-Oedipus: Capitalism and Schizophrenia*, Minneapolis: University of Minnesota Press.
Deleuze, G. and Parnet, C. (2002), *Dialogues II*, London: Athlone.
Dennison, S. and Lim, S.H. (eds) (2006), *Remapping World Cinema: Identity, Culture and Politics in Film*, London: Wallflower Press.
Desjardins, C. (2005), *Outlaw Masters of Japanese Film*, London: I.B. Tauris & Co.
Deutsch, K. W (1966), *Nationalism and Social Communication: An Inquiry into the Foundations of Nationality*, 2nd edn, London: The MIT Press.
Ďurovičová, N. and Newman, K. (eds) (2010), *World Cinemas, Transnational Perspectives*, Oxon: Routledge.
Esfandiary, S. (2012), 'Banal Transnationalism: On Mohsen Makh Malbaf's "Borderless" Filmmaking', in S.M. Bâ S and W. Higbee (eds), *De-Westernizing Film Studies*, 101–12, Oxon: Routledge.
Ezra, E. and Rowden, T. (eds) (2006), *Transnational Cinema: The Film Reader*, Oxon: Routledge.
Faludi, S. (1999), *Stiffed: The Betrayal of the American Man*, New York: Harper Collins.
Fisher, M. (2016), *The Weird and the Eerie*, London: Repeater Books.
Freeland, C. (2000), *The Naked and the Undead: Evil and the Appeal of Horror*, Oxon: Routledge.
Freud, S. (1919), *The Uncanny*. Available online: http://web.mit.edu/allanmc/www/freud1.pdf (accessed 27 May 2020).
Galloway, A.R., Thacker, E. and Wark, M. (2014), *Excommunication: Three Enquiries in Media and Mediation*, Chicago: University of Chicago Press.
Gellner, E. (2009), *Nations and Nationalism*, 2nd edn, Oxford: Blackwell Publishing.
Gibbs, M. H. (2012), *Film and Political Culture in Postwar Japan*, New York: Peter Lang.
González, J. (2003), 'The Appended Subject: Race and Identity as Digital Assemblage', in E. Shohat and R. Stam (eds), *Multiculturalism, Postcoloniality, and Transnational Media*, 299–318, New Brunswick: Rutgers University Press.
Grant, B.K. (ed.) (2008), *Auteurs and Authorship: A Film Reader*, Oxford: Wiley-Blackwell.
Grusin, R.A. (2010), *Premediation: Affect and Mediality after 9/11*, New York: Palgrave Macmillan.
Hammer, S. (2014), 'Writing (Dirty) New Media/Glitch Composition', *Technoculture*, 4. Available online: https://tcjournal.org/vol4/hammer (accessed 18 July 2020).
Hand, R.J. (2005), 'Aesthetics of Cruelty: Traditional Japanese Theatre and the Horror Film', in J. McRoy (ed.), *Japanese Horror Cinema*, 18–28, Edinburgh: Edinburgh University Press.

Hand, R.J. and McRoy, J. (eds) (2007), *Monstrous Adaptations: Generic and Thematic Mutations in Horror Film*, Manchester: Manchester University Press.

Hantke, S. (2005), 'Japanese Horror under Western Eyes: Social Class and Global Culture in Miike Takashi's Audition', in J. McRoy (ed.), *Japanese Horror Cinema*, 54–65, Edinburgh: Edinburgh University Press.

Herbrechter, S. (2013), *Posthumanism: A Critical Analysis*, London: Bloomsbury Academic.

Herzog, A. (2012), 'Fictions of the Imagination: Habit, Genre and the Powers of the False', in W. Brown and D. Martin-Jones (eds), *Deleuze and Film*, 137–54, Edinburgh: Edinburgh University Press.

Higbee, W. (2012), 'De-Westernizing National Cinema: Reimagined Communities in the Films of Férid Boughedir', in S.M. Bâ and W. Higbee (eds), *De-Westernizing Film Studies*, 83–100, Oxon: Routledge.

Higson, A. (1989), 'The Concept of National Cinema', *Screen*, 30 (4): 36–46.

Higson, A. (2000), 'The Limiting Imagination of National Cinema', in M. Hjort and S. Mackenzie (eds), *Cinema and Nation*, 63–75, London: Routledge.

Higson, A. (2006), 'The Limiting Imagination of National Cinema', in E. Ezra and T. Rowden (eds), *Transnational Cinema, The Film Reader*, 15–26, Oxon: Routledge.

Hipkins, D. and Plain, G. (eds) (2007), *Wartorn Tales: Literature, Film and Gender in the Aftermath of World War II*, Oxford: Peter Lang.

Hjort, M. and Mackenzie S. (eds) (2000), *Cinema and Nation*, Oxon: Routledge.

Hodgkins, J. (2013), *The Drift: Affect, Adaptation, and New Perspectives on Fidelity*, London: Bloomsbury Academic.

Hughes, H. J. (2000), 'Familiarity of the Strange: Japan's Gothic Tradition', *Criticism*, 42 (1): 59–89.

Iida, Y. (2002), *Rethinking Identity in Modern Japan: Nationalism as Aesthetics*, London: Routledge.

Iles, T. (2008), *The Crisis of Identity in Contemporary Japanese Film: Personal, Cultural, National*, Leiden: Brill.

Iwabuchi, K. (2002), *Recentering Globalization: Popular Culture and Japanese Transnationalism*, London: Duke University Press.

Iwabuchi, K. (2005), 'Discrepant Intimacy: Popular Culture Flows in East Asia', in S.K. Chua and J.K. Erni (eds), *Asian Media Studies: Politics of Subjectivities*, 19–36, Oxford: Blackwell.

Iwabuchi, K. (2010), 'De-Westernization and the Governance of Global Cultural Connectivity: A Dialogic Approach to East Asian Media Cultures', *Postcolonial Studies*, 13 (4): 403–19.

Iwabuchi, K. (2015), *Resilient Borders and Cultural Diversity: Internationalism, Brand Nationalism, and Multiculturalism in Japan*, London: Lexington Books.

Japan-guide (2016), 'Bunraku – Japanese Puppet Theatre', *Japan-guide*. Available online: http://www.japan-guide.com/e/e2092.html (accessed 28 May 2020).

Kennedy, B.M. (2000), *Deleuze and Cinema: The Aesthetics of Sensation*, Edinburgh: Edinburgh University Press.

Kermode, M. (2003), 'Dread and Dripping', *The Observer Online*, 8 June. Available online: https://www.theguardian.com/film/2003/jun/08/features.review (accessed 8 August 2020).

Khorana, S. (ed.) (2013), *Crossover Cinema: Cross-Cultural Film from Production to Reception*, Oxon: Routledge.

Kinnia, Y.S-T. (2009), 'Psychological, Cultural, and Social Perspectives for Understanding the Representation of Women in Miike Takashi's Box', *Asian Cinema*, 20 (1): 203–18.

Ko, M. (2004), 'The Break-up of the National Body: Cosmetic Multiculturalism and the Films of Miike Takashi', *New Cinemas: Journal of Contemporary Film*, 2 (1): 29–39.

Kobayashi, H.H. (2013), 'The Miko and the Itako: The Role of Women in Contemporary Shinto Ritual', *Senior Capstone Projects*, 160. Available online: http://digitalwindow.vassar.edu/cgi/viewcontent.cgi?article=1159&context=senior_capstone (accessed 15 June 2020).

Kristeva, J. (1982), *Powers of Horror: An Essay on Abjection*, Chichester: Columbia University Press.

Kusina, J.M. (2008), 'Difference, Repetition, Disappearance, and Death: A Deleuzian Consideration of Kiyoshi Kurosawa's Kairo', *Rhizomes*, 16. Available online: http://rhizomes.net/issue16/kusina/index.html (accessed 14 July 2020).

Leitch, T. (ed.) (2017), *The Oxford Handbook of Adaptation Studies*, Oxford: Oxford University Press.

Lessig, L. (2017), 'Laws That Choke Creativity', *TED Talks*. Available online: https://www.youtube.com/watch?v=7Q25-S7jzgs (accessed 02 July 2020).

Lewis, G. (2005), 'Pinocchio 964, Death Powder and the Post-Human Condition', in J. McRoy (ed.), *Japanese Horror Cinema*, 120–9, Edinburgh: Edinburgh University Press.

Lim, B.C. (2009), *Translating Time: Cinema, the Fantastic, and Temporal Critique*, Durham: Duke University Press.

Livesey, G. (2010), 'Assemblage', in A. Parr (ed.), *The Deleuze Dictionary*, 18–19, Edinburgh: Edinburgh University Press.

Manovich, L. (2001), *The Language of New Media*, Cambridge: MIT Press.

Mantzavinos, C. (2016), 'Hermeneutics', *Stanford Encyclopedia of Philosophy*. Available online: http://plato.stanford.edu/entries/hermeneutics/ (accessed 8 August 2020).

Marks, L.U. (2000), *The Skin of the Film: Intercultural Cinema, Embodiment, and the Senses*, London: Duke University Press.

Marks, L. U. (2002), *Touch: Sensuous Theory and Multisensory Media*, Minneapolis: University of Minnesota Press.

Martin, D. (2009), 'Japan's Blair Witch: Restraint, Maturity, and Generic Canons in the British Critical Reception of Ring', *Cinema Journal*, 48 (3): 35–51.

Martin-Jones, D. (2006), *Deleuze, Cinema and National Identity: Narrative Time in National Contexts*, Edinburgh: Edinburgh University Press.

Martin-Jones, D. (2011), *Deleuze and World Cinemas*, London: Continuum Publishing.

Massumi, B. (2002), *Parables for the Virtual: Movement, Affect, Sensation*, London: Duke University Press.

McDonald, K.I. (2006), *Reading a Japanese Film: Cinema in Context*, Honolulu: University of Hawaii Press.

McGray, D. (2002), 'Japan's Gross National Cool', *Foreign Policy*, Available online: http://homes.chass.utoronto.ca/~ikalmar/illustex/japfpmcgray.htm (accessed 23 May 2020).

McRoy, J. (2005), 'Case Study: Cinematic Hybridity in Shimizu Takashi's Ju-On: The Grudge', in J. McRoy (ed.), *Japanese Horror Cinema*, 175–84, Edinburgh: Edinburgh University Press.

McRoy, J. (ed.) (2005), *Japanese Horror Cinema*, Edinburgh: Edinburgh University Press.

McRoy, J. (2008), *Nightmare Japan: Contemporary Japanese Horror Cinema*, Amsterdam: Rodopi.

Miéville, C. (2008), 'M.R. James and the Quantum Vampire Weird; Hauntological: Versus and/or and and/or or?', in R. Mackay (ed.), *Collapse Volume IV Concept Horror*, 105–26, Falmouth: Urbanomic.

Moussavi, G. (2013), 'My Tehran for Sale: A Coproduction with Poetry at Stake', in S. Khorana (ed.), *Crossover Cinema: Cross-cultural Film from Production to Reception*, 14–26, Oxon: Routledge.

Mulvey, L. (1975), 'Visual Pleasure and Narrative Cinema', in L. Braudy and M. Cohen (eds) (2004), *Film Theory and Criticism*, 6th edn, 837–48, Oxford: Oxford University Press.

Murphy, T, S. and Noys, B. (2016), 'Introduction: Old and New Weird', *Genre*, 49 (2): 117–34.

Nagib, L. (2006), 'Towards a Positive Definition of World Cinema', in S. Dennison and S.H. Lim (eds), *Remapping World Cinema: Identity, Culture and Politics in film*, 30–7, London: Wallflower Press.

Nakagawa, C. (2014), 'Desire for the Past: The Supernaturalization of *Yatsuhaka-mura*', in D. Och and K. Strayer (eds), *Transnational Horror across Visual Media: Fragmented Bodies*, 30–43, Oxon: Routledge.

Napier, S.J. (2005), *Anime from Akira to Howl's Moving Castle: Experiencing Contemporary Japanese Animation*, New York: Palgrave Macmillan.

Ndalianis, A. (2012), *The Horror Sensorium: Media and the Senses*: Jefferson, NC: McFarland.

Ng, A.H-S. (ed.) (2008), *Asian Gothic: Essays on Literature, Film and Anime*, NC: McFarland & Co.

Nichols, B. (ed.) (1985), *Movies and Methods Volume II*, Berkeley: University of California.

Nunes, M. (ed.) (2011), *Error: Glitch, Noise, and Jam in New Media Cultures*, London: Continuum Publishing.

Nussbaum, M.C. (1999), *Cultivating Humanity: A Classical Defense of Reform in Liberal Education*. Cambridge, MA: Harvard University Press.

Nussbaum, M. (2010), *Not for Profit. Why Democracy Needs the Humanities*. Princeton: Princeton University Press.

Och, D. and Strayer, K. (eds) (2014), *Transnational Horror across Visual Media: Fragmented Bodies*, Oxon: Routledge.

Parikka, J. and Tiainen, M. (2012), 'The Primacy of Movement: Variation, Intermediality and Biopolitics in Tero Saarinen's Hunt', in E. Barrett and B. Bolt (eds), *Carnal Knowledge: New Materialism through the Arts*, 205–24, London: I. B. Tauris & Co.

Picard, R. (1997), *Affective Computing*, Cambridge, MA: MIT Press.

Powell, A. (2005), *Deleuze and Horror Film*, Edinburgh: Edinburgh University Press.

Powell, A. (2007), *Deleuze, Altered States and Film*, Edinburgh: Edinburgh University Press.

Powell, A. (2012), 'The Daemons of Unplumbed Space: Mixing the Planes in Hellboy', in W. Brown and D. Martin-Jones (eds), *Deleuze and Film*, 173–91, Edinburgh: Edinburgh University Press.
Raine, M. (2014), 'Adaptation as "Transcultural Mimesis" in Japanese Cinema', in D. Miyao (ed.), *The Oxford Handbook of Japanese Cinema*, 101–23, Oxford: Oxford University Press.
Reyes, X.A. (2012), 'Beyond Psychoanalysis: Post-millennial Horror Film and Affect Theory', *Horror Studies*, 3 (2): 243–61.
Reyes, X.A. (2016), *Horror Film and Affect: Towards a Corporeal Model of Viewership*, London: Routledge.
Richards, A. (2010), *Asian Horror*, Harpenden: Kamera Books.
Richie, D. (1971), *Japanese Cinema: Film Style and National Character*, New York: Doubleday and Company.
Richie, D. (2005), *A Hundred Years of Japanese Film*, Tokyo: Kodansha.
Rio, E, D. (2008), *Deleuze and the Cinemas of Performance: Powers of Affection*, Edinburgh: Edinburgh University Press.
Robertson, J. (2010), 'The Erotic Grotesque Nonsense of Superflat: "Happiness" as Pathology in Japan Today', *Michigan Quarterly Review*, XLIX (1).
Rodrigues, L. (2012), 'Seeing Immanent Difference: Lorna Simpson and the Face's Affect', *Rhizomes*, 23. Available online: http://www.rhizomes.net/issue23/rodrigues/rodrigues.html (accessed 14 July 2020).
Rose, N. (2007), *The Politics of Life Itself: Biomedicine, Power and Subjectivity in the Twenty-First Century*, Princeton, NJ: Princeton University Press.
Said, E.W. (2003), *Orientalism*, London: Penguin.
Schlesinger, P. (2000), 'The Sociological Scope of National Cinema', in M. Hjort and S. Mackenzie (eds), *Cinema and Nation*, 19–31, Oxon: Routledge.
Schneider, S.J. (ed.) (2004), *Horror Film and Psychoanalysis: Freud's Worst Nightmare*, Cambridge: Cambridge University Press.
Schodt, F. (1996), *Dreamland Japan: Writing on Modern Manga*, Berkeley: Stone Bridge Press.
Shaviro, S. (1993), *The Cinematic Body*, London: University of Minnesota Press.
Shaviro, S. (2010), *Post Cinematic Affect*, Ropley: Zero Books.
Shin, C-Y. (2009), 'The Art of Branding: Tartan "Asia Extreme" Films', in J. Choi and M. Wada-Marciano (eds), *Horror to the Extreme: Changing Boundaries in Asian Cinema*, 85–100, Aberdeen, Hong Kong: Hong Kong University Press.
Shohat, E. and Stam, R. (1994), *Unthinking Eurocentrism: Multiculturalism and the Media*, London: Routledge.
Shohat, E. and Stam, R. (eds) (2003), *Multiculturalism, Postcoloniality, and Transnational Media*, New Brunswick: Rutgers University Press.
Silverberg, M. (2009), *Erotic, Grotesque, Nonsense: The Mass Culture of Japanese Modern Times*, Berkeley: University of California Press.
Singer, B. (2014), 'Triangulating Japanese Film Style', in D. Miyao (ed.), *The Oxford Handbook of Japanese Cinema*, 33–60, Oxford: Oxford University Press.
Sky Movies, (2011), 'Quentin Tarantino's Favourite movies from 1992 to 2009', *Sky Movies*. Available online: https://www.youtube.com/watch?v=Zv0WlHbBhdc (accessed: 29 June 2020).
Smith, A.D. (2001), *Nationalism: Theory, Ideology, History*, Cambridge: Polity Press.

Smith, A.D. (2007), 'Nations in Decline? The Erosion and Persistence of Modern National Identities', in A. Sturm, M. Young and E. Zuelow (eds), *Nationalism in a Global Era: The Persistence of Nations*, 16–29, London: Taylor and Francis.

Stadler, J. (2010), 'Cultural Value and Viscerality in Sukiyaki Western Django: Towards a Phenomenology of Bad Film', *Continuum: Journal of Media and Cultural Studies*, 24 (5): 679–91.

Stam, R. and Raengo, A. (eds) (2005), *Literature and Film: A Guide to the Theory and Practice of Film Adaptation*, Oxford: Blackwell Publishing.

Standish, I. (2006), *A New History of Japanese Cinema: A Century of Narrative Film*, London: Continuum.

Standish, I. (2012), 'The Ephemeral as Transcultural Aesthetic: A Contextualization of the Early Films of Ozu Yasujirō', *Journal of Japanese and Korean Cinema*, 4 (1): 3–14.

Stern, N. (2013), *Interactive Art and Embodiment: The Implicit Body as Performance*, Canterbury: Glyphi.

Taylor-Jones, K.E. (2007), 'From "Wise Mother" to Prostitute: Women as Duality in Postwar Japan', in D. Hipkins and G. Plain (eds), *Wartorn Tales: Literature, Film and Gender in the Aftermath of World War II*, 123–42, Oxford: Peter Lang.

Taylor-Jones, K.E. (2013), *Rising Sun, Divided Land: Japanese and South Korean Filmmakers*, London: Wallflower Press.

Tezuka, Y. (2012), *Japanese Cinema Goes Global: Filmworkers' Journeys*, Aberdeen, Hong Kong: Hong University Press.

Thacker, E. (2003), 'Data Made Flesh: Biotechnology and the Discourse of the Posthuman', *Cultural Critique*, 53 (1): 72–97.

Thacker, E. (2004), *Biomedia*, Minneapolis: University of Minnesota Press.

Thacker, E. (2014), 'Dark Media', in A.R. Galloway, E. Thacker and M. Wark (eds), *Excommunication: Three Enquiries in Media and Mediation*, 77–150, Chicago: University of Chicago Press.

The-Noh.com (no date), 'Noh Plays DataBase: Kanawa (Iron Trivet) Synopsis and Highlight', *The-Noh.com*. Available online: http://www.the-noh.com/en/plays/data/program_026.html (accessed 28 May 2020).

The-Noh.com (no date), 'Noh Plays DataBase: Koi no Omoni (the deadweight of love): Synopsis and Highlight', *The-Noh.com*. Available online: http://www.the-noh.com/en/plays/data/program_064.html (accessed 28 May 2020).

Turkle, S. (2012), 'Connected, but Alone?' *TED Talks*. Available online: http://www.ted.com/talks/sherry_turkle_alone_together?language=en (accessed 18 July 2020).

Verbeek, P, P. (2011), *Moralizing Technology: Understanding and Designing the Morality of Things*, Chicago: University of Chicago Press.

Vitali, V. and Willemen, P. (eds) (2006), *Theorising National Cinema*, London: British Film Institute.

Wada-Marciano, M. (2009), 'J-Horror: New Media's Impact on Contemporary Japanese Horror Cinema', in J. Choi and M. Wada-Marciano (eds), *Horror to the Extreme: Changing Boundaries in Asian Cinema*, 15–38, Aberdeen, Hong Kong: Hong Kong University Press.

Walter, B.S.G. (2014), 'Spectres of History. Ghastly Transmissions: The Horror of Connectivity and the Transnational Flow of Fear', in D. Och and K. Strayer

(eds), *Transnational Horror across Visual Media: Fragmented Bodies*, 17–29, New York: Routledge.
White, E. (2005), 'Case Study: Nakata Hideo's Ringu and Ringu 2', in J. McRoy (ed.), *Japanese Horror Cinema*, 38–50, Edinburgh: Edinburgh University Press.
William (2016), 'Will 2016 See the Return of Japanese Horror Movies?', *Japan Trends*. Available online: http://www.japantrends.com/2016-japanese-horror-movies-revival/ (accessed 25 July 2020).
Williams, L. (2002), 'When the Woman Looks', in M. Jancovich (ed.), *Horror, the Film Reader*, 61–6, London: Routledge.
Wolfe, C. (2009), *What Is Posthumanism?*, Minneapolis: University of Minnesota Press.
Wollen, P. (1969), 'The Auteur Theory', in L. Braudy and M. Cohen (eds) (2004), *Film Theory and Criticism*, 6th edn, 565–80, Oxford: Oxford University Press.
Wood, R. (1985), 'An Introduction to the American Horror Film', in B. Nichols (ed.), *Movies and Methods Volume II*, 195–219, Berkeley: University of California.
Yoshimoto, M. (2000), *Kurosawa: Film Studies and Japanese Cinema*, Durham Duke University Press.
Youth Arts New York. (2013), 'Who Are the Hibakusha?' *Youth Arts New York*. Available online: http://www.hibakushastories.org/who-are-the-hibakusha/ (accessed 28 May 2020).
Zahlten, A. (2014), 'Media Mix and the Metaphoric Economy of World', in D. Miyao (ed.), *The Oxford Handbook of Japanese Cinema*, 438–56, Oxford: Oxford University Press.
Zuern, J. (1998), *Lacan: The Mirror Stage*, University of Hawai'i. Available online: http://www.english.hawaii.edu/criticallink/lacan/ (accessed 26 May 2020).

FILMOGRAPHY

A Nightmare on Elm Street (1984), [Film] Dir. Wes Craven, USA: New Line Cinema.
Alien: Covenant (2017), [Film] Dir. Ridley Scott, USA: Twentieth Century Fox.
Apartment 1303 (2007), [Film] Dir. Oikawa Ataru, Japan: 3G Communications.
Audition (1999), [Film] Dir. Miike Takashi, Japan: Art Port.
Bakushū (Early Summer) (1951), [Film] Dir. Ozu Yasujirō, Japan: Shōchiku.
Battle Royale (2000), [Film] Dir. Fukasaku Kinji, Japan: Toei Company.
Boarding Gate (2007), [Film] Dir. Olivier Assayas, France: MK2 Diffusion.
Carrie (1976), [Film] Dir. Brian De Palma, USA: United Artists.
Chakushin Ari (One Missed Call) (2003), [Film] Dir. Miike Takashi, Japan: Toho Film Company.
Chūgoku no chōjin (The Bird People in China) (1998), [Film] Dir. Miike Takashi, Japan: Excellent Film, Sedic.
Citizen Kane (1941), [Film] Dir. Orson Welles, USA: RKO Radio Pictures.
Cloverfield (2008), [Film] Dir. Matt Reeves, USA: Paramount Pictures.
Dark Water (2005), [Film] Dir. Walter Salles, USA: Buena Vista Pictures.
Destruction Babies (2016), [Film] Dir. Tetsuya Mariko, Japan: Tokyo Theatres K.K.
Dial M for Murder (1954), [Film] Dir. Alfred Hitchcock, USA: Warner Bros.
Django Unchained (2012), [Film] Dir. Quentin Tarantino, USA: The Weinstein Company.
Friday the 13th (1980), [Film] Dir. Sean S. Cunningham, USA: Paramount Pictures.
Gabal (The Wig) (2005), [Film] Dir. Shin-Yeon Won, South Korea: Korea Entertainment.
Gojira (Godzilla) (1954), [Film] Dir. Honda Ishirō, Japan: Toho Film Company.
Gokudō Kuroshakai (Rainy Dog) (1997), [Film] Dir. Miike Takashi, Japan: Daiei.
Gokudō Sengokushi: Fudō (Fudoh: The New Generation) (1996), [Film] Dir. Miike Takashi, Japan: Artsmagic.
Greatful Dead (2013), [Film] Dir. Eiji Uchida, Japan: Ark Entertainment.
Halloween (1978), [Film] Dir. John Carpenter, USA: Aquarius Releasing, Compass International Pictures.
Hostel (2005), [Film] Dir. Eli Roth, USA: Lions Gate Films.
House (1977), [Film] Dir. Ôbayashi Nobuhiko, Japan: Toho Film Company.
House on Haunted Hill (1959), [Film] Dir. William Castle, USA: Allied Artists Pictures.
Hyōryū Gai (The City of Lost Souls) (2000), [Film] Dir. Miike Takashi, Japan: Daiei.
I Spit on Your Grave (1978), [Film] Dir. Meir Zarchi, USA: Cinemagic.

Jisatsu Saakuru (Suicide Club) (2001), [Film] Dir. Sono Sion, Japan: Earthrise.
Ju-On: Origins (2020-), [TV]. USA: Netflix.
Ju-On: The Grudge (2002), [Film] Dir. Shimizu Takashi, Japan: Lions Gate Films.
Jūsan-nin no Shikaku (13 Assassins) (2010), [Film] Dir. Miike Takashi, Japan: Toho Film Company.
Kaibyo Otama-ga-ike (The Ghost Cat of Otama Pond) (1960), [Film] Dir. Ishikawa Yoshihiro, Japan: Shintōhō.
Kairo (Pulse) (2001), [Film] Dir. Kurosawa Kiyoshi, Japan: Toho Film Company.
Kawaki (The World of Kanako) (2014), [Film] Dir. Nakashima Tetsuya, Japan: GAGA.
Kill Bill: Vol. 1 (2003), [Film] Dir. Quentin Tarantino, USA: Miramax.
Koroshiya 1 (Ichi the Killer) (2001), [Film] Dir. Miike Takashi, Japan: Prénom H Co. Ltd.
Kuriipii: Itsuwari no rinjin (Creepy) (2016), [Film] Dir. Kurosawa Kiyoshi, Japan: Shochiku.
La Passion de Jeanne d'Arc (The Passion of Joan of Arc) (1928), [Film] Dir. Carl Theodor Dreyer, France: Gaumont.
Marebito (2004), [Film] Dir. Shimizu Takashi, Japan: Euro Space.
Nagai Yume (Long Dream) (2000), [Film] Dir. Higuchinsky, Japan: SPO.
One Missed Call (2008), [Film] Dir. Eric Valette, USA: Toho Film Company.
Project Zero (2001–) [Video game series] Dev. Koei Tecmo, Japan: Koei Tecmo.
Psycho (1960), [Film] Dir. Alfred Hitchcock, USA: Shamley Productions, Paramount Pictures.
Rasen (Spiral) (1998), [Film] Dir. Iida Jōji, Japan: Toho Film Company.
Rear Window (1954), [Film] Dir. Alfred Hitchcock, USA: Paramount Pictures.
Rings (2017), [Film] Dir. F. Javier Gutiérrez, USA: Paramount Pictures.
Ringu (1998), [Film] Dir. Nakata Hideo, Japan: Toho Film Company.
Ringu 2 (1999), [Film] Dir. Nakata Hideo, Japan: Toho Film Company.
Saw (2004), [Film] Dir. James Wan, USA: Lions Gate Pictures.
Southland Tales (2006), [Film] Dir. Richard Kelly, USA: Destination Films.
Sukiyaki Western Django (2007), [Film] Dir. Miike Takashi, Japan: Sony Pictures Entertainment.
Sweet Home (1989), [Film] Dir. Kurosawa Kiyoshi, Japan: Toho Film Company.
The Birds (1963), [Film] Dir. Alfred Hitchcock, USA: Universal Pictures.
The Blair Witch Project (1999), [Film] Dirs. Daniel Myrick, Eduardo Sanchez, USA: Artisan Entertainment.
The Grudge (2004), [Film] Dir. Shimizu Takashi, USA: Sony Pictures Entertainment.
The Grudge (2020), [Film] Dir. Nicolas Pesce, USA: Sony Pictures Releasing.
The Grudge 2 (2006), [Film] Dir. Shimizu Takashi, USA: Columbia Pictures.
The Grudge 3 (2009), [Film] Dir. Toby Wilkins, USA: Sony Pictures Home Entertainment.
The Haunting (1963), [Film] Dir. Robert Wise, UK: Metro-Goldwyn-Mayer.
The Innocents (1961), [Film] Dir. Jack Clayton, UK: Twentieth Century Fox.
The Mist (2007), [Film] Dir. Frank Darabont, USA: Metro-Goldwyn-Mayer.
The Ring (2002), [Film] Dir. Gore Verbinski, USA: DreamWorks.
The Ring 2 (2005), [Film] Dir. Nakata Hideo, USA: DreamWorks.

The Walking Dead (2010–), [TV]. USA: AMC.
Tōkaidō Yotsuya Kaidan (*Ghost Story of Yotsuya in Tōkaidō*) (1959), [Film] Dir. Nakagawa Nobuo, Japan: Shintōhō.
Tōkyō Monogatari (*Tokyo Story*) (1953), [Film] Dir. Ozu Yasujirō, Japan: Shōchiku Eiga.
Tomie: Re-birth (2001), [Film] Dir. Shimizu Takashi, Japan: Planet Entertainment.
Tonari no Totoro (*My Neighbor Totoro*) (1988), [Film] Dir. Miyazaki Hayao, Japan: Toho Film Company.
Ugetsu Monogatari (*Tales of Moonlight and Rain*) (1953), [Film] Dir. Mizoguchi Kenji, Japan: Daiei.
Uzumaki (*Spiral*) (2000), [Film] Dir. Higuchinsky, Japan: Tidepoint Pictures.
Visitor Q (2001), [Film] Dir. Miike Takashi, Japan: CineRocket.
Yabu no Naka no Kuroneko (*Kuroneko*) (1968), [Film] Dir. Shindō Kaneto, Japan: Toho Film Company.
Zan'e: Sunde wa ikenai heya (*The Inerasable*) (2016), [Film] Dir. Nakamura Yoshihiro Japan: Shochiku.

INDEX

a-temporal *See also* time-image
   in *Audition* 9, 109–10, 112–13, 133–4, 142, 144–5, 150–2, 155
   in Deleuzian philosophy 2, 4, 57, 59, 61
   in *Ju-On: The Grudge* 8, 75–9, 81–4, 86–9, 96, 102, 106, 198, 210–11
   in *Kairo* (*Pulse*) 156, 164, 199
abject
   and glitches/errors 191
   and Japan 36–7, 39–40
   femininity 32–3, 35, 38–40, 71, 91–3, 169
   theory 32, 35–6, 38–40, 71, 196
action-image 53–5, 58, 155
   large form action-image/SAS 2, 52, 54, 62
   small form action-image/ASA 52, 54
adaptation
   and *Audition* 109–11, 122, 127, 212
   and *Ju-On: The Grudge* 89, 124–5
   theory 5–6, 9, 110, 122–7, 212
affect
   and adaptation 126–7, 130, 133–7, 142, 212
   and audience subjectivity/experience 6, 26–8, 39–41, 57–8, 75, 79, 82–3, 86, 95, 98–9, 103, 109–10, 121–2, 126–7, 136–7, 141–2, 144, 147, 149, 161–2, 166, 192, 201
   and glitches/errors 192, 195
   and national, transnational and global discourse 24, 26–8, 50, 64, 69, 87–9, 128, 157–8, 180, 197, 199, 207, 215
   and the auteur 110, 113, 116, 118–22
   and the celebrity 38, 118
   and the horror genre 3, 38–40, 70–1
   and woman 39–40, 92, 99 (*see also* becoming-woman)
   in *Audition* 109–10, 113, 116, 118–22, 126–8, 130, 133–7, 139, 141–2, 144, 147, 149
   in cosmic/weird horror 172
   in Deleuzian philosophy 2–6, 39–41, 44–6, 49–50, 53–4, 56–60, 116, 207–8
   in *Ju-On: The Grudge* 75–7, 79, 81–4, 86–9, 92, 95–101, 103
   in *Kairo* (*Pulse*) 156–63, 166–7, 170, 172, 180, 188, 191–3, 195–7, 199, 201
   in premediating texts 195–6
   in Shaviro 26–8, 40, 50, 118, 195–6
affection-image 53–4, 56–7, 83, 99, 116
Alien: Covenant (Scott) 176
Allison, Anne 24, 64, 79, 199
Anderson, Benedict O'Gorman Richard 16–19, 62
Anthropocene 175–6, 213–14
anti-environment 196–8
any-person-whoever 79, 99, 105, 161 *See also* body without organs
any-space-whatever
   amorphous set 57
   in *Audition* 110, 112, 134, 156
   in Deleuzian philosophy 56–9, 62, 71, 180, 207

in Japanese society 64, 176–77, 193, 195, 207, 209
in *Ju-On: The Grudge* 76, 79, 81–2, 84–5, 87, 90, 99, 102, 106, 210–11
in *Kairo (Pulse)* 157, 160, 162, 172, 175, 177, 193, 200, 213
Apartment 1303 (Oikawa) 29
Appadurai, Arjun 20, 26
art of dosages 5, 41, 48, 71–2, 81, 180, 186, 208
assemblage
  adaptation, intertextuality and assemblage 110, 120–7, 132–4, 136–7, 142, 144, 149, 154–6, 210, 212
  and *Audition* 9, 107, 136–7, 147, 153, 210
  and film characters 8–9, 57, 59, 75–6, 83, 91, 95, 98–9, 102, 105–6, 137, 153, 156, 158–62, 166–8, 176, 188, 193–5, 197, 199, 203, 205, 210–11, 213
  and *Ju-On: The Grudge* 76, 78, 82–3, 86–8, 91, 95–6, 98–9, 102, 105–6, 210–11
  and *Kairo (Pulse)* 157–62, 166–8, 176, 183, 186–8, 193–7, 199–201, 203, 205, 213–14
  and technology 67, 156, 159–60, 181–3, 185–8, 197, 201, 203, 205, 213–14
  and the audience 8, 40, 49, 57, 59, 66, 75–6, 78–9, 82–3, 86, 95, 98–9, 102, 106, 118, 121, 127, 142, 147, 160, 162, 165–7, 195, 197, 199, 208, 210
  and the auteur 9, 110–22
  and the celebrity 118
  and the horror genre 38, 69–70, 125
  and the national, cultural and social 25, 61, 63, 66–7, 69, 76, 78–9, 87–8, 123, 157, 165, 179–83, 185, 193, 195–6, 200, 203, 205, 208
  and woman 72 (*see also* becoming-woman)

in Deleuzian and Guattarian philosophy 4–5, 9, 13, 44–7, 49–50, 53, 56–9, 79, 116, 179, 194, 208, 210
industrial assemblage 112–14, 117–18, 123, 208, 212, 214
Aum Shinrikyō 67–8, 175, 180, 197, 203, 214
auteur
  and Miike 9, 109–12, 114–16, 119–21, 212
  and Murakami 9, 110–11, 119–21, 212
  and Ozu 112
  and Tarantino 114–16
  theory 5–6, 9, 111–19, 121–2, 212
author-function 117, 121

Bakushū (Early Summer) (Ozu) 56–7
Balmain, Collette 1, 14, 28, 30–1, 36, 92, 94, 154
Battle Royale (Fukasaku) 1, 30
becoming
  and adaptation, transmedia storytelling and intertextuality 87–90, 110, 124–6, 132–4, 136–7, 142, 144
  and audience 6, 8, 26–7, 38, 40, 44, 49, 55, 57–9, 62–3, 65–6, 70–1, 75–6, 79, 82–6, 90, 95–6, 98–9, 102, 106, 109–10, 147, 149, 157, 159–61, 167, 175, 185, 193–202, 210 (*see also* deterritorialize)
  and glitches/errors 194–5
  and posthumanism and transhumanism 10, 180–1, 186–7, 195, 201, 203, 205, 213–14
  and premediating texts 196
  and the auteur 113, 115–22
  and the celebrity 118
  and the cosmic/weird 173–5, 177, 194
  in *Audition* 110, 113, 128, 130, 132–7, 139, 142, 144, 147, 151, 153, 155
  in Deleuzian and Guattarian philosophy 5, 25, 36, 45, 47–9, 55–7, 59, 65, 71–2, 208, 210

in *Ju-On: The Grudge* 76, 79, 81–4, 86–93, 95–102, 104–6, 198
in *Kairo* 156, 158–61, 163–5, 167–8, 170, 176, 183, 187–91, 193–8, 201, 203, 205, 213–14
becoming-animal 93–4
becoming-machine 10, 159–60, 167, 187–91, 193–4, 197, 203, 213–14
becoming-other *See* becoming
becoming-woman
  in *Audition* 134, 151–6, 212
  in Deleuzian and Guattarian philosophy 8, 40, 71–2, 91
  in *Ju-On: The Grudge* 75, 90–106, 211
Bergson, Henri 50–1
Birds, The (Hitchcock) 33, 53
Blair Witch Project, The (Myrick, Sanchez) 31
blocs of affect *See* affect; in Shaviro
Boarding Gate (Assayas) 27
body without organs 44–6, 48, 55, 72, 79, 91, 106, 159, 163, 167, 213
Braidotti, Rosi 174–6, 178–9, 181–2, 186–9
break (in linear time)
  and 9/11 195
  and the cosmic/weird 160, 177, 213
  and the First World War 177
  and the Second World War and post-war 3, 39–40, 57–63
  economic crash and related, contemporary events 3, 8, 41, 61–3, 65–6, 68–9, 90, 129, 149, 157, 160, 176–8, 182–3, 193, 197, 200, 202, 205, 207, 209, 213
  in Deleuzian philosophy 3, 53, 55, 57–61, 207, 209
  in *Ju-On: The Grudge* 84, 95
  in *Kairo* (*Pulse*) 165, 176–8, 182–3, 193, 195, 197, 200, 202, 205
Brown, Steven 158, 166, 188, 193, 197, 200
Brown, William 55, 79
Buddhism 14, 28, 32

Carrie (De Palma) 33
Chakushin Ari (*One Missed Call*) (Miike) 1, 6, 29
Chaudhuri, Shohini 14, 19
Chūgoku no chōjin (*The Bird People in China*) (Miike) 119
Citizen Kane (Welles) 59
Clover, Carol 101, 105–6, 125, 211
Cloverfield (Reeves) 176
Coates, Jennifer 38–40, 60, 62, 71
cosmic horror 5, 10, 160, 167, 170–8, 192, 202, 211, 213–14
Creed, Barbara 32–5, 92, 196
crystal-image 55–8 *See also* time-image *and* duration
Culp, Andrew 91, 187, 194, 214

Deamer, David 8, 37, 40–1, 116
Deleuze, Gilles 4, 7–10, 25–6, 28, 38, 40–1, 43–4, 60–2, 69–72, 77, 90–2, 110–11, 116–17, 122–6, 159, 173, 177, 179, 186–7, 194, 208, 210–12, 214–15
  Cinema 1: The Movement-Image 2, 3, 48–57, 83, 116, 122
  Cinema 2: The Time-Image 2, 3, 27, 49–52, 55–61, 71–2, 84–5, 116, 122
  Difference and Repetition 39
Deleuze, Gilles and Guattari, Félix 26, 49–50, 180, 187, 208
  A Thousand Plateaus: Capitalism and Schizophrenia 5, 45–8, 71, 81, 162, 186, 208
  Anti-Oedipus: Capitalism and Schizophrenia 36, 38, 44–5, 47, 71, 179
Deleuze, Gilles and Parnet, Claire
  Dialogues II 105
Dennison, Stephanie and Lim, Song Hwee 21, 25
Desjardins, Chris 111–12
Destruction Babies (Tetsuya) 35
deterritorialize
  and humanism, posthumanism/transhumanism 175–6, 178–81, 193, 200, 205, 213
  and the auteur 111, 116

in *Audition* 9, 110, 121, 128–9, 132–5, 139, 141, 144–5, 147, 149–53, 155–6, 212
in contemporary society 8, 15–16, 19, 27–8, 64, 66, 68–9, 76, 79, 90, 113, 129, 149, 157, 165, 175–6, 179, 181–2, 193, 195, 200, 205, 209–10
in cultural products 24, 27–8, 50, 195
in Deleuzian and Guattarian philosophy 5, 7, 38, 45–50, 53, 55, 57–9, 69, 72, 81, 92, 125, 163, 179–80, 208–11
in *Ju-On: The Grudge* 8, 75–6, 79, 81–8, 90–1, 94, 96, 99, 102–3, 105–6, 109, 167, 209–11
in *Kairo* 9–10, 156–7, 159–63, 167, 176–7, 199–202, 205, 213
in the cosmic/weird 173–7
Dial M for Murder (Hitchcock) 53
Django Unchained (Tarantino) 114
duration 3, 48–9, 51–2, 54–9, 71, 208
and *Ju-On: The Grudge* 76, 85, 89
and *Audition* 121–2, 156

electronic presence 193, 197
enjo kōsai 66, 180, 202
Ezra, Elizabeth and Rowden, Terry 19–21, 25, 28

final girl 75, 101, 105–6, 211–12
Fisher, Mark 170–1, 177
Freud, Sigmund 32–3, 35–6, 92, 154
Friday the 13th (Cunningham) 31

Gabal (The Wig) (Shin-Yeon) 88–9
Galloway, Alexander, Thacker, Eugene and Wark, McKenzie 192–4, 198–9, 214
Gellner, Ernest 16, 18–19, 62
globalization
and consumer culture 23–4, 118, 179–80
and film studies 19–28
and glocalization 22–3
and national society 15, 19–28, 37, 50, 61–4, 68–9, 79, 81, 118, 158, 174–5, 177–80, 182–3, 195, 209, 213
and renderings in horror 37, 50, 61, 77, 79, 81, 158, 174–5, 177, 182–3, 193, 200, 205, 209, 213
and subjectivity 26–8, 62–4, 68–9, 79, 81, 118, 158, 174–80, 182–3, 194–5, 200, 205, 209, 213
Gojira (Godzilla) (Honda) 37
Gokudō Kuroshakai (Rainy Dog) (Miike) 115
Gokudō Sengokushi: Fudō (Fudoh: The New Generation) (Miike) 114
gothic horror 31–2, 160, 169–70, 172–3
Greatful Dead (Eiji) 35
ground *See* reterritorialize
Grudge, The (Pesce) 6, 89
Grudge, The (Shimizu) 1
Grudge 2, The (Shimizu) 88
Grudge 3, The (Wilkins) 88
Grusin, Richard 192, 195–6

Halloween (Carpenter) 31
Hammer, Steven 195–6
Hand, Richard 29–30
Haunting, The (Wise) 31
Heisei recession 3, 63, 199 *See also* break (in linear time)
Herbrechter, Stefan 201–2
hermeneutics *See also* molar
and horror genre studies 38, 40, 70–1
and national, transnational and world cinema 15, 22, 25–7
definition 1–2, 207–8
in *Audition* 9, 109, 118, 124, 128–9, 134–5, 138, 142, 150, 154–5, 209
in Deleuzian philosophy 2–8, 26–7, 38, 40–1, 43, 45–8, 51, 70–1, 208, 215
in *Ju-On: The Grudge* 75–6, 78, 81, 83–4, 103, 105, 209, 210–11
in *Kairo (Pulse)* 9–10, 160–1, 167–8, 173, 178
hibakusha 36–7
Higson, Andrew 20–1

hikikomori 158, 160, 166, 182, 214
Hjort, Mette and Mackenzie, Scott 13, 15–16, 21
Hodgkins, John 110, 122–4, 126, 212
Hostel (Roth) 70
House (Ôbayashi) 31
House on Haunted Hill (Castle) 31
humanism 18, 113, 174–6, 178–81, 186
Hyōryū Gai (The City of Lost Souls) (Miike) 115

I Spit on Your Grave (Zarchi) 33
Iida, Yumiko 63–8, 128–9, 175, 202–3, 211
Iles, Timothy 63, 129
immanence 47, 83, 118, 133, 149, 188
indetermination (centre of) 2–3, 6, 21, 39–40, 54, 56, 208–9
  in *Audition* 110
  in *Ju-On: The Grudge* 78–9, 84, 91, 98
  in *Kairo (Pulse)* 159–63, 170, 193, 197
Innocents, The (Clayton) 31
intensity *See* affect
intensive series 57
Iwabuchi, Kōichi
  De-Westernization and the Governance of Global Cultural Connectivity: A Dialogic Approach to East Asian Media Cultures 22
  Discrepant Intimacy: Popular Culture Flows in East Asia 25
  Recentering Globalization: Popular Culture and Japanese Transnationalism 21–2, 24, 62
  Resilient Borders and Cultural Diversity: Internationalism, Brand Nationalism and Multiculturalism in Japan 19–21, 23–4, 28, 30, 63, 68–9

J-cool 23–4, 69
Jisatsu Saakuru (Suicide Club) (Sono) 30
Ju-On: Origins (Netflix) 89

Jūsan-nin no Shikaku (13 Assassins) (Miike) 114

Kabuki theatre 14, 28–30
Kaibyō Otama-ga-ike (The Ghost Cat of Otama Pond) (Ishikawa) 94
Kawaki (The World of Kanako) (Nakashima) 35
Kennedy, Barbara 44, 48, 72
Kill Bill: Vol.1 (Tarantino) 114–15
Kinnia, Yau Shuk-ting 28, 77–8
Ko, Mika 37, 119, 149–50
Kogyaru (kogal) 65–6, 135–6
kokutai 17, 37, 66, 149 *See also* national; ideology *and* national; culture and identity (Japan)
Koroshiya 1 (Ichi the Killer) (Miike) 114, 119, 121
Kristeva, Julia 32–3, 39, 196
Kuriipii: Itsuwari no rinjin (Creepy) (Kurosawa) 6
Kusina, Jeanne Marie 163–6, 182

La Passion de Jeanne d'Arc (The Passion of Joan of Arc) (Dreyer) 83
Leitch, Thomas 123–4
Lim, Bliss Cua 55, 61
line of flight 1, 46–50, 54, 70, 121, 124, 131, 163, 170, 194 *See also* molecular
line of segmentarity 45–8, 69–70, 91, 110, 132, 134, 156, 163, 166, 208 *See also* molar
Lovecraft, Howard, Phillips 170–3, 177

macro-politics 44–6, 51 *See also* molar
Marebito (Shimizu) 31
Marks, Laura 43, 59
Martin-Jones, David 7, 28, 52, 58, 60, 62, 84, 90–1, 208
McDonald, Keiko 14, 29
McRoy, Jay 1, 28, 31, 76–7, 149
mental-image 53–4
micro-politics 44–5, 50 *See also* molecular
Miéville, China 173–5, 177

mirror phase 33, 72
Mist, The (Darabont) 176
molar
   and becoming-woman 72, 91–2, 105, 211
   and societal conditions 26–8, 41, 50, 59, 69, 160, 187, 209–10
   and the auteur 9
   and the cosmic/weird 160, 174–5
   and the horror genre 69–70
   in *Audition* 9, 110, 127, 129–30, 132–4, 141–2, 144, 149–50, 152, 154, 156, 212
   in Coates 40
   in Deleuzian and Guattarian philosophy 5, 41, 44–8, 50–1, 54–7, 59, 69, 71–2, 81, 84, 91–2, 180, 187, 208–10
   in *Ju-On: The Grudge* 75–6, 78–9, 81, 83–6, 88–9, 91, 95, 98, 104–5
   in *Kairo* 156, 159–61, 163, 193, 199, 205, 213
   in Shaviro 27–8, 40, 79
molecular
   and becoming-woman 72
   and consumer culture 65
   and societal conditions 27–8, 41, 50, 60, 69, 79, 209
   and the auteur 9, 118–19
   and the horror genre 70
   in *Audition* 9, 110, 132–4, 144, 156
   in Coates 40
   in Deleuzian and Guattarian philosophy 5, 41, 44–8, 50, 69, 72, 81, 92, 208–10, 215
   in *Ju-On: The Grudge* 91
   in *Kairo* 156, 163, 202, 205, 213
   in Shaviro 27–8, 40, 118
monstrous-female 8, 33–5, 38, 75, 92, 95, 105, 128, 155–6, 169, 209, 211–12
movement-image 2–3, 50–5, 57, 59, 62, 84, 112, 208
multifaceted *See also* multiplicity
   cinema 77, 118, 120, 125, 132, 134, 137, 156

society 15, 19, 24, 62, 69, 78–9, 131, 177, 200, 209
subjectivity 5, 8, 38, 44, 78, 132, 135, 137, 142, 151, 179, 193, 200
multiplicity 36, 38–40, 46–7, 49, 51, 70–1, 78, 86, 95, 105, 179, 183, 189, 198, 208
multipotentiality 2, 48–9, 54–9, 76, 84, 110–11, 116, 150, 154, 167, 189, 194
Murphy, Timothy and Noys, Benjamin 170–1, 173–6
mutable *See* becoming *and* deterritorialize

national
   cinema 5, 8, 13–22, 25, 28, 36–7, 39, 60–2, 76, 78–9, 82, 87–8, 90–2, 114–16, 118, 128–30, 149–50, 159–61, 182–3, 209–10
   culture and identity (Japan) 16–25, 28, 35–7, 39–40, 46, 60–9, 71, 78–9, 92, 114–16, 128–32, 149–50, 158, 177, 180, 182–3, 195, 209–10, 213–14
   differences 16–21, 23, 25, 35–6, 60, 62, 69
   ideology 7, 14–25, 28, 32, 35–7, 39–40, 46, 60–71, 76, 78–9, 82, 87–8, 90–2, 114, 116, 118, 129–32, 149–50, 159–61, 177, 180, 182–3, 207–10, 212–13, 215
   studies 5–6, 13–22, 25, 28, 39–40, 43, 66–7, 69
   time 18–21, 25, 40, 60–9, 79, 90–1, 128, 130–1, 149–50
nation branding 23–4, 68–9
new weird 173–5, 213
Nightmare on Elm Street, A (Craven) 31
Nihonbunkaron (uniqueness of Japanese culture) 17, 66
Nihonjinron (uniqueness of Japanese people) 17, 66
Noh theatre 14, 28–9, 77
Nunes, Mark 191, 194–5

Oedipus complex 32–3, 36, 46
One Missed Call (Valette) 1
opsign 58–9, 70, 97, 141
orientalism 24, 111, 114, 116
  self-orientalism 24
  techno-orientalism 158
otaku 65–6
out-of-field 48–9, 53, 69

perception-image 53–4
posthumanism
  analytic posthumanism 181–2
  and *Kairo* 6, 10, 67, 158–9, 162, 176–8, 183, 189, 193, 195, 200–2, 205, 209, 213–14
  and the cosmic/weird 174–7
  critical posthumanism 178–81
  theory 159, 174–6, 178–82, 185–7, 189, 193, 195, 201–2, 213–14
Powell, Anna 38, 44, 49, 70–2, 91, 93–4, 208
power of the false 23, 40, 48–9, 51, 53–6, 58, 62, 72, 81, 84, 136–7, 144, 147, 149, 151, 155–6, 211
premediation 195–6
Psycho (Hitchcock) 33
psychoanalysis
  and Deleuzian and Guattarian philosophy 36–41, 43, 45–6, 70–2, 210–12
  in *Ju-On: The Grudge* 8, 75, 92–3, 210–11
  in *Kairo* 160, 169–70, 196
  theory 7, 13, 15, 28, 32–7, 196, 207
pure optical and sound situation/image 3, 57–60, 79, 84, 86

Rear Window (Hitchcock) 53
recollection-image
  in *Audition* 122, 147
  in *Ju-On: The Grudge* 84–7, 99–100, 210
  in *Kairo* 161
relational *See* assemblage
reterritorialize
  and humanism, posthumanism/transhumanism 180, 186–7, 193, 203, 205

  and the auteur 9, 110, 115, 117–18, 121, 150
  and woman 40, 72, 92, 106, 135, 137, 211
  in *Audition* 115, 121, 130–2, 134–5, 137, 139, 144, 149, 150–1, 154–6, 212
  in contemporary society 23, 28, 58–9, 65–6, 69, 76, 180, 193, 209–10
  in Deleuzian and Guattarian philosophy 5, 45–8, 56–8, 64, 69, 79, 208–10
  in *Ju-On: The Grudge* 76, 79–81, 83–6, 90–1, 94, 101–2, 106, 211
  in *Kairo* 156, 158–9, 161, 163, 166–7, 176, 193, 203, 205, 214
return of the repressed 35, 154, 169, 172, 205, 210
Reyes, Xavier Aldana 70–1
rhizome
  and adaptation, transmedia storytelling and intertextuality 125
  and the horror genre 125
  in Deleuzian and Guattarian philosophy 44, 46–8, 50, 59, 208
  in *Ju-On: The Grudge* 8, 75, 77, 88–9, 95, 125, 211
  in *Kairo* 156, 170, 188, 190
Ring, The (Verbinski) 1
Rings (Gutiérrez) 6
Ringu (Nakata) 1, 6, 29, 31, 35, 37, 157, 169
Ringu 2 (Nakata) 37
ryōsaikenbo (good wife, wise mother) 81, 92, 129–30, 152

Saw (Wan) 70
schizophrenization 83–4, 86, 144, 149
Schlesinger, Philip 17–18
Second World War 3, 34, 36–9, 57, 63, 67, 128, 130
sensation *See* affect
sensory-motor schemata 3, 27, 53–4, 57–8, 79, 84–5, 99
Shaviro, Steven

Post Cinematic Affect 26–8, 40–1, 50, 64, 70, 77, 79, 117–18, 195–6
The Cinematic Body 70
Shintōism 14, 28–9, 32
Smith, Anthony 15–18
sonsign 58–9, 70, 97–100, 103, 147, 172, 188
Southland Tales (Kelly) 118
Stam, Robert, and Raengo, Alessandra 110, 122–6, 212
Standish, Isolde 60, 113
Sweet Home (Kurosawa) 31

tactisign 58–9, 70, 141
Taylor-Jones, Kate 17, 30, 38, 72, 111, 113–15, 120
technologization 20, 26, 37, 79, 156–8, 160, 166, 174, 177, 181–3, 185–7, 189, 193–5, 197, 200, 202–3, 205, 213–14
Thacker, Eugene 185–7, 192, 198–9, 214
time-image 2–3, 5–6, 50, 54–62, 69, 71, 84, 110, 155, 195, 207–10
Tōkaidō Yotsuya Kaidan (Ghost Story of Yotsuya in Tōkaidō) (Nakagawa) 14
Tōkyō Monogatari (Tokyo Story) (Ozu) 112
Tomie: Re-birth (Shimizu) 31
Tonari no Totoro (My Neighbor Totoro) (Miyazaki) 131
transformative *See* becoming *and* deterritorialize
transhumanism 6, 10, 67, 159, 180, 186–7, 201–3, 214
transmedia *See* adaptation

transnational
and *Ju-On: The Grudge* 87, 89–90, 210
and *Kairo* 158, 160, 177, 193, 213
and the auteur 114
studies 5–7, 13–15, 19–21, 25–6, 28, 43, 61, 207–8, 215
theory 8, 15, 19–22, 24–7, 69, 92

Ugetsu Monogatari (Tales of Moonlight and Rain) (Mizoguchi) 31
uncanny 35, 101, 169–70, 172, 192, 210
unground *See* deterritorialize

virtuality 50, 53, 55, 58, 84–6, 119, 152
Visitor Q (Miike) 119
voyeurism 34, 138–9, 141

Walking Dead, The (AMC) 176
White, Eric 37, 157
Williams, Linda 105, 109
Wood, Robin 35, 172
world cinema
studies 5–7, 13, 19, 21, 25, 28, 60, 207–8, 212, 215
theory 19, 21, 25, 28, 43, 60–1, 208, 212

Yabu no Naka no Kuroneko (Kuroneko) (Shindō) 94
Yoshimoto, Mitsuhiro 113, 115, 117

Zan'e: Sunde wa ikenai heya (The Inerasable) (Nakamura) 6

www.ingramcontent.com/pod-product-compliance
Lightning Source LLC
Chambersburg PA
CBHW062132300426
44115CB00012BA/1899